T0290628

FINANCIAL REPORTING UNDER GASB STATEN

AND

ASBO INTERNATIONAL CERTIFICATE
OF
EXCELLENCE IN FINANCIAL REPORTING

by

Gary Heinfeld, CPA, CGFM

Association of School Business Officials International

Financial Reporting Under GASB Statement No. 34 and ASBO International Certificate of Excellence in Financial Reporting by Gary Heinfeld, CPA, CGFM
© 2002, Association of School Business Officials International, Reston, Virginia. All rights reserved.
ISBN 0-910170-83-5

2002 CERTIFICATE OF EXCELLENCE (COE) COMMITTEE

Chair
Janice R. Klein, RSBA
Director of Fiscal Services
Mt. Lebanon School District
7 Horsman Drive
Pittsburgh, PA 15228-1107
E-mail: jklein@mtlsd.net

Paul E. Glick
Consultant
Post Office Box 109
Orange Lake, FL 32681-0109
E-mail: pglick@mindspring.com

Gary Heinfeld, CPA, CGFM
Managing Partner
Heinfeld, Meech & Co., P.C.
6740 North Oracle Road, Suite 100
Tucson, AZ 85704-5618
E-mail: gary@heinfeldmeech.com

Ric King
Controller
Schaumburg CCSD 54
524 East Schaumburg Road
Schaumburg, IL 60194-3597
E-mail: fredricking@sd54.k12.il.us

Rebecca McClain
Interim CFO
Savannah/Chatham BOE
208 Bull Street
Savannah, GA 31401
E-mail: Rebecca.mcclain@savannah.chatham.k12.ga.us

Phillip W. Saurman, CPA
CPA - Auditor
HAN&C, PC
910 Lucerne Drive, SE
Grand Rapids, MI 49546-7175
E-mail: psaurman@hanc.com

Meritorious Budget Awards Committee Liaison
Wilson H. Hatcher, CPA
District Fiscal Officer
Academy School District Twenty
7610 North Union Boulevard
Colorado Springs, CO 80907
E-mail: whatcher@d20.co.edu

Board Liaison
Bert E. Huszcza, MBA, RSBA
Director of Business Services
Canon City Schools RE-1
101 N. 14th Street
Canon City, CO 81212
E-mail: huszczb@canon.k12.co.us

Staff Liaison
Pam Geswein
Professional Recognition Coordinator
ASBO International
11401 North Shore Drive
Reston, VA 20190
E-mail: pgeswein@asbointl.org

David A. Ritchey, CAE
Interim Executive Director
ASBO International
11401 North Shore Drive
Reston, VA 20190
E-mail: dritchey@asbointl.org

ASBO International wishes to thank the following school systems for their contributions to this book:

Board of Education of the City of New York
Brooklyn, New York

Carteret County Public School System
Beaufort, North Carolina

Catalina Foothills Unified School District No. 16
Tucson, Arizona

Dublin City School District
Dublin, Ohio

Edgecombe County Schools
Tarboro, North Carolina

Glendale Union High School District No. 25
Glendale, Arizona

Goose Creek Consolidation Independent School District
Baytown, Texas

Grant Parish School Board
Colfax, Louisiana

Lincoln County Board of Education
Lincolnton, North Carolina

Mesa Unified School District No. 4
Mesa, Arizona

Neshaminy School District
Langhorne, Pennsylvania

Richardson Independent School District
Richardson, Texas

School District of Kettle Moraine
Wales, Wisconsin

Tucson Unified School District
Tucson, Arizona

Vancouver Public Schools
Vancouver, Washington

TABLE OF CONTENTS

Page   Exhibit

TABLE OF CONTENTS
(Continued)

TABLE OF CONTENTS
(Concluded)

Preface

The new reporting model, Governmental Accounting Standards Board (GASB) Statement No. 34 *Basic Financial Statements and Management's Discussion and Analysis – for State and Local Governments* is the most significant change to occur in governmental accounting. This new model affects all governmental entities that issue financial statements in conformity with Generally Accepted Accounting Principles (GAAP).

This publication has been prepared in response to the requests of ASBO members seeking specific examples of school system financial statement presentations. Included in this guide are GASB 34 implementation examples and discussions along with a full set of financial statements prepared under the old model and new model. (Appendices B and C) It should be noted that such examples are provided for illustrative purposes. Each school system must recognize its own accounting requirements in conjunction with the authoritative accounting literature.

ASBO's Certificate of Excellence in Financial Reporting Program was established in 1972 to promote and recognize excellence in school system's comprehensive annual financial reports. The program enables school business officials to achieve a high standard of financial reporting through the use of generally accepted accounting practices and the presentation of financial information in a concise and easily readable format.

The program is a result of a vision of a dedicated group of school business professionals and CPA's who, in the 1960's, were not satisfied with meeting the then minimum governmental reporting standards. They were seeking for their school systems the uniformity, consistency, and credibility enjoyed by preparers of financial statements of publicly held corporations whose financial statements appeared in annual reports to shareholders and public offering documents.

More than 400 school systems currently receive the Certificate of Excellence (COE) Award. Those school systems who prepare Comprehensive Annual Financial Reports (CAFRs) in accordance with such specifications as outlined in Section 2200 of the *Codification of Governmental Accounting and Financial Reporting Standards*, published by the Governmental Accounting Standards Board (GASB), and other related GASB pronouncements, and whose financial statements have been subjected to an audit with an unqualified opinion (or an opinion qualified as to consistency, or a "subject to" type of opinion) having been rendered thereon, are eligible for participation.

To assist the school system in the preparation and issuance of its CAFR, ASBO developed a Self-Evaluation Worksheet (obtain from ASBO International Web Site, www.asbointl.org). This comprehensive worksheet, in a question and answer format, details what should be included in a CAFR from cover to cover, and includes references to the aforementioned GASB Statements of Codification as well as *Governmental Accounting, Auditing, and Financial Reporting* published by the Government Finance Officers Association.

This guide is divided into six chapters. The first chapter provides background information on the COE program, offers insights on how to prepare a successful submission, and provides an explanation of the program's general requirements. The next three chapters are devoted to each of the three sections in a CAFR (i.e., Introductory, Financial, and Statistical). Each of these chapters includes examples from actual CAFRs that may be used for reference in addition to the complete CAFRs included in Appendices B and C. The guide continues with a chapter of common problems noted by Certificate of Excellence panel review members. The concluding chapter discusses how to achieve report excellence with the Financial Reporting of Governments (F.R.O.G.).

Completion of this guide would not have been possible without the assistance of the school business administrators who provided CAFR examples. Special thanks goes to ASBO International and their editorial consultants on this project.

David A. Ritchey, CAE, Interim Executive Director
Association of School Business Officials International

(This page intentionally left blank)

Chapter One

GENERAL REQUIREMENT OF THE NEW REPORTING MODEL AND BACKGROUND OF THE ASBO COE PROGRAM

This chapter will explain the general requirements of the new reporting model and the Certificate of Excellence in Financial Reporting (COE) Program, including its origin, purpose, eligibility and procedures.

GENERAL REQUIREMENTS

The GASB issued in June 1999 the new financial reporting model, GASB Statement No. 34, *Basic Financial Statements and Management's Discussion and Analysis for State and Local Governments,* which will <u>significantly</u> change the way governmental entities, including school systems, present their annual financial statements. This statement is one of the most significant changes to occur in school system financial reporting in over 20 years. *Illustration 1* provides the basic framework of the new reporting model. A summary of the basic financial statements and Required Supplementary Information (RSI) for school systems is as follows:

Illustration 1

    New Financial Reporting Model: Minimum Information Required for Fair Presentation in Conformity with Generally Accepted Accounting Principals (GAAP)

REQUIRED SUPPLEMENTARY INFORMATION
Management's Discussion and Analysis

BASIC FINANCIAL STATEMENTS

Government-wide Financial Statements
Statement of Net Assets
Statement of Activities

Fund Financial Statements
<u>Governmental Funds:</u>
Balance Sheet
Statement of Revenues, Expenditures and Changes in Fund Balances
<u>Proprietary Funds:</u>
Statement of Net Assets
Statement of Revenues, Expenses and Changes in Net Assets
Statement of Cash Flows
<u>Fiduciary Funds:</u>
Statement of Fiduciary Net Assets
Statement of Changes in Fiduciary Net Assets (not applicable to agency funds)

Notes to the Financial Statements

Required Supplementary Information
Budgetary Comparison Schedules
Notes to the Budgetary Comparison Schedule
Infrastructure assets reported using the modified approach (if any)
Pension Information (in certain situations)

---

1) **Management's Discussion and Analysis (MD&A).** The MD&A will be presented before the basic financial statements and will introduce the basic financial statements and include an analytical overview of the school system's financial activities. (This will include more data than the current transmittal letter in a CAFR.)

   a) It will provide an analysis of the school system's overall financial position and results of operations to help the users in assessing whether the school system's financial position has improved or deteriorated as a result of the year's activities. It is important to note that if the school system remains the same as the previous year (same revenues and expenses) the school system's position will actually deteriorate due to depreciation expense.

2. **Basic Financial Statements.** The basic financial statements will include:

   a) Government-wide financial statements, which will include a statement of net assets and a statement of activities. These two new statements will be presented using the economic resources measurement focus and the <u>accrual basis</u> of accounting. These statements will distinguish between the governmental and business-type activities of the school system and between the total primary government and its discretely presented component units by reporting each in separate columns. Fiduciary activities will not be included in the government-wide statements.

   It is important to note that these statements will report all capital assets, including infrastructure assets, in the net assets statement and will report depreciation expense in the statement of activities. In addition, the government-wide statement of activities will be presented in a format that reports expenses reduced by program revenues, resulting in a net (expense) revenue for each school system function.

b. Fund financial statements will consist of statements that will focus on the school system's major governmental and proprietary funds, including any blended component units. These financial statements will include the fiduciary activities whereas the government-wide will no include this activity. The financial statements o governmental funds (i.e., general, specia revenue, capital projects, debt service, and permanent funds) will be prepared using the current financial resources measurement focu and the modified accrual basis of accounting whereas the government-wide financia statements are prepared using the accrual basi of accounting. The proprietary fund (enterprise and internal service) and th fiduciary funds will be prepared using th economic resources measurement focus and th accrual basis of accounting.

To help users assess the difference between tl fund and government-wide financial statemen the school system must present a summa reconciliation to the government-wide financi statements at the bottom of the fund financi statements or in an accompanying schedule.

The fund statements will have separate colum for the general fund and for major governmen and enterprise funds. A major fund is a fu whose revenues, expenditures/expenses, asse or liabilities (excluding extraordinary items) at least 10 percent of corresponding totals for governmental or enterprise funds and at lea percent of the aggregate amount for governmental and enterprise funds. Other fu may be reported as a major fund if the sch system's officials believe it is particula important to financial statement users. All o (non-major) funds will be presented i separate column. Internal service funds also be presented in a separate column on proprietary fund statements.

Separate fiduciary fund statements will presented with the fund financial stateme Fiduciary funds are assets that are held trustee or agency capacity for others and cannot be used to support the school syste own programs. Required fiduciary statements are a statement of fiduciary net assets and a statement of changes in fiduciary net assets.

c) Notes to the financial statements are intended to communicate information that is necessary for a fair presentation. GASB Statement No. 38 was issued recently to revise current disclosure requirements to improve the information provided. In addition, Statement No. 38 addresses new disclosures required in conjunction with the new reporting model outlined in Statement No. 34.

d) Required Supplementary Information (RSI) includes budgetary comparison schedules.

These budgetary comparison schedules are used to demonstrate compliance with the school system's legally adopted budget and would include the general fund and each major special revenue fund that has a legally adopted annual budget. The budgetary comparison schedules will present both the original and the final revised budgets as well as actual inflows, outflows, and balances.

If the school system contributes to a single employer or agent multiple-employer PERS, and the required ten-year trend information is not available in a separate PERS report, the CAFR should include the ten-year trend (required supplementary) information required by GASB.

If infrastructure assets are reported using the modified approach, the school system should also include this data as Required Supplementary Information.

The implementation of GASB Statement No. 34 will be phased in over a three-year period based on the school system's total fiscal year 1998-99 revenues.

The first phase is effective for the periods beginning after June 15, 2001, for school systems with total annual revenues of $100 million or more.

The second phase is effective for the periods beginning after June 15, 2002, for school systems with total annual revenues of $10 million or more but less than $100 million.

The third phase is effective for the periods beginning after June 15, 2003, for school systems with total annual revenues of less than $10 million.

A new Self-Evaluation Worksheet will be designed by ASBO to meet the new reporting model requirements and this worksheet will be required to be submitted as part of the application material in the first year of a school system's implementation of GASB Statement No. 34.

BACKGROUND OF ASBO COE PROGRAM

The Certificate of Excellence in Financial Reporting Program was designed by ASBO International to encourage and recognize excellence in the preparation and issuance of school system Comprehensive Annual Financial Reports (CAFRs). Upon completion of a technical review, the panel members conclude whether the school system's CAFR has met the criteria for excellence in financial reporting. The Certificate of Excellence Award is the highest form of recognition in school financial reporting issued by ASBO International.

The COE Program was established in 1972 and currently receives applications from more than 400 school systems and community-supported educational institutions from throughout the United States. Since Certificates are granted based on a particular fiscal year's report, a school system must resubmit its financial report annually to maintain its Certificate.

Benefits To Participants In The Certificate Of Excellence Program

Prestigious National Award
Since its inception, the program has gained the distinction of being a prestigious national award recognized by:
- Accounting Professionals
- Bond Counsel
- Underwriters
- Securities Analysts
- Bond Rating Agencies
- Educational, Teacher and Citizen Groups
- Federal and State Agencies

Validated Fiscal Credibility

Receipt of a Certificate of Excellence validates a school system's fiscal and financial management credibility with its various reporting constituencies, including:

- School Board Members, Superintendents
- School System Management
- State and Local Government Offices
- Oversight Entities
- State and Federal Granting Agencies
- Education, Taxpayer and Teacher Organizations

Enhanced Report Presentations

Inclusion of a Certificate of Excellence enhances a school system's financial presentations in:

- Annual Reports
- Bond Issuance Official Statements
- Presentations to the Media
- Budget Presentations and Hearings
- Continuing Disclosure Requirements

A Measure of Uniformity

Adherence to the formatting and terminology as promulgated by the appropriate standard setting bodies (GASB, AICPA, etc.) allows for comparability between:

- School systems
- School system reports from year to year

Individual Recognition and Development

Receipt of a Certificate of Excellence provides a school system's board and superintendent with a measure of the integrity and technical competence of the system's fiscal administration.

The program stimulates personal technical development through:

- Use of technical materials and attendance at professional seminars
- Completion of ASBO's Self-Evaluation Worksheet
- Networking between peers, consultants and CPA's
- Implementation of comprehensive comments from the Panel of Review

The program promotes professional development by documenting technical proficiency. The recognition afforded by receipt of the Certificate is personally stimulating and satisfying.

Submitting A CAFR For Review

Participating school systems submit their CAFR and application materials within six months of their fiscal year end. The application must include:

- One copy of the Official Certificate of Excellence Application Form
- Three copies of the school system's CAFR
- Three copies of the school system's responses to the prior year's comments (if applicable)
- Three copies of the Self-Evaluation Workshee **(Submitting the worksheet is optional for school systems that received the award for the prior fiscal year. New applicants, past conditional awards, first year GASB 34, and past denial are required to complete and submit three copies of the worksheet.)**
- Payment based on the total revenue of all funds

Send application, with materials and payment, to ASBO International, Certificate of Excellence Program, 11401 North Shore Drive, Reston, VA 20190-4200.

To request program information and application materials, contact ASBO International, 11401 North Shore Drive, Reston, VA 20190-4200 / Phone : (703) 478-0405 / Fax: (703) 478-0205 / Website www.asbointl.org.

Panel of Review And The Review Process

ASBO Panel of Review

A typical Panel of Review is composed of professionals experienced in governmental accounting and auditing who volunteer to review CAFR's submitted by school systems. Panel members include professionals in the field of higher education, school system financial management, consulting and certified public accountants. All votes and comments are reviewed by ASBO's technical consultants.

The Review Process

Each panel member performs a review, prepares relevant comments, and concludes whether to issue deny the certificate award. Panel members are totally independent of the school systems on which they perform reviews. For example, a member of a CPA firm cannot review a report that has been audited by the firm even if the audit was performed by a distant office. In addition, the names of the panel members who performed a particular school system's review are held strictly confidential by ASBO.

Self-Evaluation Worksheet

School systems that submit their financial reports for the Certificate of Excellence Program should complete a "Self-Evaluation Worksheet". The worksheet is a comprehensive document in a question and answer format. Each question requires a specific response of either a "yes", "no" or "not applicable". A "comments" section is provided to explain "no" and "not applicable" answers. For example a question might ask: Are columns captioned with fund titles? If the answer is "no" or "not applicable", an explanation is required. The worksheet provides a school system with a valuable tool in the preparation of the financial report and serves as a checklist in the review process.

Notification of results are sent to the school system. Every applicant receives confidential comments from a trained professional regarding the CAFR. Award recipients also receive a personalized award plaque and certificate, and are recognized in ASBO International's newsletter, *ASBO Accents,* and professional journal, *School Business Affairs.* ASBO also provides a press release that the school system can distribute to its local news media.

ASBO Arbitration Review Panel

The Certificate of Excellence Program includes a cadre of preeminent governmental accounting and auditing experts who function as an Arbitration Review Panel. This panel's responsibility is to review cases in which a school system's CAFR has been denied a certificate and the school system strongly disagrees with the review panel's decision. The decision of the Arbitration Review Panel is final.

Annual Financial Reporting

As stated by GASB, every governmental entity should prepare and publish, as a matter of public record, a *Comprehensive Annual Financial Report* (CAFR) that encompasses governmental activities and all fund activity of the primary government, including its blended component units. The CAFR should also encompass all discretely presented component units of the reporting entity. The CAFR should contain:

a. The basic financial statements.
b. Combining statements for the non-major funds of the primary government, including its blended component units.
c. Combining statements for the discretely presented component units.
d. Individual fund statements and schedules for the funds of the primary government, including its blended component units.

The CAFR is the school system's official annual report and should also contain introductory information, schedules necessary to demonstrate compliance with finance-related legal and contractual provisions, and statistical data.

School systems may also issue basic financial statements separately from the CAFR. However, the basic financial statements should not substitute for the issuance of a CAFR.

A school system's basic financial statements may be issued for inclusion in official statements for bond offerings and for widespread distribution to users requiring less detailed information about the school system's finances than what is contained in the CAFR. A transmittal letter from the school accompanying the separately issued basic financial statements should inform users of the availability of the CAFR for those requiring more detailed information.

The major differences between the basic financial statements and the other statements in the CAFR relate to the reporting of school focus and the reporting on finance-related legal and contractual provisions that differ from GAAP. The CAFR includes (a) both individual major fund and aggregate data of non-major funds included in the basic financial statements, and individual fund data of the non-major funds included in the combining statements for the primary government, including its blended component units; (b) additional introductory, supplementary, and statistical information throughout the CAFR; and (c) schedules essential to demonstrate compliance with finance-related legal and contractual provision. The general outline and minimum content of the CAFR of a school system is as follows:

INTRODUCTORY SECTION

(1) Table of contents,

(2) Letter(s) of transmittal

(3) Other material deemed appropriate by management.

FINANCIAL SECTION

(1) Independent Auditor's Report

(2) Management's Discussion and Analysis (MD&A)

(3) Basic Financial Statements
   (See Illustration 1 on page 1)

(4) Combining and Individual Fund Financial Statements and Schedules
   a. Combining Statements
      (i) By non-major fund – when a primary government (including its blended component units) has more than one non-major fund of either governmental of business-type activities.
      (ii) By Discretely Presented Component Units – when the reporting entity has more than one component unit.
      (iii) By Internal Service Fund – when government entity has more than one internal service fund.

   b. Individual Fund Statements – when a primary government (including its blended component units) chooses to present prior-year and budgetary comparisons for individual funds.

   c. Schedules
      (i) Schedules necessary to demonstrate compliance with finance-related legal and contractual provisions.
      (ii) Schedules to summarize information presented throughout the statements that can be brought together and shown in greater detail (for example, taxes receivable, including delinquent taxes; long-term debt; investments; etc.)

      (iii) Schedules to present information in greater detail (for example, revenue by sources and expenditures by object or by school).

STATISTICAL SECTION

Statistical tables present comparative data for several periods of time, often ten years, or contain data from sources other than the school system's accounting records. Examples of such nonaccounting information are assessed and estimated actual value of taxable property, property tax rates, ratio of net general bonded debt to assessed value and net bonded debt per capita, legal debt margin, direct and overlapping debt, principal taxpayers, and economic and population data.

There are numerous reference materials that can be used when preparing a school system's CAFR. Some include:

A. Statements, interpretations, exposure drafts and discussion memorandums issued by the Governmental Accounting Standards Board (GASB)

B. Guide to Audits of State and Local Government Units issued by the AICPA

C. What You Should Know About Your School District's Finances issued by GFOA

D. Guide to Implementation of GASB Statement on Basic Financial Statements and Management Discussion and Analysis – For State and Local Governments – Questions and Answers, issued by GFOA (GASB)

E. GASB Statement No. 34 Implementation Recommendations for School Districts issued by ASBO

F. Governmental Accounting, Auditing and Financial Reporting (GAAFR) issued by GFOA

G. GAAFR Review published by GFOA

H. GFOA financial reporting releases

I. ASBO International Self-Evaluation Worksheet

Chapter Two

INTRODUCTORY SECTION

The "Introductory Section" is the first section of a CAFR. As the name implies, this section introduces the reader to the CAFR. It includes the following:

- Cover
- Title Page
- Table of Contents
- Transmittal Letter
- Certificate of Excellence Award (if applicable)
- Listing of Board Members and Administrators
- Organizational Chart

Transmittal Letter

The Transmittal Letter describes the school system's organizational and management structure as well as general policies and procedures. Information regarding major initiatives, forecasts and accomplishments will be included. **The transmittal letter should not include information already presented in the MD&A.**

In addition, a school system may want to supplement these basic items with other relevant information that is not covered elsewhere in the CAFR.

The COE Program criteria that follows is established in the ABSO self-evaluation worksheet.

1. Is the transmittal letter:
    a. presented on the letterhead stationery of the school system?
    b. dated on or after the date of the auditor's report?
    c. signed by <u>both</u> the chief financial officer and the chief executive officer (may include others at the school's option)?

2. Is the transmittal letter sufficiently comprehensive in scope? For example, it <u>should</u> include the following subjects without duplicating information presented in the MD&A:
    a. Profile of school system
    b. Explanation of CAFR
    c. Definition of the reporting entity
    d. Economic condition and outlook of local economy
    e. Long-term planning
    f. Major initiatives undertaken by school system
    g. Internal controls
    h. Budgetary controls
    i. Cash management
    j. Risk management
    k. Certificate of Excellence
    l. Acknowledgments
    m. Service Efforts and Accomplishments

3. Are the amounts and data reported in the transmittal letter consistent with those in the other sections of the CAFR?

Exhibits 2-1 and 2-2 are examples of covers.

Exhibit 2-3 is an example of a transmittal letter.

The COE Award is valid for only one year. Thus, if a school has received the Certificate of Excellence in Financial Reporting for its preceding CAFR, the Introductory Section should include a copy of that year's certificate. See Exhibit 2-4.

Listing of Board Members, Administrators and Organizational Chart

The listing of Board Members and Administrators and Organizational Chart can be displayed in a number of ways. Exhibit 2-5 is an example of a simple listing of board members and administrators. Exhibit 2-6 is more elaborate and includes a photograph. Exhibit 2-7 is an example of an organizational chart.

Exhibit 2-1

COMPREHENSIVE ANNUAL FINANCIAL REPORT

Fiscal Year Ended
June 30, 2000

Glendale Union High School District No. 205
7650 North 43rd Avenue
Glendale, Arizona 85301

Exhibit 2-2

CATALINA FOOTHILLS UNIFIED SCHOOL DISTRICT NO. 16
COMPREHENSIVE ANNUAL FINANCIAL REPORT
FOR THE FISCAL YEAR ENDED JUNE 30, 2000

2101 East River Road - Tucson, AZ 85718

10

Exhibit 2-3 Transmittal Letter

School District of Kettle Moraine

District Office
P.O. Box 901 · 563 A. J. Allen Circle · Wales, WI 53183
(414) 968-6300 · Fax (414) 968-6391

December 30, 2000

Members of the Board of Education
Citizens of the School District of Kettle Moraine

We are pleased to submit the sixth Comprehensive Annual Financial Report (CAFR) of the School District of Kettle Moraine for the year ended June 30, 2000. Responsibility for both the accuracy of the data and completeness and fairness of the presentation, including all disclosures, rests with management. To the best of our knowledge and belief the enclosed data are accurate in all material respects and are reported in a manner that presents fairly the financial position and results of operation of the district as a whole and of its various funds. This report is a complete disclosure of all financial activities of the district.

This report is prepared in conformance with generally accepted accounting principles (GAAP) for governments as promulgated by the Government Accounting Standards Board (GASB). This report is consistent with legal reporting requirements of the State of Wisconsin. In addition to meeting legal requirements, this report is intended to present a comprehensive summary of significant financial data to meet the needs of citizens, taxpayers, employees, financial institutions, intergovernmental agencies, creditors, and the School Board.

The comprehensive annual financial report is presented in four sections:

1. The *INTRODUCTORY SECTION* contains the Table of Contents, this Letter of Transmittal, and the Certificate of Excellence in Financial Reporting presented by the Association of School Business Officials for last year's CAFR. The letter of transmittal includes a list of principal officers and an organizational chart. The introductory section is not audited.

2. The *FINANCIAL SECTION* begins with the independent auditor's report. This section includes the management's discussion and analysis, basic financial statements, notes to the basic financial statements, combining and individual fund statements, and required budgetary supplemental information. All reports of the financial section are audited.

3. *SINGLE AUDIT* – the school district is required to undergo an annual single audit in conformity with the provisions of the Single Audit Act Amendments of 1996, and the U. S. Office of Management and Budget, Circular A-133, Audits of State, Local Governments, and Non-profit Organizations. Information related to this single audit, including the schedules of state and federal assistance, the independent auditor's reports on internal controls, and compliance with applicable laws and regulations is included in this section of the report.

4. The *STATISTICAL SECTION*, which is not audited, includes selected financial, demographic and economic data, generally presented on a multi-year basis. This section also includes all disclosures, not contained elsewhere in the CAFR, to comply with the Securities and Exchange Commission continuing disclosure requirements for general obligation debt issues.

Exhibit 2-3 (continued)

THE REPORTING ENTITY

The legal name of the district is the School District of Kettle Moraine. The school district was established in 1967. The district is located in western Waukesha County and eastern Jefferson County approximately half way between Milwaukee and Madison on Interstate Highway 94. The district includes all or part of the City of Delafield, the Villages of Dousman, North Prairie and Wales, and portions of the Townships of Delafield, Eagle, Genesee, Ottawa, and Summit of Waukesha County and a portion of the Township of Sullivan in Jefferson County.

The district is an independent entity governed by an elected seven member School Board. The Board has the power and duty to set budgets, certify tax levies, issue debt and perform other tasks necessary to the operation of the district. The district is subject to the general oversight of the Wisconsin Department of Public Instruction. This oversight generally includes an approval process that reviews compliance to standards enacted by legislative mandate.

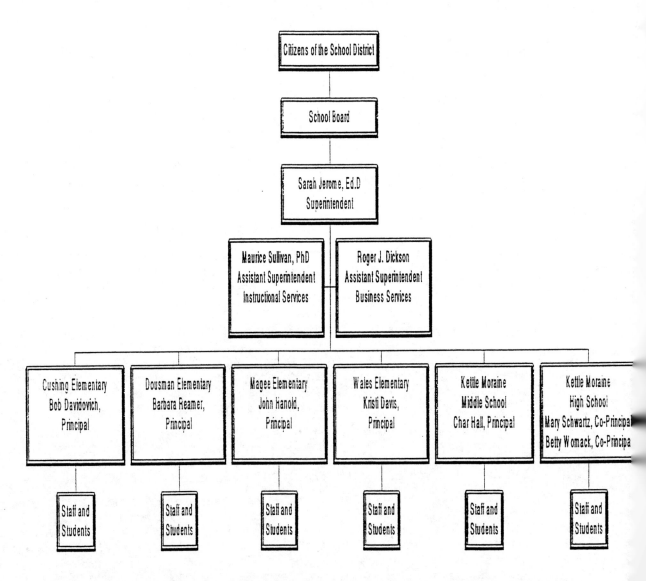

The district serves a general population of approximately 22,000 in an area of about 90 square miles. The district operates four elementary schools (grades PK-5), one middle school (grades 6-8), one high school (grades 9-12), and a senior citizen center. In addition to education for students between the ages of 3 and 21 (unless graduated from high school), the district operates a school food service program, which primarily serves lunch to regular day school students, and a community service program that operates educational classes for adults and recreational programs for students and adults.

Exhibit 2-3 (continued)

The district office is housed in a separate facility. In addition, the district leases, as lessor, a one-room schoolhouse to a private firm for a day care center. The district leases classroom space in the Village of Dousman for an alternative school. At the end of the school year, the district served 4,404 pupils in its regular day program.

The school district enjoys a favorable economic environment and local indicators point to continued growth. Residential development continues in the district at a pace that is both constant and manageable. Although the district is primarily residential, significant commercial development has taken place during the past several years and will continue. Unemployment for the county is among the lowest in the state. Western Waukesha County enjoys full employment, continued residential development and well-planned commercial development.

MANAGEMENT SYSTEMS and CONTROLS

Kettle Moraine is committed to developing, maintaining, and improving effective management systems and controls. The district makes conscientious efforts to employ highly qualified employees through active recruitment and thorough reference evaluations. Further, operations are annually evaluated to assure they function effectively and provide appropriate levels of supervision and segregation of duties.

Budget Adoption

Budgetary control is decentralized to managers of each operating unit. Overall administrative responsibility rests with the Assistant Superintendent of Business Services under the direction of the Superintendent and consistent with School Board policy. Board policy allows for re-appropriation of budgets within an operating unit by authority of operating unit managers. Re-appropriation of budget amounts between and among operating units requires authorization of the Assistant Superintendent. School Board approval is required to change appropriations at the fund level. Wisconsin statutes require that any budget change authorized by the School Board must be approved by a 2/3 vote of the total board. The change is not effective until published in the district's official newspaper, within 10 days of the Board action.

The budget process starts each year in December. Starting in December and ending in April, operating unit managers prepare budget requests for the upcoming year. The Business Office compiles requests and tentative recommendations, consistent with annual strategies and goals, which are recommended to the Administrative Council. The Administrative Council will modify the budget request and submit to the School Board's Building and Finance Committee for review and possible further modification. The Building and Finance Committee will recommend an interim budget to the full School Board in April. The School Board adopts the interim budget in May and submits a recommended tentative property tax levy to the annual meeting of electors. The original budget is adopted in October following an official enrollment count, adjustment of estimates made the previous spring and certification of general state aid.

Risk Management

The School District of Kettle Moraine maintains a risk management program that includes a comprehensive insurance program specifically designed to meet school district needs, casualty and benefit insurance consultation, active safety committees oriented to identification and avoidance of risk, annual independent safety evaluations, and periodic review of contracts and policies to assure regulatory compliance and adherence to legal constructs. The Assistant Superintendent for Business Services oversees risk management for the district.

Independent Audit

Kettle Moraine policy and state law requires an annual audit of the financial statements of the district by an independent certified public accountant. This requirement has been complied with and the auditor's opinion is included in this report. Kettle Moraine does not maintain an internal audit staff.

Exhibit 2-3 continued

Financial Reporting

This is the first year the School District of Kettle Moraine has prepared the CAFR in conformance with GASB Statement No. 34, Basic Financial Statements – and Management's Discussion and Analysis – for State and Local Governments. GASB Statement 34 is an all encompassing and sweeping change to financial reporting requirements for governments. Public school districts of the size of Kettle Moraine are required to implement GASB Statement 34 for fiscal years beginning after June 15, 2002. The district chose earlier implementation to take advantage of the significant improvements in financial disclosure afforded by Statement 34. GASB 34 creates the following financial statements that had not previously been published:

- Statement of net assets to report all assets and liabilities of the district as a whole,
- Statement of activities to report all revenues and expenses of the district as a whole, and
- Budgetary comparison statements to inform readers of changes in the budget during the fiscal year as well as compare year-end results with the final budget.

The Association of School Business Officials International awarded a Certificate of Excellence in Financial Reporting to the district for its comprehensive annual financial report for the year ended June 30, 1999. This was the fifth year the district has received this prestigious award. In order to be awarded a Certificate of Excellence, the district published an easily readable and efficiently organized comprehensive annual financial report. The CAFR satisfies both generally accepted accounting principles and applicable legal requirements.

A Certificate of Excellence is valid for a period of one year only. We believe that the current comprehensive annual financial report continues to meet the Certificate of Excellence Program's requirements and will submit it to the ASBO International to determine it's eligibility for another certificate.

ACCOMPLISHMENTS

The School District of Kettle Moraine takes pride in its comprehensive instructional, co-curricular, and support programs. Taxpayers have shown their support for the present educational programs. They have voiced their desire for the existing programs to continue and for resources to be provided to future students on the same comparable basis as provided to current and prior students.

The district has developed and adopted various long-range plans for maintenance of facilities, incorporation of technology into education, improvement of education, and streamlining of operations. Plans are reviewed periodically and updated as needed. Implementation of technology, replacement of equipment, maintenance of facilities, and instructional improvement plans throughout the district continue on schedule.

The district currently has one computer for every four students and full internet access in all buildings. Staff development is provided on a regular and scheduled basis. Plans have been developed and allocations made to provide for distance learning capabilities.

Individual schools annually review strategies necessary to implement the district mission. Allocation of resources is based on annual identification of tasks necessary to meet goals.

Student achievement highlights for the 1999-2000 school year include:
- The Wisconsin Manufacturers and Commerce Association named Kettle Moraine Schools as Best in Class in the top 10% out of 426 school districts in the state based on test scores and effective budgeting practices.
- The Wisconsin Taxpayers Alliance ranked Kettle Moraine High School as one of 27 Best High Schools in the State of Wisconsin in July 1999.
- 270 elementary and middle school students qualified for the Midwest Talent Search based on their standardized test scores in the top 5% nationwide.
- 80% of Kettle Moraine High School graduates will attend a 2 or 4-year college or university.

14

Exhibit 2-3 (continued)

- 15 school business partnerships have been established with Kettle Moraine schools and area businesses with every school having a partnership with Junior Achievement.
- 74% of Kettle Moraine High School students taking the Advanced Placement Exams passed with scores of 3's, 4's, or 5's.
- The U.S. Department of Education has designated five of Kettle Moraine's six schools as National Blue Ribbon Schools of Excellence.
- Kettle Moraine music programs received state and national recognition and has established an innovative music program for kindergarten students.
- Kettle Moraine School District was ranked 4th out of 35 school districts by the Milwaukee Public Policy Forum based on state and national test scores as reported by The Milwaukee Journal.
- The National Merit Scholar Program recognized six seniors as semifinalists.
- The Advanced Placement Scholars Program recognized five students.

The school district continues to provide an above average education to students for a cost that is below the statewide average. In performance measures the district out performs state averages. Data for 1999-2000 demonstrates student performance on state tests:

	DISTRICT	STATE
a. Attendance Rate	95.50%	94.03%
b. High School Graduation Rate	100.00%	89.00%
c. Third Grade Reading Test	89.50%	70.01%
d. Average Composite ACT Score	23.2	22.3
e. Percent Passing Advanced Placement Exams	82%	75%

The table below provides other measures of resource allocation for 1997-98:

	DISTRICT	STATE
a. Number of pupils per licensed instructional staff	13.92	13.29
b. Number of pupils per all staff members	9.19	8.39
c. Expenditures per pupil (as calculated by Wisconsin Department of Public Instruction)	$ 7,322	$ 7,539

LOOKING AHEAD

The district will continue to provide a high quality, effective education within reasonable costs for students who attend district schools. Schools will continue to review and update strategic plans and prioritize strategies and tasks for implementation.

The district continues to closely monitor student enrollment. The district purchased a site for a future high school in Dousman and one for a future elementary and middle school in the Town of Delafield. The need for an additional high school is not anticipated for 20 years

The superintendent and instructional staff continue to explore and implement research-based instructional methodology to improve instructional delivery. Projects underway include continuing to study the impact of music on temporal-spatial reasoning, brain research instructional models, improved programs for gifted and talented students, improved mathematics instruction, and emphasis on writing and technology. Review of reading and writing methodologies was conducted and implementation of program changes is underway in 1999-2000.

The School District of Kettle Moraine is in good financial condition. Recent legislation will assure increased state funding of public schools and will be used to reduce reliance on local property taxes. The additional state support, effective long-range planning and supportive electorate will contribute to continued improvement in the financial condition of Kettle Moraine.

Exhibit 2-3 (concluded)

In addition to individual schools continuing to develop and implement strategic plans, school goals are published annually. Major themes apparent in 2000-01 goals are:

- Improve communications and relations with community, including expanded adult education opportunities
- Improve writing skills across the curriculum.
- Increase use of, and competence with, technology.
- Monitor and improve academic achievement across the curriculum.
- Continue to provide safe and inviting learning environments.
- Provide for needs of growing enrollments and maintain facilities prepared for the 21st century Educational demands.

Concerns

Although the district's educational program and finances are in good condition, the following concerns for the future have been identified:

- The amount of property taxes and state formula aid (general aid) a school district is permitted to receive is limited by state statute. Permitted revenue limit increases are based on a per pupil amount that is adjusted each year for inflation. Kettle Moraine's student enrollment has historically increased; therefore the district has been able to raise sufficient revenues to continue to offer the comprehensive programs desired by residents. Enrollment projections for future years show a stabilizing or slight decrease. If enrollment decreases faster than projected, program constraints may become necessary.

- State statutes prevent unions representing certified employees from seeking binding interest arbitration if the school board offers a minimum total compensation package with an increase of at least 3.8%, calculated in accordance with promulgations of the Wisconsin Employment Relations Council. If the district experiences a decline in enrollment, it is possible that the 3.8% increase in compensation could exceed the permitted revenue limit increase. The district believes teacher retirements, allowing the hiring of less experienced and therefore less expensive staff will moderate any negative impact.

- The district is continuing to study and receive public comment on facilities. A facilities project with a cost greater than $15 million is expected to be presented to the taxpayers for approval during the 2000-2001 fiscal year.

ACKNOWLEDGEMENTS

We express our appreciation to Kettle Moraine's dedicated staff and Feld, Schumacher and Company, certified public accountants, for their many hours assisting with preparation of the report. Particular appreciation is extended to Susan Graham, Accountant, for her dedication and diligence in gathering, editing, and verifying data and the actual preparation of this report.

Respectfully submitted,

Sarah Jerome, Ed.D
Superintendent

Roger J. Dickson
Assistant Superintendent

Exhibit 2-4 Certificate of Excellence Award

ASSOCIATION OF SCHOOL BUSINESS OFFICIALS

INTERNATIONAL

This Certificate of Excellence in Financial Reporting is presented to

SCHOOL DISTRICT OF KETTLE MORAINE

For its Comprehensive Annual Financial Report (CAFR)
For the Fiscal Year Ended June 30, 1999

Upon recommendation of the Association's Panel of Review which has judged that the Report substantially conforms to principles and standards of ASBO's Certificate of Excellence Program

Pam Deering
President

Don A. Kugan
Executive Director

17

Exhibit 2-5 Listing of Board Members and Administrators

THE SCHOOL DISTRICT OF KETTLE MORAINE

Comprehensive Annual Financial Report

For the fiscal year ended June 30, 2000

MEMBERS OF THE BOARD

Michael Wagner	President
Gerald Powell	Vice-President
Jacqueline Offerman	Clerk
Gary Vose	Treasurer
Gregory J. Cook	Member
Patricia Millichap	Member
Dave Wentworth	Member

ADMINISTRATORS

Dr. Sarah D. Jerome	Superintendent
Dr. Maurice Sullivan	Assistant Superintendent - Instructional Services
Roger J. Dickson	Assistant Superintendent - Business Services

OFFICIALS ISSUING REPORT

Dr. Sarah D. Jerome	Roger J. Dickson

REPORT PREPARED BY

Roger J. Dickson	Assistant Superintendent - Business Services
Susan A. Graham	Accountant

TECHNICAL SUPPORT PROVIDED BY

Business Office	Communication Services

Exhibit 2-6 Listing of Board Members and Administrators

Board of Education Members and Principal Officers

Board of Education Members, seated from left, Ellen Piner, Chairman Roger Newby, Vice Chairman Kim Willis, and , standing from left, Mike Hodges, Cathy Neagle, June Fulcher and Arnold Stone

Superintendent
Dr. David K. Lenker Jr.

Assistant Superintendent
John A. Welmers

Assistant Superintendent
Jane R. Alexander

19

Exhibit 2-7 Organizational Chart

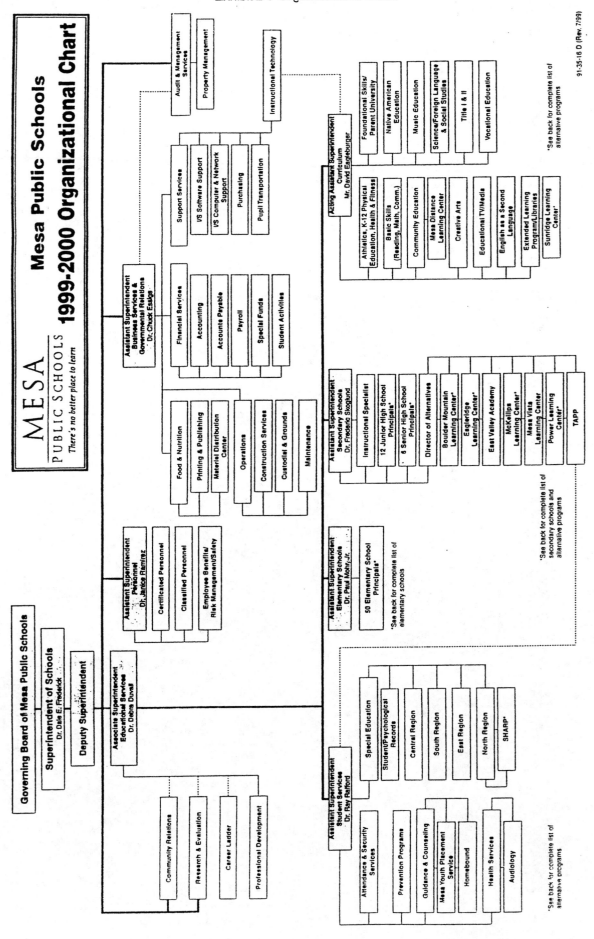

20

Chapter Three

FINANCIAL SECTION

The focus of this section is the school system's financial statements for the year. The Auditor's Report **must** be unqualified to meet the minimum COE criteria. The financial statements must be presented in accordance with generally accepted accounting principals and include the following statements and disclosures along with the Independent Auditor's Report.

FINANCIAL SECTION

. Independent Auditor's Report

I. Management's Discussion and Analysis is limited to the paragraph 11, items d-h in GASB 34. (Exhibit 3-1)
  a. Brief discussion of the Basic Financial Statements
  b. Condensed financial information derived from government-wide financial statements
  c. Financial Analysis of the Government's overall financial position and results of operations
  d. Analysis of balances and transactions individual funds
  e. Budgetary Highlights
  f. Capital Assets and Debt Administration
  g. A discussion by governments that use the modified approach
  h. A description of current known facts, decisions, or conditions that are expected to have a material effect on the financial statement.

. Basic Financial Statements
  a. Government-wide Financial Statements (including discretely presented component units)
    1. Statement of Net Assets (Exhibit 3-2)
    2. Statement of Activities (Exhibit 3-3)
  b. Fund Financial Statements
    1. Balance Sheet – Governmental Funds (Exhibit 3-4)
    2. Statement of Revenues, Expenditures, and Changes in Fund Balances – Governmental Funds (Exhibit 3-5)
    3. Reconciliation of Statement of Revenues, Expenditures, and Changes in Fund Balances of Governmental Funds to the Statement of Net Activities (Exhibit 3-6)
    4. Statements of Net Assets – Proprietary Funds (Exhibit 3-7)
    5. Statements of Revenues, Expenses, and Changes in Net Assets – Proprietary Funds (Exhibit 3-8)
    6. Statements of Cash Flows – Proprietary Funds (Direct method) (Exhibit 3-9)
    7. Statement of Fiduciary Net Assets (Exhibit 3-10)
    8. Statement of Changes in Fiduciary Net Assets (Exhibit 3-10)
  c. Notes to the Financial Statements. (See CAFR Appendix C, pages 28 to 44)

IV. Additional Required Supplementary Information
  a. Budgetary Comparison Schedules for Major Governmental Funds (Exhibit 3-11)
    1. Include the revenue and expenditure budgets for the general fund and each major Special Revenue Fund with a legally adopted budget.
    2. Include the original budget and the final revised budget.
    3. Include variance columns to either the original and/or final revised budget

4. Include Budget Comparison reconciliation (Exhibit 3-12)
b. If the school system contributes to a <u>single employer</u> or <u>agent multiple-employer</u> PERS, and the required ten-year trend information is not available in a separate PERS report, the CAFR should include the ten-year trend (required supplementary) information required by GASB.
c. Infrastructure assets reported using the modified approach.
d. Claims development trend data

V. Combining Statements and Schedules
a. By Non-Major Fund Type-when a primary government (including its blended component units) has more than one non-major fund of either a governmental or business-type activity. (Exhibit 3-13 & 14)
b. For Discretely Presented Component Units-when the reporting entity has more than one component unit.
c. For Internal Service Funds when the reporting entity has more than one fund.
d. Individual Fund Statements when a primary government (including its blended component units) has only one fund of a given type and chooses to present prior-year and budgetary comparisons. (Exhibit 3-15)
e. Schedules
1. Schedules necessary to demonstrate compliance with finance-related legal and contractual provisions.
2. Schedules to summarize information presented throughout the statements that can be brought together and shown in greater detail (for example, taxes receivable, including delinquent taxes; long-term debt; investments; and cash receipts, disbursements, and balances).

3. Schedules to present in greater detail information reported in the statement (for example, additional revenue source and detail of expenditures by object o school).

Complete financial statements using both th current and new reporting models are include in the Appendix B and C.

Due to the complexity of the Financial Sectio see the Self Evaluation Worksheet for th Certificate of Excellence Award criter required.

(Exhibit 3-1)

Management's Discussion and Analysis (MD&A)

Exhibit 3-1 continued

School District of Kettle Moraine
Management's Discussion and Analysis
For the Year Ended June 30, 2000

The discussion and analysis of the School District of Kettle Moraine's financial performance provides an overall review of financial activities for the fiscal year. The analysis focuses on school district financial performance as a whole. Efforts have been made to provide comparison to prior year data when such data is available. In subsequent years comparison to prior year data will be provided for all key financial information.

FINANCIAL HIGHLIGHTS

- The District's financial status, as reflected in total net assets, improved by $1.7 million. Net assets of governmental activities increased $1.6 million as a result of reduction in liabilities from 1999. Business-type activities also reported an increase in net assets for the current fiscal period.

- Business-type activities had a net increase in capital assets of $79,000 as a result of acquisition of new equipment outpacing depreciation. In governmental activities, capital assets declined by $585,000 reflecting depreciation expense greater than the cost of acquisitions.

- The district reduced its overall liabilities by $2.6 million. $2 million of the reduction is repayment of long-term notes and bonds. The district also reduced the amount of outstanding short-term notes by $600,000.

- Program revenues, in the form of charges for services and operating grants and contributions, accounted for $4.2 million of total revenues of $39 million. General revenues accounted for $34.8 million, including $19.3 million of property taxes and $15 million of general state aid. General revenues account for 89% of all revenues.

- In governmental activities the district had a total of $36.1 million of expenses, of which $2.9 was financed with program revenues.

- The school food service program, the district's only business-type activity, had $1.2 million in total expenses and $1.275 million in revenues.

- In governmental funds, total fund balance increased $187,000. The general fund had an increase of $461,000 with a decrease of $235,000 in the debt service fund and $39,000 in non-major funds. The debt service decrease was planned and budgeted.

OVERVIEW OF THE FINANCIAL STATEMENTS

This section of the comprehensive annual financial report consists of three parts—management's discussion and analysis, basic financial statements (district-wide and fund statements) including notes to the financial statements, and other required supplementary information.

The basic financial statements consist of two kinds of statements that present different views of the districts' financial activities.

- The *statement of net assets* and *statement of activities* provide information on a district-wide basis. The statements present an aggregate view of the district's finances. District-wide statements contain useful long-term information as well as information for the just-completed fiscal year.

- The remaining statements are *fund financial statements* that focus on individual parts of the district. Fund statements generally report operations in more detail than the district-wide statements.

Exhibit 3-1 continued

School District of Kettle Moraine
Management's Discussion and Analysis
For the Year Ended June 30, 2000

The *notes to the financial statements* provides further explanation of some of the information in the statements and provides additional disclosures so statement users have a complete picture of the district's financial activities and position.

Required supplementary information further explains and supports the financial statements by including a comparison of the district's budget data for the year.

The major features of the district's financial statements, including the portion of the activities reported and the type of information contained is shown in the following table.

Major Features of the District-wide and Fund Financial Statements

	District Wide Statements	Fund Financial Statements		
		Governmental	Proprietary	Fiduciary
Scope	Entire district (except fiduciary funds).	The activities of the district that is not proprietary or fiduciary, such as instructional, support services, and community services.	Activities the district operates similar to private business. The district's food service program is its only proprietary operation.	Assets held by the district on behalf of someone else. Student and other organizations that have funds on deposit with the district are reported here.
Required financial statements	Statement of net assets, and Statement of activities.	Balance sheet, and Statement of revenues, expenditures and changes in fund balance.	Statement of net assets, and Statement of revenues, expenses and changes in net assets, and Statement of cash flows.	Statement of fiduciary net assets, and Statement of changes in fiduciary net assets.
Basis of accounting and measurement focus	Accrual accounting. Economic resources focus.	Modified accrual accounting. Current financial resources focus.	Accrual accounting. Economic resources focus.	Accrual accounting. Economic resources focus.
Type of asset and liability information	All assets and liabilities, both financial and capital, short-term and long-term.	Generally assets expected to be used up and liabilities that come due during the year or soon thereafter. No capital assets or long-term liabilities included.	All assets and liabilities, both financial and capital; short-term and long-term.	All assets and liabilities, both financial and capital; short-term and long-term. These funds do not currently contain any capital assets, although they can.
Type of inflow and outflow information	All revenues and expenses during the year, regardless of when cash is received or paid.	Revenues for which cash is received during or soon after the end of the year; expenditures when goods or services have been received and the related liability are due and payable.	All revenues and expenses during the year, regardless of when cash is received or paid.	All additions or deductions during the year, regardless of when cash is received and paid.

Exhibit 3-1 continued
School District of Kettle Moraine
Management's Discussion and Analysis
For the Year Ended June 30, 2000

District-wide Statements

The district-wide statements report information about the district as a whole using accounting methods similar to those used by private-sector companies. The two district-wide statements report the district's *net assets* and how they have changed. Net assets, the difference between the district's assets and liabilities, are one way to measure the district's overall financial position.

- Increases or decreases in the district's net assets are one indicator of whether its financial position is improving or deteriorating, respectively.

- To assess the overall financial condition of the district additional non-financial factors, such as changes in the district's property tax base and the condition of school buildings and other facilities, should be considered.

In the district-wide financial statements, the district's activities are divided into two categories:

- *Governmental activities*—Most of the district's basic services are included here, such as regular and special education, transportation, support services, community programs and administration. Property taxes and state formula aid finance most of these activities.

- *Business-type activities*—The district charges fees and received federal and state reimbursements to cover the costs of its food service operation. The financial activity of this program is reported as a business-type activity.

Fund Financial Statements

The fund financial statements provide more detailed information about the district's *funds*, focusing on its most significant or "major" funds — not the district as a whole. Funds are accounting devices the district uses to keep track of sources of funding and spending on particular programs and to demonstrate compliance with various regulatory requirements.

- Some funds are required by state law and by bond covenants.

- The district establishes other funds to control and manage money for particular purposes (like repaying its long-term debt) or to show that it is properly using certain revenues (like capital project funds).

The District has three kinds of funds:

- *Governmental funds*—Most of the district's basic services are included in governmental funds, which generally focus on (1) how cash and other financial assets that can readily be converted to cash flow in and out and (2) the balances left at year-end that are available for funding future basic services. Consequently, the governmental funds statements provide a detailed short-term view that helps determine whether there are more or fewer financial resources that can be spent in the near future to finance the district's programs. Governmental fund information does not report on long-term commitments as is reported on the district-wide statements. Therefore an explanation of the differences between the governmental funds and the district-wide statements is included either at the bottom of the governmental funds statements or as a separate statement.

- *Proprietary funds*—The food service fund, an activity for which the district charges a fee and for which revenues are expected to cover all expenses is reported as a proprietary fund. Proprietary funds are reported in the same way as the district-wide statements.

Exhibit 3-1 continued

School District of Kettle Moraine
Management's Discussion and Analysis
For the Year Ended June 30, 2000

- *Fiduciary funds*—The district serves as a trustee, or *fiduciary*, for student and parent organizations. The assets of these organizations belong to the organization, and not the district. The district is responsible for ensuring that the assets reported in these funds are used only for their intended purposes and only by those to whom the assets belong. These activities are excluded from the district-wide financial statements because the district cannot use these assets to finance its operations.

FINANCIAL ANALYSIS

The District as a Whole

Net Assets. Table I, below, provides a summary of the district's net assets for the year ended June 30, 2000 compared to 1999.

	Governmental Activities		Business-type Activities		Total School District		% Change
	1999	2000	1999	2000	1999	2000	1999-2000
Current and other assets	$11,822.80	$ 10,453.8	$ 481.7	$ 489.5	$ 12,304.5	$ 10,943.3	-11.1%
Capital assets	29,430.5	28,845.0	348.3	427.6	29,778.8	29,272.6	-1.7%
Total assets	41,253.3	39,298.9	829.9	917.0	42,083.2	40,215.9	-4.4%
Long-term debt outstanding	23,606.7	21,587.6	-	-	23,606.7	21,587.6	-8.6%
Other liabilities	8,161.6	6,575.3	58.7	64.8	8,220.3	6,640.1	-19.2%
Total liabilities	31,768.3	28,162.9	58.7	64.8	31,827.0	28,227.6	-11.3%
Net assets							
Invested in capital assets, net of related debt	13,156.4	11,074.6	348.3	427.6	13,504.7	11,502.2	-14.8%
Restricted	1,188.1	953.1	422.9	424.7	1,611.0	1,377.8	-14.5%
Unrestricted	(1,358.0)	(891.7)	-	-	(1,358.0)	(891.7)	-34.3%
Total net assets	$ 9,485.0	$ 11,136.0	$ 771.2	$ 852.3	$ 10,256.2	$ 11,988.3	16.9%

Table 1
Condensed Statement of Net Assets
(in thousands of dollars)

Note: totals may not add due to rounding.

The district's combined net assets increased by 16.9 percent to $11,988,300. Most of this improvement in the financial position came from governmental activities, the net assets of which grew $1,650,955. The net assets of the district's business-type activities increased $81,100. While the dollar growth was smaller, it nonetheless represented an increase of more than 10 percent. The district's improved financial position is due primarily to reduction in both long-term and short-term debt.

The district continues to report a negative unrestricted net asset amount of $891,700. This is a reduction of $460,300 from 1999. The calculation of net assets uses an historical cost of school buildings that may not accurately reflect the true value. Kettle Moraine's buildings are in excellent condition as a result of sufficient annual operating funds appropriated for maintenance and repair. The district does not have any deferred maintenance on buildings.

Further, the district has $2,230,000 outstanding long-term debt incurred to refinance a prior-service retirement obligation. Since this debt is not supported by capital assets its impact on the district's financial position does not reflect the strategic purpose of refinancing, which was to reduce long-term interest costs.

Exhibit 3-1 continued

School District of Kettle Moraine
Management's Discussion and Analysis
For the Year Ended June 30, 2000

As illustrated in the chart below, as net assets have increased, negative unrestricted net assets have also been reduced.

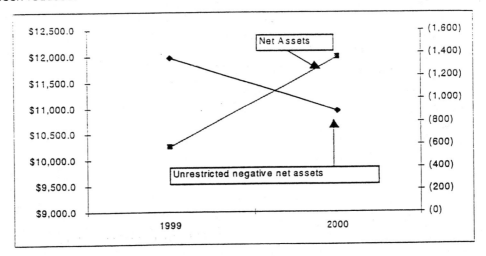

Changes in net assets. Table 2 shows the changes in net assets for the fiscal year 2000. Since this is the first year for preparation of financial statements in accordance with GASB Statement 34, revenue and expense comparisons to fiscal year 1999 are not available. Comparison data will be presented in subsequent years.

	Govn't Activities 2000	Business Type Activities 2000	Total 2000
Table 2			
Changes in Net Assets from Operating Results			
(in thousands of dollars)			
Revenues:			
Program revenues			
Charges for services	$ 581.0	$ 1,085.0	$ 1,666.0
Operating grants & contributions	2,325.3	172.1	2,497.4
General revenues			
Property taxes	19,281.4		19,281.4
State formula aid	14,967.8		14,967.8
Other	617.9	18.1	636.1
Total revenues	37,773.4	1,275.2	39,048.6
Expenses:			
Instruction	22,241.6		22,241.6
Pupil & instructional services	2,967.0		2,967.0
Administration and business	2,596.8		2,596.8
Maintenance and operations	2,674.6		2,674.6
Transportation	1,787.1		1,787.1
Community service	344.2		344.2
Interest on debt	1,402.9		1,402.9
Other	2,108.2	1,194.1	3,302.3
Total expenses	36,122.4	1,194.1	37,316.6
Increase in net assets	$ 1,651.0	$ 81.1	$ 1,732.0

Note: totals may not add due to rounding.

Exhibit 3-1 continued

School District of Kettle Moraine
Management's Discussion and Analysis
For the Year Ended June 30, 2000

As shown in Table 2, general revenues provide 92% of the funding required for governmental programs and nearly 99% of the funding for business-type activities. Kettle Moraine relies on property taxes for 51% of its governmental activities..

The district's had total revenues of $39 million of which $37.8 million was for governmental activities and $1,275,200 was for the district's food service operation.

Total revenues surpassed expenses, increasing net assets $1,732,000, over last year. Both the governmental and business-type activities contributed to the district's improved financial position.

Governmental Activities

Revenues for governmental activities were $37.8 million, while total expenses amounted to $36.1 million. Governmental activities contributed $1.65 million to the increased net assets.

The improvement in the district's financial position can be credited both to increased student enrollment and effective fiscal management:

- Student enrollment increased by 43 full-time equivalent students enabling the district to increase revenues to support additional programs and staffing.

- The district changed from a self-funded health insurance plan to a fully insured plan in January 2000. The district had benefited financially from the self-funded plan for many years. However, changing demographics and changes in the health insurance market made a switch to a fully insured plan prudent at this time.

- The district sought and received additional competitive federal grants in 2000. These grants allowed the district to initiate new programs. Federal grants contributed over $27,800 to indirect costs for the 1999-2000 year.

- The district has improved efficiency in purchasing through more cooperative arrangements with other area governments, allowing sites greater discretion in purchasing decisions and taking advantage of "off-season" purchasing.

- Long-range facility maintenance plans and long-range equipment replacement plans have allowed the district to achieve cost savings through better planning.

- Investment programs were reviewed and several changes made to enhance earnings of investment of temporarily idle cash.

Table 3 presents the cost of eight major district activities: instruction, pupil and instructional services, administration and business, maintenance and operations, transportation, community services, interest on debt and other (see Chart 2 below). The table also shows each activity's net cost (total cost less fees generated by the activities and intergovernmental aid provided for specific programs). The net cost shows the financial burden that was placed on the district's taxpayers by each of these functions.

Exhibit 3-1 continued

School District of Kettle Moraine
Management's Discussion and Analysis
For the Year Ended June 30, 2000

	Table 3		
	Net Cost of Governmental Activities		
	(in thousands of dollars)		
	Total Cost		**Net Cost**
	of Services		**of Services**
	2000		**2000**
Instruction	$	22,241.6	$ 20,147.0
Pupil & instructional services		2,967.0	2,575.3
Administration and business		2,596.8	2,596.8
Maintenance and operations		2,674.6	2,628.8
Transportation		1,787.1	1,606.5
Community service		344.2	152.1
Interest on debt		1,402.9	1,402.9
Other		2,108.2	2,106.8
Total	$	36,122.4	$ 33,216.2

Note: totals may not add due to rounding.

- The cost of all governmental activities this year was $36.1 million.

- Individuals who directly participated or benefited from a program offering paid for $581,000 of costs.

- Federal and state governments subsidized certain programs with grants and contributions of $2.3 million.

- Net cost of governmental activities ($33.2 million), were financed by general revenues, which are made up of primarily property taxes ($19.3 million) and general state aid ($15 million). Miscellaneous and investment earnings accounted for $617,900 of funding.

- The composition of governmental revenues by source is illustrated in the Chart 1 below.

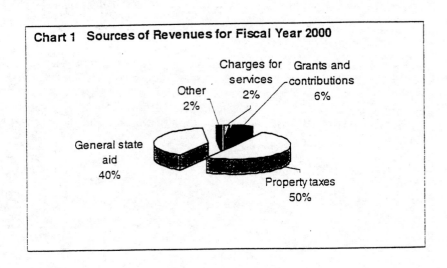

Chart 1   Sources of Revenues for Fiscal Year 2000

Exhibit 3-1 continued

School District of Kettle Moraine
Management's Discussion and Analysis
For the Year Ended June 30, 2000

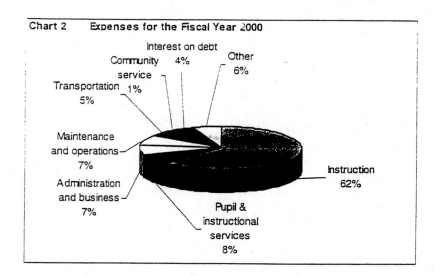

Chart 2   Expenses for the Fiscal Year 2000

Interest on debt 4%
Community service 1%
Transportation 5%
Other 6%
Maintenance and operations 7%
Administration and business 7%
Instruction 62%
Pupil & instructional services 8%

Business-Type Activities

Revenues for the district's business-type activities (food service program) were comprised of charges for services, federal and state reimbursements and investment earnings (See Table 2).

- Food services revenues exceeded expenses by $81,100. Kettle Moraine raised school lunch prices 5 percent across the board in mid-year with the intent of building resources for anticipated higher expenses in future years.

- Charges for services represent $1,085,000 of revenue. This represents amounts paid by patrons for daily food service.

- Federal and state reimbursement for meals, including payments for free and reduced lunches, was $172,100.

- During the year the district purchased nearly $102,000 of new equipment and furniture.

Governmental Funds

The strong financial performance of the district is also reflected in its governmental funds. The district completed the year with a total governmental fund balance of $4,222,920, $187,533 over last year's ending fund balance of $4,035,387.

- The general fund had an increase in fund balance of $460,000. This was due to a one-time transfer of excess fund balance from the debt service fund of $339,000 and revenues for medical assistance payments that were $120,000 greater than anticipated.

- The debt service fund had a decrease of $235,000 as a result of the transfer to the general fund. The fund balance of the debt service fund will fluctuate each year because the fund balance must be at least equal to the amount of debt service payments scheduled prior to the following January 20. Normally the district only makes interest payments prior to January 20 with an additional interest and principal payment occurring in March of each year.

- Non-major funds reported a decrease in fund balance of $39,000. The community service fund decreased $32,000 due to changes in staffing for the year and the TEACH fund decreased $7,000. The TEACH fund is reserved for technology purchases for which the district receives

Exhibit 3-1 continued

School District of Kettle Moraine
Management's Discussion and Analysis
For the Year Ended June 30, 2000

money each year from the state. To assure these funds are expended properly the district will withhold spending these funds until sufficient instructional goals are submitted and approved.

As mentioned, the food service program (business-type activity) also did well financially.

- Participation in the program increased from 71% to 73% during the year.

- A mid-year price increase allowed the program to continue to build reserves for equipment replacement in kitchens and cafeterias and to absorb anticipated increases in the cost of operation. The district has begun a policy to charge the food service program for all costs of operation. This will result in charges in future years for utilities, trash removal, custodial and maintenance services, and cafeteria supervision.

- The equipment used by food services is old and, in some cases, obsolete. The district purchased $82,000 of new equipment in the 1998-1999 school year and another $102,000 in 1999-2000. Most kitchen equipment is now up-to-date. In future years the district will begin to replace cafeteria furniture.

General Fund Budgetary Highlights

The district adopts an interim budget in May for the subsequent year. Consistent with current state statutes and regulations an *original* budget is adopted in October following determination of official enrollment and certification of general state aids. Generally the original budget is rarely modified. The district modified its original budget in 1999-2000 to reflect:

- Extraordinary personnel changes resulting from an unusually high number of employees seeking long-term disability.

- Modification in federal grants.

While the district's final budget for the general fund anticipated that revenues and expenditures would be roughly equal, the actual results for the year show a $460,000 surplus, as explained above.

CAPITAL ASSET AND DEBT ADMINISTRATION

Capital Assets

By the end of fiscal year 2000, the district had invested over $42 million in a broad range of capital assets, including buildings, sites, library books, and equipment. (See Table 4.) This amount represents a net increase of $647,000 in governmental activities from last year. (More detailed information about capital assets can be found in Note 4-D to the financial statements.) Total accumulated depreciation on these assets exceeded $13.3 million for governmental activities and $148,000 for business-type activities.

- Asset acquisitions for governmental activities totaled $724,560 and $101,979 for the food service program.

- The district disposed of $77,368 of assets for governmental activities during the year.

- The district recognized depreciation expense of $1.3 million dollars for governmental activities and $23,000 for the food service program.

Exhibit 3-1 continued
School District of Kettle Moraine
Management's Discussion and Analysis
For the Year Ended June 30, 2000

	Governmental Activities		Business-type Activities		Total School District		Total % Change
Table 4 Capital Assets (net of depreciation, in thousands of dollars)	1999	2000	1999	2000	1999	2000	1999-2000
Land	$ 1,389.4	$ 1,389.4	-	-	$ 1,389.4	$ 1,389.4	0.0%
Site improvements	76.2	89.4	-	-	$ 76.2	$ 89.4	17.3%
Buildings & building improvements	35,449.8	35,630.6	-	-	$ 35,449.8	$ 35,630.6	0.5%
Equipment & furniture	4,605.0	5,058.3	$ 473.9	$ 575.8	$ 5,078.8	$ 5,634.1	10.9%
Accumulated depreciation	(12,089.9)	(13,322.6)	$ (125.6)	$ (148.3)	$ (12,215.5)	$ (13,470.8)	10.3%
Total	$ 29,430.5	$ 28,845.0	$ 348.3	$ 427.6	$ 29,778.8	$ 29,272.6	-1.7%

Note: totals may not add due to rounding.

Long-Term Debt

At year-end the district had $21.6 million in general obligation bonds and other long-term debt outstanding—a reduction of 8.6% from last year (see Table 5). (More detailed information about the District's long-term liabilities is presented in Note 5-B to the financial statements).

Table 5 Outstanding Long-Term Obligations (in thousands of dollars)	Total School District		Total Percentage Change
	1999	2000	1999-2000
General obligation debt	$ 21,911.4	$ 20,000.4	-8.7%
Other	1,695.3	1,587.2	-6.4%
Total	$ 23,606.7	$ 21,587.6	-8.6%

- The district retired $1.6 million of outstanding bonds and notes related to capital projects and $280,000 of debt for refinancing the prior service obligation.
- The district reduced its capital lease obligations by $9,700 during the year.

Debt of the district is secured by an irrepealable tax levy adopted by the School Board at the time of issuance. Wisconsin state statutes require that the first property tax receipts be segregated for use for annual debt service payments. Kettle Moraine complies with all statutory requirements.

Exhibit 3-1 concluded

School District of Kettle Moraine
Management's Discussion and Analysis
For the Year Ended June 30, 2000

FACTORS BEARING ON THE DISTRICT'S FUTURE

Currently known circumstances that will impact the districts financial status in the future are:

- The existing labor agreement for teachers expires June 30, 2001. The agreement provides for 3.8% increase in total compensation for the 2000-2001 school year. This will increase expenses $781,000.

- The State of Wisconsin has an open enrollment law that allows students to attend the school district of their choice with few restrictions. The state adjusts each district's general state aid payment based on the number of students who transfer. Kettle Moraine expects to have a net gain of 15 to 20 students that will provide an additional $70,500 to $94,000 of revenue in 2000-2001.

CONTACTING THE DISTRICT'S FINANCIAL MANAGEMENT

This financial report is designed to provide our citizens, taxpayers, customers, and investors and creditors with a general overview of the district's finances and to demonstrate the district's accountability for the money it receives. If you have questions about this report or need additional financial information, contact Susan Graham, Accountant, School District of Kettle Moraine, 563 A. J. Allen Circle, Wales, WI 53183-0901.

Government-wide Financial Statements

Exhibit 3-2

SCHOOL DISTRICT of KETTLE MORAINE
Statement of Net Assets
As of June 30, 2000

	Governmental Activities	Business-type Activities	Total
Assets			
Current assets:			
Cash and investments	$ 5,079,038	$ 75	$ 5,079,113
Receivables:			
Taxes	4,486,753		4,486,753
Accounts	75,132		75,132
Due from other funds		418,762	418,762
Due from other governments	611,195	3,258	614,453
Inventories and prepaid items	201,700	67,363	269,063
Total current assets	10,453,818	489,458	10,943,276
Noncurrent assets:			
Land	1,389,423		1,389,423
Site improvements	89,352		89,352
Buildings and building improvements	35,630,564		35,630,564
Furniture and equipment	5,058,271	575,841	5,634,112
Less: Accumulated depreciation	(13,322,566)	(148,269)	(13,470,835)
Total noncurrent assets	28,845,044	427,572	29,272,616
Total assets	39,298,862	917,030	40,215,892
Liabilities			
Current liabilities:			
Accounts payable	840,405		840,405
Short-term notes payable	4,400,000		4,400,000
Accrued Liabilities			
Payroll, payroll taxes, insurance	142,378		142,378
Claims incurred but not reported	42,993		42,993
Interest	481,011		481,011
Deferred revenue	16,684	64,753	81,437
Due to other funds	651,855		651,855
Current portion of long-term obligations	2,306,969		2,306,969
Total current liabilities	8,882,295	64,753	8,947,048
Noncurrent liabilities:			
Noncurrent portion of long-term obligations	19,280,588		19,280,588
Total non-current liabilities	19,280,588	-	19,280,588
Total liabilities	28,162,883	64,753	28,227,636
Net Assets			
Invested in capital assets, net of related debt	11,074,637	427,572	11,502,209
Restricted for:			
Debt service	953,053		953,053
Other activities		424,705	424,705
Unrestricted (deficit)	(891,711)		(891,711)
Total net assets	11,135,979	852,277	11,988,256
Total liabilities and net assets	$ 39,298,862	$ 917,030	$ 40,215,892

See accompanying notes to the basic financial statements.

36

Exhibit 3-3

SCHOOL DISTRICT of KETTLE MORAINE
Statement of Activities
For the Year ended June 30, 2000

| Functions/Programs | Expenses | Program Revenues | | Net (Expense) Revenue and Changes in Net Assets | | |
		Charges for Services	Operating Grants and Contributions	Government Activities	Business-Type Activities	Total
Governmental activities:						
Instruction:						
Regular instruction	$ 16,187,490	$ 169,732	$ 316,505	$ (15,701,253)		$ (15,701,253)
Vocational instruction	917,921	9,459	11,567	(896,895)		(896,895)
Special education instruction	3,341,643	2,720	1,389,907	(1,949,017)		(1,949,017)
Other instruction	1,794,553	166,228	28,500	(1,599,825)		(1,599,825)
Total Instruction	22,241,607	348,139	1,746,479	(20,146,989)		(20,146,989)
Support services:						
Pupil services	1,659,890		186,619	(1,473,271)		(1,473,271)
Instructional staff services	1,307,109		205,117	(1,101,992)		(1,101,992)
General administration services	355,566			(355,566)		(355,566)
School administration services	1,720,040			(1,720,040)		(1,720,040)
Business services	521,216			(521,216)		(521,216)
Operations & maintenance of plant	2,674,592	40,744	5,071	(2,628,777)		(2,628,777)
Pupil transportation services	1,787,111		180,628	(1,606,483)		(1,606,483)
Central services	1,136,690		1,337	(1,135,353)		(1,135,353)
Insurance	131,512			(131,512)		(131,512)
Other support services	6,943			(6,943)		(6,943)
Community services	344,199	192,133		(152,066)		(152,066)
Interest on debt	1,402,934			(1,402,934)		(1,402,934)
Depreciation - unallocated*	833,022			(833,022)		(833,022)
Total Support Services	13,880,824	232,877	578,771	(13,069,176)		(13,069,176)
Total governmental activities	36,122,431	581,016	2,325,250	(33,216,165)		(33,216,165)
Business-type activities:						
School food service program	1,194,142	1,084,966	172,117		62,941	62,941
Total school district	$ 37,316,573	$ 1,665,982	$ 2,497,367	(33,216,165)	62,941	(33,153,224)

	Government Activities	Business-Type Activities	Total
General revenues:			
Property taxes:			
General purposes	15,955,654		15,955,654
Debt services	3,199,812		3,199,812
Community services	125,960		125,960
State and federal aids not restricted to specific functions:			
General	14,967,776		14,967,776
Other	162,883		162,883
Interest and investment earnings	314,245	18,137	332,382
Miscellaneous	140,790		140,790
Total general revenues	34,867,120	18,137	34,885,257
Change in net assets	1,650,955	81,078	1,732,033
Net assets - beginning of year	9,485,024	771,199	10,256,223
Net assets - end of year	$ 11,135,979	$ 852,277	$ 11,988,256

*This amount excludes the depreciation that is included in the direct expenses of the various functions. See Note 4-D.

See accompanying notes to the basic financial statements.

Fund Financial Statements

Exhibit 3-4

SCHOOL DISTRICT of KETTLE MORAINE
Balance Sheet
Governmental Funds
As of June 30, 2000

	General Fund	Special Education Fund	Debt Service Fund	Other Gov't Funds	Total Gov't Funds
Assets					
Cash and investments	$ 4,984,301		$ 94,712	$ 25	$ 5,079,038
Receivables:					
Taxes	4,486,753				4,486,753
Accounts	75,132				75,132
Due from other funds			858,341	221,780	1,080,121
Due from other governments	487,575	123,620			611,195
Inventories and prepaid items	200,873			827	201,700
Total assets	10,234,634	123,620	953,053	222,632	11,533,939
Liabilities and Fund Balances					
Liabilities:					
Short-term notes payable	4,400,000				4,400,000
Accounts payable	840,405				840,405
Accrued Liabilities					
Payroll, payroll taxes, insurance	138,586	1,458		2,334	142,378
Claims incurred but not reported	42,993				42,993
Interest	136,584				136,584
Deferred revenue	3,202			13,482	16,684
Due to other funds	1,609,814	122,162			1,731,976
Total liabilities	7,171,584	123,620	-	15,816	7,311,020
Fund Balances:					
Reserved for:					
Inventories and prepaids	200,873			827	201,700
Special revenue funds				205,989	205,989
Debt Service			953,053		953,053
Unreserved:					
Designated	2,862,178				2,862,178
Total fund balances	3,063,051	-	953,053	206,816	4,222,920
Total liabilities and fund balances	$ 10,234,635	$ 123,620	$ 953,053	$ 222,632	

Total net assets reported for governmental activities in the statement of net assets are different from the amount reported above as total governmental funds fund balance because:

Capital assets used in government activities are not financial resources and therefore are not reported in the fund statements. Amounts reported for governmental activities in the statement of net assets:

Governmental capital asset	42,167,610	
Governmental accumulated depreciation	(13,322,566)	28,845,044

Long term liabilities, including bonds and notes payable, are not due in the current period and therefore are not reported in the fund statements. Long-term liabilities reported in the statement of net assets that are not reported in the funds balance sheet are:

General obligation debt	(20,000,407)	
Accrued interest on general obligation debt	(344,428)	
Vested employee benefits	(1,587,150)	(21,931,985)

Total net assets - governmental activities $11,135,979

Exhibit 3-5

SCHOOL DISTRICT of KETTLE MORAINE
Statement of Revenues, Expenditures and Changes in Fund Balances
Governmental Funds
For the Year Ended June 30, 2000

	General Fund	Special Education Fund	Debt Service Fund	Other Gov't Funds	Total Gov't Funds
Revenues:					
Property taxes	$ 15,955,654 *		$ 3,199,812	$ 125,960	$ 19,281,426
Other local sources	680,453		42,216	192,133	914,802
Intermediate sources	111,673	71,979			183,652
State sources	15,198,825	1,143,339		117,265	16,459,429
Federal sources	405,305	362,118			767,423
Other sources	166,654				166,654
Total revenues	32,518,564	1,577,436	3,242,028	435,358	37,773,386
Expenditures:					
Instruction:					
Regular instruction	15,862,296	3,461		107,226	15,972,983
Vocational instruction	884,033	3,135			887,168
Special instruction	254,157	3,104,763			3,358,920
Other instruction	1,805,039				1,805,039
Total instruction	18,805,525	3,111,359	-	107,226	22,024,110
Support Services:					
Pupil services	1,074,171	601,804			1,675,975
Instructional staff services	1,110,784	148,142		16,742	1,275,668
General administration services	355,566				355,566
Building administration services	1,655,794				1,655,794
Business services	519,262				519,262
Operations and maintenance	2,834,249	8,877		1,089	2,844,215
Pupil transportation	1,488,604	291,794			1,780,398
Central services	1,084,694	1,527			1,086,221
Insurance	131,512				131,512
Community service				348,698	348,698
Principal and interest	191,121		3,152,542		3,343,663
Other support services	543,536		1,235		544,771
Total support services	10,989,293	1,052,144	3,153,777	366,529	15,561,743
Total expenditures	29,794,818	4,163,503	3,153,777	473,755	37,585,853
Excess (deficiency) of revenues over expenditures	2,723,746	(2,586,067)	88,251	(38,397)	187,533
Other Financing Sources (Uses):					
Transfer to special education fund	(2,586,067)	2,586,067			
Transfer to debt service fund	(16,035)		16,035		
Transfer (from) debt service fund	339,280		(339,280)		-
Net Change in Fund Balances	460,924	-	(234,994)	(38,397)	187,533
Fund balances - beginning of year	2,602,127	-	1,188,047	245,213	4,035,387
Fund balances - end of year	$ 3,063,051	$ -	$ 953,053	$ 206,816	$ 4,222,920

See accompanying notes to the basic financial statements.

Exhibit 3-6

SCHOOL DISTRICT of KETTLE MORAINE
Reconciliation of Statement of Revenues, Expenditures and Changes in Fund Balance
of Governmental Funds to the Statement of Activities
For the Year Ended June 30, 2000

Net change in fund balances - total governmental funds $ 187,533

Amounts reported for governmental activities in the statement of activities are different because:

The acquisition of capital assets are reported in the governmental funds as expenditures. However, for governmental activities those costs are shown in the statement of net assets and allocated over their estimated useful lives as annual depreciation expenses in the statement of activities.

Capital outlay reported in governmental fund statements 724,560

Depreciation expense reported in the statement of activities (1,310,014)

Amount by which capital outlays are greater (less) than depreciation in the current period. (585,454)

Vested employee benefits are reported in the government funds when amounts are paid. The statement of activities reports the value of benefits earned during the year.

Special termination benefits paid in current year 537,828

Special termination benefits earned in current year (429,681)

Amounts paid are greater (less) than amounts paid by 108,147

Repayment of principal on long-term debt is reported in the governmental funds as an expenditure, but is reported as a reduction in long-term debt in the statement of net assets and does not affect the statement of activities.

The amount of long-term debt principal payments in the current year is: 1,910,973

In governmental funds interest payments on outstanding debt are reported as an expenditure when paid. In the statement of activities interest is reported as it accrues.

The amount of interest paid during the current period 1,251,277

The amount of interest accrued during the current period (1,221,521)

Interest paid is greater (less) than interest accrued by 29,756

Change in net assets - governmental activities $ 1,650,955

Exhibit 3-7

SCHOOL DISTRICT of KETTLE MORAINE
Statements of Net Assets
Proprietary Funds
As of June 30, 2000 and 1999

	Food Service Fund	
	2,000	1999
Assets		
Current Assets:		
Cash and investments	$ 75	$ 75
Due from other funds	418,762	403,634
Due from other governments	3,258	14,548
Inventories and prepaid items	67,363	63,398
Total current assets	**489,458**	**481,655**
Non-current Assets:		
Furniture and equipment	575,841	473,862
Less accumulated depreciation	(148,269)	(125,586)
Total non-current assets	**427,572**	**348,276**
Total assets	**917,030**	**829,931**
Liabilities		
Current Liabilities:		
Deferred revenue	64,753	58,733
Total liabilities	**64,753**	**58,733**
Net Assets		
Invested in capital assets, net of related debt	427,572	348,276
Restricted for food service	424,705	422,922
Total net assets	**852,277**	**771,198**
Total liabilities and net assets	**$ 917,030**	**$ 829,931**

Exhibit 3-8

SCHOOL DISTRICT OF KETTLE MORAINE
Statements of Revenues, Expenses and Changes in Net Assets
Proprietary Funds
For the Years Ended June 30, 2000 and 1999

	Food Service Fund	
	2000	1999
Revenues:		
Food sales	$ 1,084,966	$ 1,006,051
State sources	17,466	16,528
Federal sources	101,102	114,583
Federal commodities	53,549	47,814
Total revenues	1,257,083	1,184,976
Operating Expenses:		
Salaries and wages	344,783	315,604
Employer paid benefits	172,492	135,790
Purchased services	17,999	33,239
Supplies, food and materials	634,611	548,009
Other	1,574	446
Depreciation	22,683	17,941
Total operating expenses	1,194,142	1,051,029
Operating gain	62,941	133,947
Non-operating revenues:		
Investment earnings	18,138	17,284
Total non-operating revenues	18,138	17,284
Change in net assets	81,079	151,231
Net Assets - beginning of year	771,199	619,968
Net Assets - end of year	$ 852,278	$ 771,199

See accompanying notes to the basic financial statements.   43

Exhibit 3-9

SCHOOL DISTRICT of KETTLE MORAINE
Statements of Cash Flows
Proprietary Funds
For the Year Ended June 30, 2000 and 1999

	Food Service Fund	
	2000	1999
Cash Flows from Operating Activities		
Cash received from user charges	$ 1,069,838	$ 937,431
Cash received from other government payments	129,858	116,563
Cash payments to employees for services	(517,275)	(451,595)
Cash payments for utilities and other purchased services	(17,999)	(33,239)
Cash payments to suppliers for goods and services	(579,008)	(503,555)
Cash payments for other operating expenses	(1,573)	(446)
Net cash provided by operating activities	83,841	65,159
Cash Flows from Capital and Related Financing Activities		
Cash payments for acquisition of capital assets	(101,979)	(82,443)
Net cash used by capital and related financing activities	(101,979)	(82,443)
Cash Flows from Investing Activities		
Interest on investments	18,138	17,284
Net cash provided by investing activities	18,138	17,284
Net increase in cash and cash equivalents	-	-
Cash and cash equivalents - beginning of year	75	75
Cash and cash equivalents - end of year	75	75
Reconciliation of operating income to net cash provided by operating activities		
Operating income	62,941	133,947
Adjustments to reconcile operating income to net cash provided by operating activities:		
Depreciation	22,683	17,941
Changes in assets and liabilities:		
due to (from) other governments	11,290	(14,548
due to (from) other funds	(15,128)	(68,620
accrued payroll		(20
inventories	(3,965)	(9,779
deferred revenue	6,020	6,419
Net cash provided by operating activities	$ 83,841	$ 65,15
Noncash Noncapital Financing Activities		
During the year the district received commodities from the US Department of Agriculture in the amount of:	$ 59,568	$ 53,75

Exhibit 3-10

Illustrative Statements of Fiduciary Net Assets
and Illustrative Statement of Changes in Fiduciary Net Assets

ASBO, International School District
Statement of Fiduciary Net Assets
As of June 30, 2002

	Private-Purpose Trust	Agency Funds
ASSETS		
Cash and cash equivalents	$ 280,087	$ 101,959
Due from other governments	—	100,242
Accrued interest	23,853	—
Due from other funds	321,026	1,272,211
Total assets	624,966	1,474,412
LIABILITIES		
Accounts payable	1,450	14,911
Due to student groups	—	1,239,739
Due to other governments	—	219,762
Total liabilities	1,450	1,474,412
NET ASSETS		
Reserved for scholarships	585,221	
Unreserved	38,295	
Total Net Assets	$ 623,516	

ASBO, International School District
Statement of Changes in Fiduciary Net Assets
For the Year Ended June 30, 2002

	Private-Purpose Trusts
ADDITIONS	
Private donations	$ 24,480
District contribution	5,000
Interest	32,487
Total additions	61,967
DEDUCTIONS	
Scholarships awarded	36,644
Change in net assets	25,323
Net Assets--Beginning	598,193
Net Assets--Ending	$ 623,516

See accompanying notes to the basic financial statements.

Exhibit 3-11

ASBO, International School District
Budgetary Comparison Schedule for the General Fund
For the Year Ended June 30, 2002

	Budgeted Amounts		Actual	Variances-- Positive (Negative)	
	Original	Final	(GAAP Basis)	Original to Final	Final to Actual
Revenues:					
Property Taxes	$ 149,617,343	$ 151,571,192	$ 153,862,367	$ 1,953,849	$ 2,291,175
Other Local Sources	8,330,157	8,318,808	8,404,240	(11,349)	85,432
Intermediate Sources	1,773,000	1,885,500	2,106,451	112,500	220,951
State Sources	189,720,000	187,073,000	188,019,530	(2,647,000)	946,530
Federal Sources	2,137,500	2,250,000	2,284,748	112,500	34,748
Other Sources	364,500	364,500	395,088	-	30,588
Total revenues	351,942,500	351,463,000	355,072,424	(479,500)	3,609,424
Expenditures:					
Instruction:					
Regular Instruction	147,577,920	147,152,460	146,067,673	425,460	1,084,787
Special Instruction	34,288,430	34,189,580	33,937,539	98,850	252,041
Other Instruction	27,231,945	27,153,438	26,953,263	78,507	200,175
Total Instruction	209,098,295	208,495,478	206,958,475	602,817	1,537,003
Support Services:					
Pupil Services	34,413,082	34,694,864	34,010,001	(281,782)	684,863
Instructional Staff Services	12,185,382	12,411,520	12,579,165	(226,138)	(167,645)
General Administration Services	10,252,023	9,627,845	9,290,149	624,178	337,696
Building Administration Services	18,314,271	18,654,150	18,906,114	(339,879)	(251,964)
Business Services	6,442,400	6,442,400	6,047,066	-	395,334
Operations & Maintenance	35,078,360	35,432,695	33,258,353	(354,335)	2,174,342
Pupil Transportation	17,138,286	17,376,467	16,310,144	(238,181)	1,066,323
Central Services	1,725,361	1,721,536	1,691,107	3,825	30,429
Principal and Interest	1,531,812	1,531,812	1,538,918	-	(7,106)
Other Support Services	5,059,000	5,059,000	922,537	-	4,136,463
Total Support Services	142,139,977	142,952,289	134,553,554	(812,312.00)	8,398,735
Total expenditures	351,238,272	351,447,767	341,512,029	(209,495)	9,935,738
Excess (deficiency) of revenues over expend	704,228	15,233	13,560,395	(688,995)	13,545,162
SPECIAL ITEM					
Proceeds from sale of unimproved land	2,610,000	2,610,000	2,601,908	—	(8,092)
Net change in fund balances	3,314,228	2,625,233	16,162,303	(688,995)	13,537,070
Fund balance--Beginning	54,938,434	54,938,434	54,938,434	—	—
Fund balance--Ending	$ 58,252,662	$ 57,563,667	$ 71,100,737	$ (688,995)	$ 13,537,070

Exhibit 3-12

Illustrative Budgetary Comparison Reconciliation

Note A—Explanation of Differences between Budgetary Inflows and Outflows and GAAP Revenues and Expenditures for ASBO, International School District

	General Fund	Special Revenue Fund
Sources/inflows of resources		
Actual amounts (budgetary basis) "available for appropriation" from the budgetary comparison schedule	$92,370,775	$ 4,349,914
Differences—budget to GAAP:		
The fund balance at the beginning of the year is a budgetary resource but is not a current-year revenue for financial reporting purposes.	(2,742,799)	(1,618,441)
revenues for financial reporting purposes.	(129,323)	—
The proceeds from the sale of the park land are budgetary resources but are regarded as a *special item,* rather than revenue, for financial reporting purposes.	(3,476,488)	—
changes in fund balances—governmental funds.	$86,022,165	$ 2,731,473
Uses/outflows of resources		
Actual amounts (budgetary basis) "total charges to appropriations" from the budgetary comparison schedule.	$90,938,522	$ 3,314,572
Differences—budget to GAAP:		
Encumbrances for supplies and equipment ordered but not received is reported in the year the order is placed for *budgetary* purposes, but in the year the supplies are received for *financial reporting* purposes.	(186,690)	(16,037)
expenditures for financial reporting purposes.	(2,034,659)	(344,146)
Total expenditures as reported on the statement of revenues, expenditures, and changes in fund balances—governmental funds.	$88,717,173	$ 2,954,389

Exhibit 3-13

SCHOOL DISTRICT of KETTLE MORAINE
Combining Balance Sheet
Nonmajor Governmental Funds
As of June 30, 2000

	Special Revenue Funds		Total Non-Major Gov't Funds
	TEACH Fund	Community Service Fund	
Assets			
Cash and investments		$ 25	$ 25
Due from other funds	129,566	92,214	221,780
Inventories and prepaid items		827	827
Total assets	**129,566**	**93,066**	**222,632**
Liabilities and Fund Balances			
Liabilities:			
Payroll and payroll taxes		2,334	2,334
Deferred revenue		13,482	13,482
Total liabilities	**-**	**15,816**	**15,816**
Fund Balances:			
Reserved for:			
Inventories and prepaids		827	827
Special revenue funds	129,566	76,423	205,989
Total fund balances	**129,566**	**77,250**	**206,816**
Total liabilities and fund balances	**$ 129,566**	**$ 93,066**	**$ 222,632**

Exhibit 3-14

SCHOOL DISTRICT of KETTLE MORAINE
Combining Statement of Revenues, Expenditures and Changes in Fund Balances
Nonmajor Governmental Funds
For the Year Ended June 30, 2000

	Special Revenue Funds		
	TEACH Fund	Community Service Fund	Total Gov't Funds
Revenues:			
Property taxes		$ 125,960	$ 125,960
Other local sources		192,133	192,133
State sources	117,265		117,265
Total revenues	117,265	318,093	435,358
Expenditures:			
Instruction:			
Regular instruction	107,226		107,226
Total Instruction	107,226	-	107,226
Support Services:			
Instructional staff services	16,742		16,742
Operations and maintenance		1,089	1,089
Community services		348,698	348,698
Total support services	16,742	349,787	366,529
Total expenditures	123,968	349,787	473,755
Net Change in Fund Balances	(6,703)	(31,694)	(38,397)
Fund balances - beginning of year	136,269	108,944	245,213
Fund balances - end of year	$ 129,566	$ 77,250	$ 206,816

Exhibit 3-15

SCHOOL DISTRICT of KETTLE MORAINE
Comparative Statements of Revenues, Expenditures and Changes in Fund Balance
General Fund
For the Years Ended June 30, 2000 and 1999

	2000			1999		
	FINAL BUDGET	ACTUAL	VARIANCE FAVORABLE (UNFAVORABLE)	FINAL BUDGET	ACTUAL	VARIANCE FAVORABLE (UNFAVORABLE)
Revenues:						
Property taxes	$ 15,955,654	$ 15,955,654		$ 15,891,110	$ 15,892,313	$ 1,203
Other local sources	736,527	680,453	(56,074)	683,013	717,590	34,577
Intermediate sources	140,670	111,673	(28,997)	73,387	61,730	(11,657)
State sources	15,128,966	15,198,825	69,859	13,694,402	13,703,926	9,524
Federal sources	397,503	405,305	7,802	389,724	339,754	(49,970)
Other sources	163,102	166,654	3,552	101,364	300,320	198,956
Total revenues	32,522,422	32,518,564	(3,858)	30,833,000	31,015,633	182,633
Expenditures:						
Instruction:						
Regular instruction	15,889,526	15,862,296	27,230	14,801,470	14,880,609	(79,139)
Vocational instruction	871,448	884,033	(12,585)	860,522	866,793	(6,271)
Special instruction	247,989	254,157	(6,168)	227,219	227,390	(171)
Other instruction	1,692,506	1,805,039	(112,533)	1,719,744	1,734,801	(15,057)
Total instruction	18,701,469	18,805,525	(104,056)	17,608,955	17,709,593	(100,638)
Support Services:						
Pupil services	1,167,252	1,074,171	93,081	1,070,090	1,102,688	(32,598)
Instructional staff services	1,062,824	1,110,784	(47,960)	1,059,757	1,103,669	(43,912)
General administration services	318,397	355,566	(37,169)	306,393	380,280	(73,887)
Building administration services	1,664,735	1,655,794	8,941	1,601,562	1,662,040	(60,478)
Business services	685,601	519,262	166,339	628,527	638,136	(9,609)
Operations and maintenance	3,102,104	2,834,249	267,855	3,004,101	3,012,905	(8,804)
Pupil transportation	1,439,408	1,488,604	(49,196)	1,395,358	1,362,779	32,579
Central services	1,092,212	1,084,694	7,518	958,675	957,321	1,354
Insurance	142,223	131,512	10,711	159,032	138,438	20,594
Principal and interest	203,435	191,121	12,314	222,847	206,547	16,300
Other support services	659,407	543,536	115,871	490,360	618,108	(127,748)
Total support services	11,537,598	10,989,293	548,305	10,896,702	11,182,911	(286,209)
Total expenditures	30,239,067	29,794,818	444,249	28,505,657	28,892,504	(386,847)
Excess (deficiency) of revenues over expenditures	2,283,355	2,723,746	440,391	2,327,343	2,123,129	(204,214)
Other Financing Sources (Uses):						
Transfer to special education fund	(2,606,600)	(2,586,067)	20,533	(2,311,308)	(2,398,647)	(87,339)
Transfer to debt service fund	(16,035)	(16,035)		(16,035)	(16,035)	
Transfer (from) debt service fund	339,280	339,280				
Proceeds from capital leases					60,723	60,723
Net Change in Fund Balance		460,924	460,924		(230,830)	(230,830)
Fund balance - beginning of year	2,602,127	2,602,127		2,832,957	2,832,957	
Fund balance - end of year	$ 2,602,127	$ 3,063,051	$ 460,924	$ 2,832,957	$ 2,602,127	$ (230,830)

Chapter Four

STATISTICAL SECTION

The last section of a school CAFR is the Statistical Section, which presents comparative data for several periods of time, most often ten years. This section may contain data from sources other than the accounting records. These sources should be indicated on each schedule. The use of graphs is beneficial to readers of this section. At a minimum, the COE Program criteria requires the following information in this section of the CAFR:

The Statistical Tables should include the following:

a. Government-wide Expenses by Function – Last 10 Fiscal Years (Exhibit 4-1)
b. Government-wide Revenues – Last 10 Fiscal Years (Exhibit 4-2)
c. General School System Expenditures by Function-Last 10 Fiscal Years *
d. General School System Revenues by Source-Last 10 Fiscal Years *
e. Property Tax Levies and Collections-Last 10 Fiscal Years
f. Assessed and Estimated Actual Value of Taxable Property-Last 10 Fiscal Years *
g. Property Tax Rates-All Direct and Overlapping Governments-Last 10 Fiscal Years *
h. Special Assessment Billings and Collections - Last 10 Fiscal Years (if any)
i. Ratio of Net General Bonded Debt to Assessed Value and Net Bonded Debt per Capita-Last 10 Fiscal Years *
j. Computation of Legal Debt Margin *
k. Computation of Direct and Overlapping Debt *
l. Ratio of Annual Debt Service Expenditures for General Bonded Debt to Total General Expenditures-Last 10 Fiscal Years *
m. Revenue Bond Coverage-Last 10 Fiscal Years (if any)
n. Demographic Statistics-Last 10 Fiscal Years *
o. Property Value, Construction, and Bank Deposits-Last 10 Fiscal Years *
p. Principal Taxpayers *
q. Miscellaneous Statistics *

Special Assessment Billings and Collections and Revenue Bond Coverage are not tables commonly found in school system's CAFRs. However, if these tables are applicable to the school system, they must be included.

If there is a valid reason for a *no answer* for some of these tables, N/A should be checked and an explanation provided in the Comments/Explanation column of the self-evaluation worksheet. In addition to the tables listed above, other information can be presented in the Statistical Section of a school system's CAFR. For example:

Annual Average FTE Student Enrollment	Exhibit 4-3
Interest Earnings on Investments	Exhibit 4-4
Food Service Operations	Exhibit 4-5
Land Use Assessments by Municipalities	Exhibit 4-6
Operational Expenditures By Pupil	Exhibit 4-7
Per Pupil Expenditure Ranking	Exhibit 4-8
Cost to Educate a 1997 Graduate	Exhibit 4-9
Property Taxes, Levies and Collections	Exhibit 4-10
Enrollment/Attendance	Exhibit 4-11
Sources of Child Nutrition Revenues and Reimbursements	Exhibit 4-12
Where Each Education Dollar Goes	Exhibit 4-13
Schedule of Insurance and Surety Bonds in Force	Exhibit 4-14

See CAFRs in Appendices B and C for examples

Exhibit 4-1

Table 1

GRANT PARISH SCHOOL BOARD
Colfax, Louisiana

Government-wide Expenses by Function
Fiscal Year Ended June 30, 2000

	2000
Governmental activities:	
Instruction:	
Regular programs	$ 7,106,182
Special programs	2,952,342
Other instructional programs	1,155,608
Support services:	
Student services	654,172
Instructional staff support	1,176,299
General administration	434,169
School administration	1,309,118
Business services	239,348
Plant services	1,639,088
Student transportation services	1,888,419
Central services	1,261
Food services	1,778,991
Community service programs	2,021
Interest on long-term debt	123,034
Total governmental activities	$ 20,460,052

Note: The above information is available only for the current year.
However, as additional years' information becomes available,
it will be added.

Table 2

Exhibit 4-2

GRANT PARISH SCHOOL BOARD
Colfax, Louisiana

Government-wide Revenues
Fiscal Year Ended June 30, 2000

	2000
Program revenues:	
Charges for services	$ 262,454
Operating grants and contributions	2,573,551
Capital grants and contributions	142,450
General revenues:	
Taxes	2,502,874
Grants and contributions not restricted	
to specific programs	14,450,467
Unrestricted investment earnings	184,561
Miscellaneous	224,099
Total governmental revenues	$ 20,340,456

Note: The above information is available only for the current year.
However, as additional years' information becomes available,
it will be added.

Exhibit 4-3 Annual Average FTE Student Enrollment

VANCOUVER PUBLIC SCHOOLS
ANNUAL AVERAGE FTE STUDENT ENROLLMENT
LAST TEN FISCAL YEARS
(Unaudited)

YEAR	K	1st - 3rd	4th - 5th	6th - 8th	9th - 12th	TOTAL DISTRICT ENROLLMENT	TOTAL STATE ENROLLMENT	DISTRICT'S % OF STATE ENROLLMENT
1987/88	629	3,721	2,248	3,504	4,383	14,485	733,850	1.97%
1988/89	636	3,843	2,304	3,626	4,149	14,558	748,420	1.95%
1989/90	646	4,063	2,567	3,449	4,240	14,965	768,356	1.95%
1990/91	678	4,144	2,636	3,692	4,334	15,484	795,404	1.95%
1991/92	712	4,260	2,769	3,858	4,551	16,150	823,040	1.96%
1992/93	721	4,539	2,945	4,105	4,762	17,072	849,759	2.01%
1993/94	771	4,637	2,917	4,258	4,896	17,479	868,298	2.01%
1994/95	785	4,740	3,002	4,324	5,149	18,000	885,609	2.03%
1995/96	825	4,843	3,169	4,449	5,230	18,516	904,289	2.05%
1996/97	847	5,094	3,195	4,690	5,479	19,305	923,271	2.09%

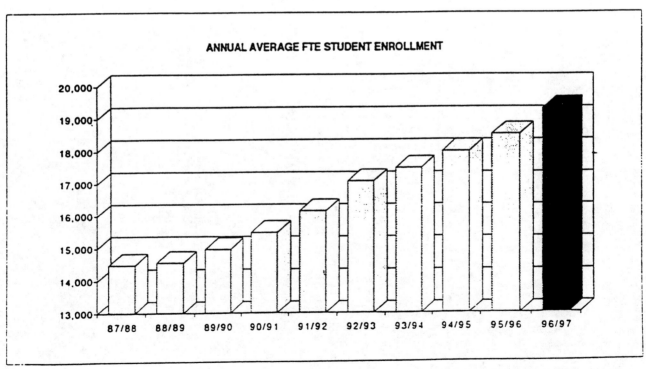

ANNUAL AVERAGE FTE STUDENT ENROLLMENT

Exhibit 4-4 Interest Earnings on Investments

VANCOUVER PUBLIC SCHOOLS
INTEREST EARNINGS ON INVESTMENTS
LAST TEN FISCAL YEARS
(Unaudited)

YEAR	GENERAL FUND	ASB PROGRAM FUND	DEBT SERVICE FUND	CAPITAL PROJECTS FUND	TRANSP. VEHICLE FUND	TOTAL
1987/88	$338,306	$22,251	$31,875	$176,024	$69,332	$637,788
1988/89	318,795	30,629	43,598	183,338	79,237	655,597
1989/90	340,156	29,667	42,205	136,322	92,643	640,993
1990/91	351,148	25,232	61,525	1,572,457	107,366	2,117,728
1991/92	372,068	22,778	69,436	1,347,011	109,311	1,920,604
1992/93	460,783	23,204	69,832	1,042,282	134,479	1,730,580
1993/94	291,106	24,260	94,903	1,095,190	93,624	1,599,083
1994/95	287,955	29,076	108,111	2,619,198	114,106	3,158,446
1995/96	306,461	33,259	110,274	6,137,678	131,041	6,718,713
1996/97	392,196	39,553	131,224	4,792,768	134,607	5,490,348

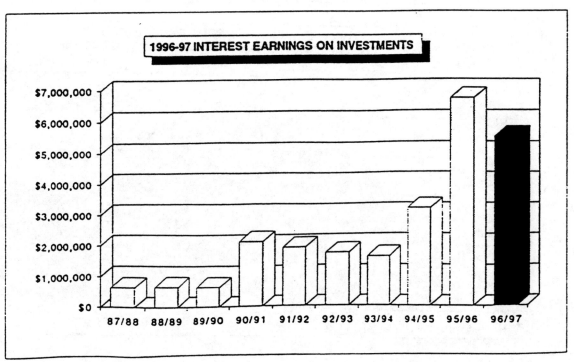

1996-97 INTEREST EARNINGS ON INVESTMENTS

55

Exhibit 4-5 Food Service Operations

VANCOUVER PUBLIC SCHOOLS
FOOD SERVICE OPERATIONS
LAST FIVE FISCAL YEARS
(Unaudited)

	1992-93	1993-94	1994-95	1995-96	1996-97
REVENUES					
STATE	$82,949	$123,692	$142,436	$138,094	$132,318
FEDERAL	1,897,553	2,077,795	2,212,182	2,351,213	2,503,789
LOCAL	1,473,558	1,534,192	1,513,715	1,467,121	1,717,587
INTEREST EARNINGS	0	4,205	9,377	7,222	5,969
TOTAL REVENUE	3,454,060	3,739,884	3,877,710	3,963,650	4,359,663
EXPENDITURES					
FOOD	1,381,645	1,414,432	1,584,742	1,726,500	1,842,783
OPERATIONS	1,881,119	1,942,245	2,077,807	2,083,838	2,349,909
SUPERVISION	168,475	185,020	190,171	217,823	202,495
TOTAL EXPENDITURES	3,431,239	3,541,697	3,852,720	4,028,161	4,395,187
EXCESS (DEFICIENCY) OF REVENUES OVER EXPENDITURES	22,821	198,187	24,990	(64,511)	(35,524)
DESIGNATED BALANCE - September 1	(29,256)	(6,435)	191,752	216,742	152,231
DESIGNATED BALANCE - August 31	($6,435)	$191,752	$216,742	$152,231	$116,707

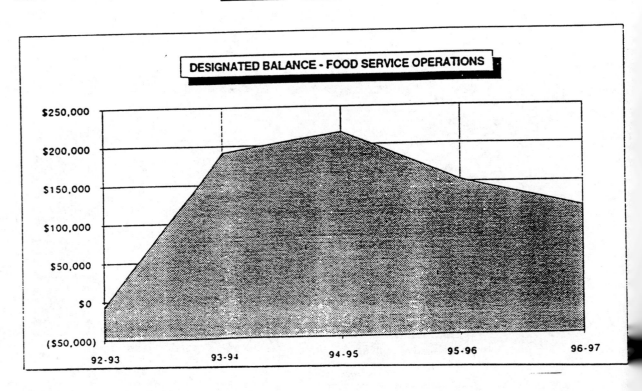

56

Exhibit 4-6 Land Use Assessments by Municipalities

Neshaminy School District

Land Use Assessments by Municipalities - Year End June 30, 1997

Distribution of Municipalities' Assessments

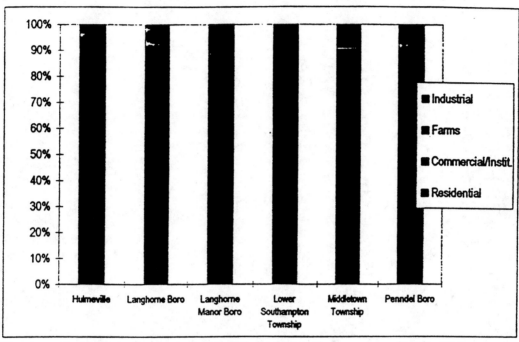

The above chart indicates how each municipality's land is used by percentage of total property.

Distribution of Land Use Classifications

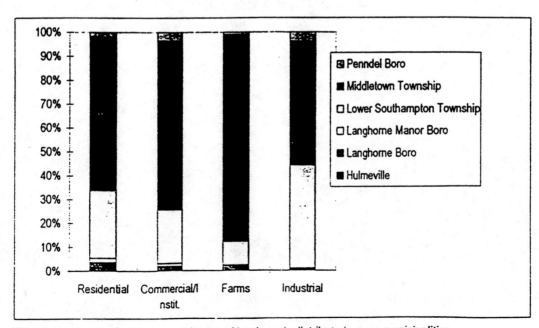

The above chart indicates how each type of land use is distributed among municipalities.

Exhibit 4-7 Operational Expenditures by Pupil

LINCOLN COUNTY BOARD OF EDUCATION
OPERATIONAL EXPENDITURES PER PUPIL
For the Last Ten Fiscal Years

Year Ended June 30	Average Daily Membership	Instructional	Pupil Support	Instructional Support	General Administration	School Administration	Business Support	Central Support	Other	Community Services	Non-Program Charges	Total
1997	9671	$ 3,038	$ 180	$ 122	$ 63	$ 218	$ 495	$ 21	$ 808	$ 10	$ 1	$ 4,957
1996	9303	2,994	163	117	55	219	438	26	1,146	10	--	5,169
1995	9015	2,922	183	114	72	218	444	25	232	5	1	4,216
1994	8875	2,735	168	111	57	207	424	20	226	7	3	3,958
1993	8836	2,847	165	89	61	219	406	20	256	6	--	3,869
1992	8639	2,445	161	95	54	221	416	15	173	5	--	3,585
1991	8573	2,513	153	98	59	216	415	13	182	6	1	3,656
1990	8577	2,364	126	92	50	213	399	15	170	6	--	3,435
1989	8635	2,177	106	88	47	198	355	8	147	5	6	3,137
1988	8690	2,045	89	73	43	167	328	--	121	2	2	2,868

NOTE:
The above operational expenditures include the General, State Public School and Federal Grant Funds.
Central Support was combined in other columns until 1989.
"Other" includes other supporting services and debt service.

Exhibit 4-7 Operational Expenditures by Pupil (continued)

LINCOLN COUNTY BOARD OF EDUCATION
OPERATIONAL EXPENDITURES PER PUPIL
For the Last Ten Fiscal Years

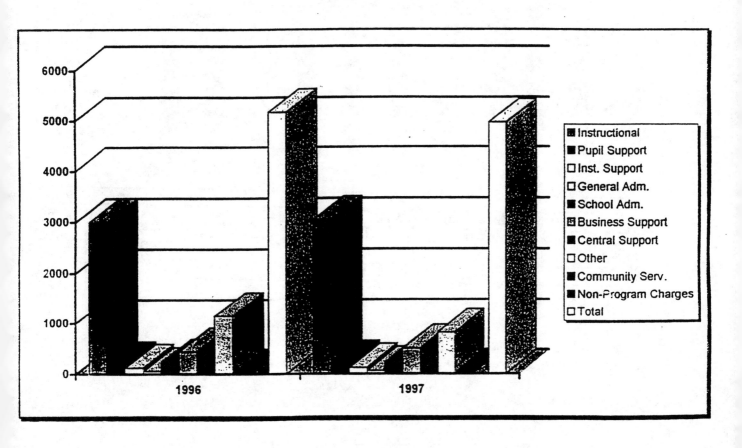

Exhibit 4-8 Per Pupil Expenditure Ranking

LINCOLN COUNTY SCHOOLS
PER PUPIL EXPENDITURE RANKING
EXCLUDES SCHOOL FOOD SERVICE EXPENDITURES
For the Last Ten Fiscal Years

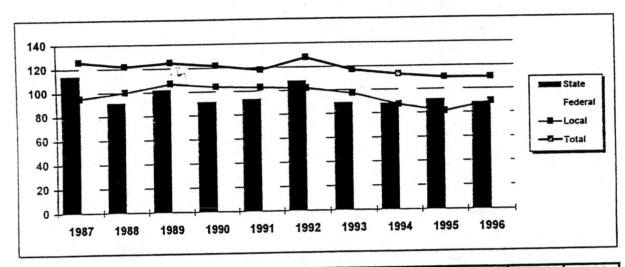

YEAR	1987	1988	1989	1990	1991	1992	1993	1994	1995	1996
State	114	91	102	91	93	108	89	88	91	88
Federal	124	121	121	114	117	114	118	108	103	90
Local	95	100	107	104	103	102	97	87	81	89
Total	126	122	125	122	118	128	117	113	110	110

NOTE:
Ranking in 1996 based on 119 school systems. Prior to 1996, the number of systems in North Carolina varied from 140 t

Source: North Carolina Public Schools Statistical Profile. Editions 1984-1997.

Exhibit 4-9 Cost to Educate a 1997 Graduate

Dublin City School District
Cost to Educate a 1997 Graduate
Dublin City Schools VS State of Ohio

School Year Ended	Grade	Dublin Annual Per Pupil Cost	State Average
1997	12	6,292	5,939
1996	11	5,984	5,284
1995	10	5,346	5,353
1994	9	5,216	5,241
1993	8	5,020	5,024
1992	7	4,625	4,473
1991	6	4,482	4,386
1990	5	4,447	4,349
1989	4	4,327	4,019
1988	3	3,729	3,622
1987	2	3,252	3,438
1986	1	2,742	3,322
1985	Kindergarten	2,658	3,080
Total Cost		$ 58,120	$ 57,530

Source :   District Financial Records
Costs per Pupil-State of Ohio Department of Education

61

Exhibit 4-10 Property Taxes Levies and Collections

RICHARDSON INDEPENDENT SCHOOL DISTRICT

PROPERTY TAX LEVIES AND COLLECTIONS
LAST TEN FISCAL YEARS (UNAUDITED)

FISCAL YEAR	TOTAL TAX LEVY	CURRENT CASH COLLECTIONS	DISCOUNT ALLOWED	TOTAL CURRENT COLLECTIONS		OTHER TAX PRIOR YEAR DELINQUENT TAXES
				TAX ROLL CREDIT	PERCENT OF CURRENT	
1989	$ 109,085,155	$ 104,902,950	$2,388,699	$ 107,291,649	98.4%	$ 3,014,856
1990	113,547,680	111,831,219	(2)	111,831,219	98.5	2,056,992
1991	121,840,885	120,114,763	(2)	120,114,763	98.6	1,631,408
1992	53,320,805(3)	52,501,349	(2)	52,501,349	98.5	1,719,816
1993	54,153,729(3)	53,423,259	(2)	53,423,259	98.7	1,040,424
1994	153,720,854	150,620,760	(2)	150,620,760	98.0	2,079,3
1995	154,943,453	153,709,031	(2)	153,709,031	99.2	1,623,84
1996	164,932,781	162,666,917	(2)	162,666,917	98.6	1,198,14
1997	177,135,692	176,243,317	(2)	176,243,317	99.5	1,805,91
1998	195,406,095	194,852,864	(2)	194,852,864	99.7	2,355,36

Notes:

(1) The District performs its own tax collection activities.

(2) The District eliminated the early payment discount option for the 1989 tax year (fiscal year 1989-1990).

(3) In 1991, a new taxing entity (County Education District) was established by the State of Texas with the stated purpose to co local property taxes and redistribute the taxes among school districts within the county. The property tax revenue amount f 1992 and 1993 includes only the tax levied by the District. Taxes levied by the County Education District are included in revenues from intermediate sources for 1992 and 1993. The legislation which created county education districts was declar unconstitutional by the Texas Supreme Court, and a new State funding method was enacted for fiscal year 1994.

Exhibit 4-11 Enrollment/Attendance

RICHARDSON INDEPENDENT SCHOOL DISTRICT

ENROLLMENT/ATTENDANCE
LAST TEN FISCAL YEARS (UNAUDITED)

FISCAL YEAR	AVERAGE DAILY ENROLLMENT	AVERAGE DAILY ATTENDANCE	PERCENTAGE
1989	31,062	29,774	95.8 %
1990	32,200	30,116	93.5
1991	32,794	30,505	93.0
1992	31,737	30,257	95.3
1993	31,774	30,634	96.4
1994	32,141	30,788	95.8
1995	32,316	30,921*	95.8
1996	32,044	30,596	95.5
1997	32,288	30,885	95.6
1998	32,406	31,075*	95.9

*Year of greatest daily attendance.

Exhibit 4-12 Sources of Child Nutrition Revenues and Reimbursements

Edgecombe County Schools
Sources of Child Nutrition Revenues and Reimbursements
For the Last Ten Fiscal Years

Year Ended June 30	Food Sales	USDA Reimbursement	Donated Commodities	Other Revenue	State Reimbursement	Total
1998	$947,774	$1,802,401	$188,397	$140,019	-	$3,078,591
1997	890,398	1,698,480	141,033	128,862	-	2,858,773
1996	903,263	1,571,893	180,829	115,503	$ 50,360	2,821,848
1995	946,600	1,569,488	186,615	89,046	125,797	2,917,546
1994	909,385	1,566,834	165,110	73,681	123,517	2,838,527
1993	726,461	1,431,677	195,353	40,960	93,007	2,487,458
1992	753,417	1,429,521	170,815	53,605	91,299	2,498,657
1991	759,990	1,306,325	173,225	81,397	N/A	2,320,937
1990	720,586	1,217,192	195,576	90,294	N/A	2,223,648
1989	744,225	1,158,342	203,916	77,463	N/A	2,183,946

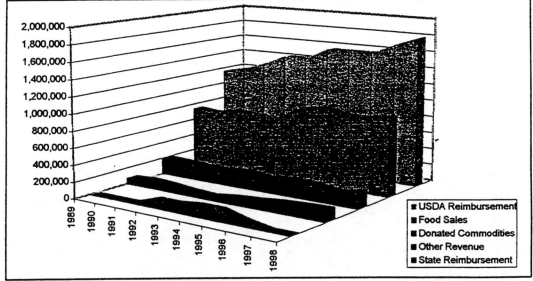

Notes:

Source: Edgecombe County Schools independent auditor.

The State reimbursements are operating transfers from the State Public School Fund.

"Other" revenues includes investment income, rentals, indirect cost not paid, and disposition of fixed assets, miscellaneous income, and State allocations restricted to Capital Outlay.

Effective July 1, 1993, Edgecombe County Schools and Tarboro City Schools merged to form Edgecombe County Schools. Fiscal years 1989-1993 have been restated for comparison.

N/A = Not available for the years 1989-1991 for State reimbursement figures.

Exhibit 4-13 Where Each Education Dollar Goes

**Board of Education
of The City of New York**

**Comprehensive Annual Financial Report
For Fiscal Year 1998**

Demographic, Financial & Other Trends (Unaudited)

Where Each Education Dollar Goes

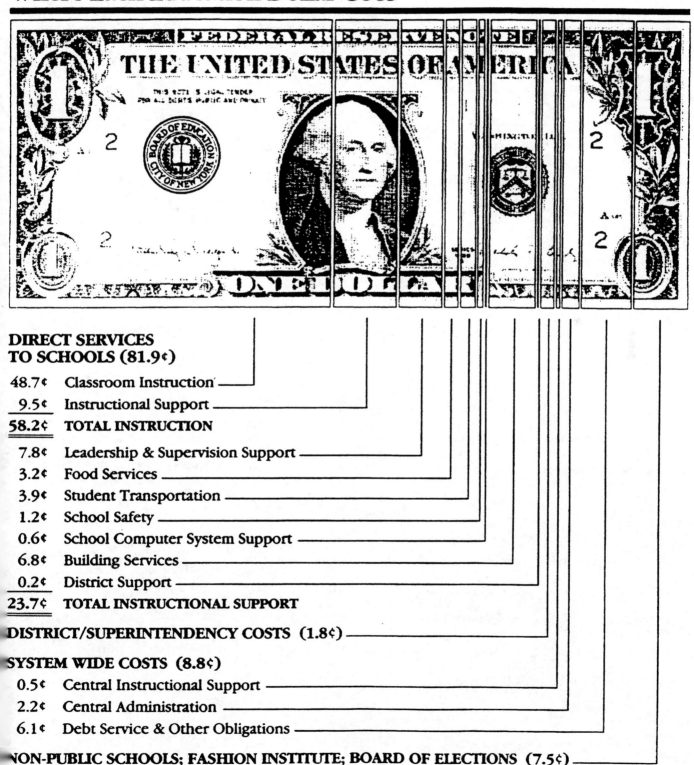

**DIRECT SERVICES
TO SCHOOLS (81.9¢)**

48.7¢	Classroom Instruction
9.5¢	Instructional Support
58.2¢	**TOTAL INSTRUCTION**
7.8¢	Leadership & Supervision Support
3.2¢	Food Services
3.9¢	Student Transportation
1.2¢	School Safety
0.6¢	School Computer System Support
6.8¢	Building Services
0.2¢	District Support
23.7¢	**TOTAL INSTRUCTIONAL SUPPORT**

DISTRICT/SUPERINTENDENCY COSTS (1.8¢)

SYSTEM WIDE COSTS (8.8¢)

0.5¢	Central Instructional Support
2.2¢	Central Administration
6.1¢	Debt Service & Other Obligations

NON-PUBLIC SCHOOLS; FASHION INSTITUTE; BOARD OF ELECTIONS (7.5¢)

Exhibit 4-14 Schedule of Insurance and Surety Bonds in Force

TUCSON UNIFIED SCHOOL DISTRICT NO. 1
SCHEDULE OF INSURANCE IN FORCE*
AS OF JUNE 30, 2000
(UNAUDITED)

Coverage	Company Name	Policy Number	Policy Period From/To	Limit of Liability	Annual Premium
Auto liability, general liability, and errors & omissions	Royal Indemnity	RHJ09003402	7/01/00-7/01/01	$25,000,000	$ 197,0
Underground storage tank	Zurich American	USC3507909-00	5/15/00-5/15/01	$1,000,000	$ 4
Asbestos abatement	Gulf Underwriters	GU0692610	11/01/00-11/01/01	$5,000,000	$ 9,7
Boiler and machinery	Hartford Steam & Boiler	FBP9937016	7/01/00-7/01/01	$50,000,000	$ 13,
Installation and builders risk	St. Paul Fire & Marine	IM08901162	8/01/00-8/01/01	$15,000,000 project limit $1,000,000 earthquake/ flood	$ 5,
Electronic data processing	American Insurance	MX198376937	7/01/00-7/01/01	$3,427,600 equipment $2,500,000 software $200,000 extra expense $10,000 transit/ temporary location	$ 5,
Crime	Kemper Insurance	3F89732603	7/01/00-7/01/01	$1,000,000 employee dishonesty $1,000,000 forgery or alteration $75,000 inside premises $1,000,000 computer fraud	$ 7.
Finance Director	Hartford Insurance	SUN00481	8/01/00-8/01/01	$24,000	$
Department of Administration	St. Paul & Marine	400J10073	9/22/00-9/22/02	$18,000	$
Excess workers' compensation	Republican Western	RSU0201064	7/1/00-7/1/01	Statutory workers' compensation $1,000,000 employer's liability	$ 34
Fidelity bond - seif-insurance trust fund	Hartford Fire	598BPEAH1566	1/28/00-1/28/01	$10,000 employee dishonesty	$
Self-insurance guaranty bond	Aetna Casualty & Surety	S100092145	1/1/00-1/1/01	$250,000	$
Property	St. Paul Guardian	CFO08900115	7/1/00-7/1/01	$688,488,275	$ 21
Non-owned aircraft	XL Specialty Insurance	NAC3000507	3/16/00-3/16/01	$5,000,000	$ 1

* The source of this information is District records.

Chapter Five

COMMON PROBLEMS

This chapter is devoted to the common problems seen in CAFRs. These problems range from overall appearance, typographical errors, completeness, technical deficiencies, consistency, response to self-evaluation worksheet and response to ASBO review comments. As the CAFR is a large, complex financial document, the chance for errors or lack of consistency is tremendous. Remember when you make last minute changes to any section of the CAFR to ask yourself if the error could affect other sections of the CAFR. The following common problems came from actual CAFR's and will be divided by the three sections of a CAFR i.e., Introductory, Financial, and Statistical) and Other information.

INTRODUCTORY SECTION

. Amounts/data in transmittal letter do not agree with amounts in the Financial or Statistical Sections.

. The last paragraph on page iii should explain the unusual policy of adopting a budget that would result in a fund deficit at the end of the year per page 6.

. 2nd paragraph on page v - the letter of transmittal should include a narration supplementing the general governmental revenue and expenditure tables. This narrative should highlight major fluctuations and indicate the reasons for their occurrence. Your discussion needs more specificity.

Risk Management Fund's losses should be discussed.

5th paragraph on page iii - the enrollment should agree with a related amount reported on page 106. The 2nd paragraph on page xii indicates the increase in enrollment was the cause for the administration and instruction expenditures. However, on page 106, only 13 more students were enrolled which is not consistent with this discussion.

FINANCIAL SECTION

1. A statement/schedule which includes only one fund and two years data should be captioned as "comparative". These statements should not be captioned as combined statements as they only include a single fund.

2. Consider deleting the reconciliation of cash and cash equivalents to the balance sheet since this amount is easily traceable.

3. 3rd paragraph on page 14 – the note indicates that the financial statements are presented on the modified accrual basis. The note should be clarified to indicate that only the governmental fund types and the agency fund are reported on the modified accrual basis.

4. 4th paragraph on page 15 – it is not clear how encumbrances can lapse. Are outstanding encumbrances canceled? Do encumbered appropriations lapse at year end?

5. 2nd paragraph on page 16 – the amount of unused commodities at balance sheet date should be reported as deferred revenue since title does not pass to the school district until the commodities are used.

6. 5th paragraph on page 16 – the compensated absences note should indicate clearly that it includes "salary related payments," if applicable.

7. Consider including a schedule of changes in general fixed assets by function and activity. If older data is not available start accumulating this data now and present all prior years data in a single caption such as "all assets acquired prior to a specific date."

FINANCIAL SECTION (Continued)

8. Excess of expenditures over budget were not explained.
9. These statements should not be captioned as combined, as they include only a single internal service fund.
10. The basis of accounting for the agency fund should be disclosed.
11. For clarity, consider adding the word "revenue" after the word "interest."
12. Construction in progress – account captions should not be presented on financial statements unless dollar amounts are reported for them.
13. Per page 23 – subsequent payments reducing capital lease liabilities should be reported as a debt service expenditure (COD. SEC. L20.114 & L20.115).
14. The special revenue fund's total budget should agree with a related amount reported in the Combining Statements.
15. The over expenditure for the Classroom Improvement Fund should have been disclosed in the notes to the financial statements.
16. Expenditures should be classified by character (current, intergovernmental, capital outlay and debt service) (COD. SEC. 180.119 & 2200.604).
17. The notes to the financial statements should disclose the difference in cash flows required to service the old debt (i.e., the refunded debt) and the new debt (i.e., the refunding debt) for transactions entered into during the year that resulted in debt being defeased through an advance refunding (GASB COD. SEC. D20.111).
18. The notes to the financial statements should disclose the economic gain or loss, (i.e., the difference between the present value of the debt service requirements for the old debt [refunded debt] and the present value of the debt service requirements for the new debt [refunding debt]) from transactions entered into during the year that resulted in debt being defeased through an advance refunding (GASB COD. SEC. D20.111).

STATISTICAL SECTION

1. The table caption "last 10 years" should b changed to "last 11 years" since 11 years of data presented.
2. Consider deleting governments that do not hav any outstanding debt.
3. 1996-97 – the total debt service expenditures do not crossfoot.
4. Consider adding the ADA and the ADA as percentage of ADM.
5. Salaries – dollar signs ($) should be include where applicable.
6. The report should indicate clearly that t unemployment rate column, presented on t demographics statistics table, is expressed as percentage.
7. The total expenditures should agree with a relat amount reported on page 8.
8. 1997 & 1996 – the total general expenditu reported in the "ratio of annual debt serv expenditures for general bonded debt to to general expenditures" table should agree with related amount reported in the "total gene governmental expenditures by function" table.

OTHER INFORMATION

1. On the self-evaluation worksheet, questions b, c h, i, j, and k on page 20 appear to be answe incorrectly.
2. The lack of a positive response to prior y comments is of concern to the review panel. Th changes must be made in the next CA submission if the school district is to continu receive a Certificate of Excellence.

Exhibit 5-1 is an example of an ASBO Panel of Rev Comments under GASB 34. The failure of a sch system to adequately respond to the comments of ASBO Panel of Review is sometimes grounds denial. These comments are a tool for the sch system to improve their CAFRs. Exhibit 5-2 i article on common deficiencies in a CAFR.

Exhibit 5-1 continued

ASBO PANEL OF REVIEW COMMENTS
EXAMPLE SCHOOL SYSTEM
FOR THE FISCAL YEAR ENDED JUNE 30, 1999

**PAGE
REFERENCE**

COMMENTS

Cover

1. The cover states for the year ended June 30, 1999, whereas the Title Page states as of and for the year ended June 30, 1999.

INTRODUCTORY SECTION

Title Page

2. The president's name on Title Page does not agree to name on letterhead.

Back of Title Page

3. Should be marked "(This page intentionally left blank)".

Table of Contents – pg. 1

4. Last line should read Notes to the Basic Financial Statements.

Table of Contents – pg. 2

5. Under Nonmajor Special Revenue Funds – should be Schedule not Statement and -Budget (Non-GAAP Basis) to Actual should be and Actual.

Table of Contents – pg. 3

6. Financial Section (Continued) should be (Concluded).

Page i

7. Under Management Responsibility – fourth line should read "to present fairly the basic financial statements", not the "financial position and results of operations of the various funds and account groups." Please note no account groups are presented under GASB Statement 34 presentations.

Page i

8. Section B. should only be discussed in MD & A.

Page i

9. Organization structure should be organization chart.

Page ii

10. Section C should only be discussed in MD & A.

Page ix

11. Under Risk Management – should include discussion on all insurance coverage.

Back of Certificates

12. No page number and not marked "(This page intentionally left blank.)"

FINANCIAL SECTION

Page 1

13. Suggest referencing to a note explaining the new statements, rather than using the auditors' report to explain the statements.

MD & A

14. MD&A should be before opinion.

Page 5

15. Fourth paragraph $.4 does not agree to $.3 on page 20 or page 11.

Page 14

16. First paragraph, last sentence should be in this report on page 55, not in our annual report on page 55.

Page 15

17. Under Capital Assets at Year-end 1998, Furniture and Equipment should be 2,100,737 not 2,329,729. Totals should be 27,063,921 not 27,292,904.

ample School Board, AZ

Exhibit 5-1 continued

PAGE REFERENCE		**COMMENTS**

FINANCIAL SECTION (Concl'd)

Page 25	18.	Should add the word Deficit-Net Change (Deficit) in Fund Balances.
Page 26	19.	Interest on long-term debt equals 8,539 however interest payable on page 23 equals 233,134.
Page 27	20.	Due to student groups includes more than student accounts.
Page 29	21.	Third paragraph states adult education programs, however no tuition is recorded in the financial statements.
Page 31	22.	Fourth paragraph, "Indirect expenses of other functions is not allocated to those functions but is recorded separately in the Statement of Activities" is not a true statement.
Pages 55, 56 and 57	23.	Not all actual amounts agree to the amounts on page 24.
Page 58	24.	First paragraph should be basic fund financial statements, not combined financial statements.
Page 60	25.	Under Non Major Funds – Special Education is listed twice.
Page 60	26.	Even though a summary of Non Major Capital Projects is presented, a Combining Non Major Capital Projects Statement is not presented.
Page 102	27.	Heading should be labeled "Schedule vs Statement".
Page 114	28.	Line item – Advance refunding escrow should be eliminated.
Page 125	29.	The 1998 column shows Advance refunding escrow expenditures; however no footnote disclosure was included for prior refunded debt outstanding.
Page 127	30.	In fiscal year 1998/99, 152,048 in outstanding delinquent taxes is shown; however taxes receiveable were not recorded on the financial statements.
Page 129	31.	1998 tax levies for School does not agree to the tax levy on page 127.
Page 134	32.	N/A: Information not available is listed twice.

OTHER INFORMATION

The GASB issued Interpretation No. 5, *Property Tax Revenue Recognition Governmental Funds* in November 1997. This statement may change how your school district recognizes property tax revenues. The provisions of interpretation are effective for fiscal years beginning after June 15, 2000 with earlier application encouraged.

The GASB issued Statement No. 32, *Accounting and Financial Reporting Internal Revneu Code Section 457 Deferred Compensation Plans* in October 1997. This statement may change how your school district accounts for reports deferred compensation. The provisions of this statement are effective fiscal years beginning after December 31, 1998 or when plan assets are held trust under the requirements of IRC Section 457, if sooner.

Exhibit 5-2

This article was published in the October 1993 issue of School Business Affairs. *It will alert you to the deficiencies that are frequently noted in reports reviewed in ASBO's Certificate of Excellence Program.*

Call For Careful CAFR Crafting
Common Certificate of Excellence Problems

By Bernard F. Gatti, CPA

Excellence is difficult to achieve and maintain; it is a continuous challenge. One way to attain excellence is to learn from our mistakes and the mistakes of others.

In the eight years that I have been the coordinator of ASBO's Certificate of Excellence in Financial Reporting by School Systems program, I have seen Comprehensive Annual Financial Reports (CAFRs) that were the epitome of excellence and some that have been just not acceptable. I also believe that those CAFRs that were not awarded a Certificate of Excellence shared similar problems. To confirm this premise, I decided to go to the people who would know — the ASBO Certificate of Excellence (COE) Panel of Review Members.

Reviewers are governmental accounting and auditing specialists who are currently school business officers, finance directors, independent certified public accountants, academicians and consultants. Most, in their own right, are currently responsible for either preparing or auditing a school system's CAFR for submission to the COE Program.

In February 1993, I asked the reviewers to provide a list of the deficiencies that concerned them the most in their reviews of CAFRs.

While we requested comments from all of the current, active panel members (approximately 160), it was not intended to be a formal sampling process. No extrapolations were performed or conclusions rendered. We just wanted to gain from them their concerns/experiences and to share them with our program participants both present and future. We did, however, provide the reviewers a list of problem areas that were gleaned from the comment letters issued over the years. The problem areas solicited were:

■ Overall appearance, cover, layout;
■ Typographical errors;
■ Poor grammar;
■ Page numbering; and
■ Consistent technical deficiencies such as not following and/or implementing suggestions from the previous year's Panel of Review.
■ Space was also provided for write-in comments.

Presentation of the CAFR

For purposes of this report I have combined the problem areas of overall appearance, typographical errors, poor grammar and page numbering under the broad classification "Presentation of the CAFR." How does the CAFR "present itself" to its readers? Does it have that "professional appearance"? Is it well written? Is it grammatically correct? Is it free of typographical errors? Is the presentation consistent? Irrespective of the technical content, does it look professional? Does it represent "excellence"?

With Total Quality Management the current buzzword you would expect that schools would set an example of excellence for their students when issuing a public document like a CAFR. Unfortunately, the COE reviewers reported that this is often not the case. On a scale of 1-5 with 5 being the most damaging to the success of the report, "Grammar" received an average score of 3.5; three panel members gave this a "5" rating. One panel member noted that it was "inexcusable for a school district's report to include poor grammar." I agree.

"Overall appearance" came in with a "3-plus rating" with very few ratings under "3" and far too many "4s." We all know that first impressions are lasting, yet the reviewers are telling us that the CAFRs are making poor first impressions.

"Typographical errors" earned a "3" rating. There was enough feedback to indicate that basic typing errors were more than just an occasional glitch. You would not expect this in an age where most word processing systems have spell checking capability.

"Page sequencing or numbering" did not, on the whole, seem to trouble the panel members. However, several reviewers did rank it in the "3" or "4" grouping.

Introductory Section

The introductory section "is intended to familiarize the reader with the organizational structure of the government, the nature and scope of the services it provides, and a summary of a government's financial activities and the factors that influence these activities..." (GFOA, 1988).

If there ever was a place to "put your best foot forward," it would be in the introductory section. However, as the following comments from the ASBO Panel of Review Members show, many school systems are missing their opportunity to make a good first impression:

■ "Inadequate transmittal letter — no economic outlook or citing of current year accomplishments."
■ "Weak/Un-information in transmittal letter."
■ "Financial analyses without explanation."
■ "Inconsistencies between transmittal letter and other sections of report."
■ "Same old boiler plate paragraphs," "Repetitive," "Boring."
■ "Figures in transmittal letter do not tie to other sections of report."

Next to GAAP deficiencies, the transmittal letter was the most frequently cited deficiency. Many reviewers graded it with a "5."

Since much of what is included in the letter of transmittal is subjective, you would expect that the reviewers would have divergent views on the subject. However, it is obvious from the comments above that the school systems are failing to adequately provide ". . . a summary of a government's financial activities and the factors that influence these activities . . . ."

The Codification of Governmental Accounting and Financial Reporting Standards (GASB - June 30, 1992) at 2200.105(a.) cites that the Introductory Section of the CAFR should contain "Table of contents, letter of transmittal and other material deemed appropriate by management." This allows the preparer significant freedom in its presentation.

However, the format of the letter of transmittal has evolved over time into a more structured format as presented in the Illustrative Comprehensive Annual Financial Report in the *Governmental Accounting, Auditing and Financial Reporting* (GFOA , 1988, pp229-237). I believe this is an excellent example for schools to follow.

Although that example may be good, your transmittal letter must be responsive to your specific school. It must tell your school's story. After all, much of the formatting of the report in Sections II and III (Financial and Statistical Tables) is structured in detail. But in Section I (Introductory Section), you have the opportunity to fully describe your school system's activities and the factors influencing those activities. Make the most of it, tell your story, and tell it well. Since your signature is on the transmittal letter, its content and display are measurements of your professionalism and credibility. What more can I say except "Just Do It."

Consistency Throughout

The reviewers were deeply concerned with the inconsistencies occurring in the CAFRs. Inconsistencies were not confined to numbers not referencing, but also to factual statements that were inconsistent and at times contradictory. The reviewers' comments with respect to inconsistencies included:

■ "Figures in transmittal letter not in agreement with financials, notes and statistical tables."
■ "Numbers in report do not tie to schedules."
■ "Comments in transmittal letter are inconsistent with notes."
■ "Items in transmittal contradict the results in the financials."

There is no question that inconsistencies are a major item of concern to the panels in their review process. The larger question is, why? That answer is easy. The CAFR is a large, complex financial presentation incorporating fiscal analysis, financial statements, note disclosures, combining and supplementary financial schedules and statistical tables. All of these items include various interrelated information.

The chance for errors of consistency is tremendous. Last minute changes must be made throughout the report. These changes sometimes affect all of the various presentations, e.g. the transmittal letter, financials, notes, schedules and statistical tables. It goes without saying that the final reviewer in the statement issuance process must be familiar with the entire report and its various inter-relationships in order to catch errors of consistency.

Once again, the final review must be done by the school business official. The review must reconcile all of the presentations and factual statements in the report. The professionalism of the accounting function, the financial officer and the school system are at stake. No less than a maximum effort is required to preclude errors of inconsistency. "Just Do It."

Response to Self-Evaluation Worksheet

The completion of ASBO's Self-Evaluation Worksheet is a point of consternation for the ASBO reviewers. Consider these comments from the reviewers:

■ "Yes answer checked, when No, or Not Applicable, applies."
■ "Comment section is rarely used."
■ "No depth to comments."
■ "Reference in comments section, where is this item presented in the report?"
■ "Disclosures in comments not consistent with CAFR."
■ "N/A items should have an explanatory comment."

I cannot stress enough the need for diligence in preparing the Self-Evaluation Worksheet. Such diligence would eliminate a number of the aforementioned deficiencies. However, I am not sure whether the submitting schools really focus on the important role the worksheet plays in the review process. It is, in effect, the "road map" which the reviewer follows in evaluating the CAFR.

The major dilemma facing the reviewers is referencing/relating the answers in the worksheet to the CAFR presentation. An example would be, "Do appropriations lapse at year end?" If the "Yes" answer is checked but not referenced, the reviewer must scan the entire report to ascertain if this is indeed true. Had the answer included a reference to where in the report this is presented, the reviewer could readily access the

Summary of the Presentation Findings

Far too many CAFRS do not pass the "Does it look professional? Is this excellence?" test. Poor grammar and typographical errors are pervasive and the COE reviewers penalize CAFRs that contain them.

The underlying problem is, regrettably, one of carelessness, along with an obvious lack of an effective quality control review mechanism. What hurts the most in these situations is that an otherwise strong technical performance in the accounting area is compromised by a lack of diligence in the report finalization and issuance process.

The solution to this dilemma is simple. The chief financial officer who signs the report for the school must take it upon himself or herself to be held totally accountable for the form and content of the school's CAFR. The response to this is, "Of course he or she is. That's the way it's always been." Perhaps, but did he or she read the entire report from cover to cover? Word by word? Did he or she reference each number in the report to its appropriate relationship? I think not.

It is no secret that school business officials are facing increasing work loads and that reviewing a CAFR can be a very time consuming project. But if the school business official does not have time to do this detailed pre-report issuance review then who shall do it? To whom should this be delegated?

I say this should not be delegated. The buck stops with you. This is your report. You are the one with signing authority. As the Nike commercial says, "Just do it!" This does not mean that the normal quality control reviews are not performed by the accounting people, the report department and the auditors, all of whom have responsibility and accountability in the report preparation and issuance process. What I am saying is that the final read-through of the report prior to its printing should be done by *you*, the school business official, the person signing the report.

This reading should be done word by word, page by page. Mentally you should be challenging each statement or phrase: "If asked a question about this, how would I respond? Does this make sense? Is it consistent throughout the report? (In the technical section of this article, consistency of figures and statements within the report is a major technical problem noted by the reviewers.) Is this professional? Is this excellence? Do I want to be professionally measured by this report?"

This reading should be done at one sitting, uninterrupted. Problems noted should be brought to the attention of the responsible employees. Staff should be apprised of any errors or omissions. You should impress upon them that allowing such errors to go undetected until reaching your desk is a serious mistake. Apprise the auditor of his or her performance in this process, if appropriate. No one is immune from being held accountable in such an important process. Personnel evaluations should measure the employee's performance in this process, if applicable.

If there ever was a time when you want to make a solid impression with your CAFR, it is the present. With all of the funding and budget problems being confronted, you don't want to be responding to format deficiencies when the substantive issues are overwhelming.

Persistent Technical Deficiencies

As would be expected from a group of highly skilled technicians, technical deficiencies were graded high by the panel members, with a diverse grouping of specific technical concerns noted. They are grouped as follows:
- Generally Accepted Accounting Principles (GAAP)
- Introductory Section
- Consistency throughout the CAFR
- Response to Self-Evaluation Worksheet
- Response to ASBO Review Comments

Generally Accepted Accounting Principles

The panelists repeatedly lamented the schools' less than strict adherence to Generally Accepted Accounting Principles (GAAP). Since many of the comments referred to "adherence to GAAP" as being deficient, but were not specific in their citation, I believe that the panel members are telling us that a return to accounting fundamentals is needed. To put it in the football vernacular, we need to return to the fundamentals of blocking and tackling.

In accounting and financial reporting, such basics include going through the ASBO Certificate of Excellence Program Self-Evaluation Worksheet line by line and diligently answering the questions. This should be augmented with appropriate referencing to the authoritative literature, namely the Codification of Governmental Accounting and Financial Reporting Standards (Codification) published by the Governmental Accounting Standards Board. Another useful reference text in this process is the publication *Governmental Accounting, Auditing and Financial Reporting (GAAFR)*, published by the Government Finance Officers Association (GFOA). While not authoritative, this text expands and illustrates what is embodied in the Codification.

Strict adherence to GAAP encompasses both accounting principles and report presentation and disclosure, all of which are detailed in the Codification, illustrated in the GAAFR, and queried in the ASBO Self-Evaluation Worksheet. Your school's CAFR should incorporate, where applicable, all of the accounting and report presentation items addressed in the Self-Evaluation Worksheet. This, I believe, will preclude both the specific and general GAAP deficiencies cited by the ASBO Panels of Review. I might add, this diligent compliance with the Worksheet's provisions applies to both the school and the independent public accountants performing the audit.

item and proceed with the evaluation. My experience in processing the panels' comments indicates that the questionnaires often appear to be prepared in an "after-the-fact" perfunctory manner. Accordingly, in addition to the school not gaining the benefits provided by the worksheet, the reviewer is forced to search through the entire report looking for items that may or may not be applicable.

The ASBO Self-Evaluation Worksheet is a valuable tool in the report preparation process. It is the product of a task force comprised of leading governmental accounting specialists who spent countless hours (on a voluntary basis) preparing it. It contains page-by-page references to the authoritative literature (Codification) so that appropriate research and documentation is readily available during the report preparation process. To not use it to the fullest extent possible is foolish as well as unprofessional.

Complete it as though *you* were performing the review. In the comments section, reference where in the report a particular item is addressed. If it is not applicable, explain why. Completing the worksheet in this manner assures you that your response is correct, and expedites and enhances the review process. This result is a win-win situation.

Keep in mind that the pursuit of excellence and professionalism are synonymous.

Response to ASBO Review Comments

A school system's failure to adequately respond to the comments of the previous ASBO Panel of Review was an obvious irritant to reviewers:
■ "Answered without thought."
■ "No depth to the answers."
■ "Not implemented. No response as to why no implementation."
■ "Repetitive deficiencies."
■ "Should be grounds for denial."

Clearly, failing to properly and adequately respond to the prior year's comments places the reviewer in a negative frame of mind for the balance of the review. But let's dismiss the impact this may have on the reviewer's approach to the review and focus on the real issue: Are we really serious in our quest for excellence?

Sometimes I hear school business officials say that "those comments are 'nit picking,'" or they reflect the reviewers' "preference in presentation and are not GAAP per se."

Let's look at the reality of the situation. A panel of professionals with proven technical competence has taken time out of their busy professional lives, on a voluntary basis, to perform an in-depth review of your school's CAFR. Each panel member works on each CAFR for six to eight hours. Using the low rate of $150 per hour for their professional time, this adds up to $3,600 for a three-member panel.

This review includes the preparation of comments for your attention. To fail to address those comments with professional diligence in effect compromises your personal professionalism and precludes your school from its deserved value received from the ASBO Certificate Program. This is a serious indictment, but deserving of thought.

With that said, there are many less incriminating reasons for failing to fully address the reviewers' comments. I would expect the most prevalent is that the school business official simply does not thoroughly understand the comment. This is certainly understandable given the fact that the reviewer is performing a "cold review"; he or she has no prior knowledge or experience with the school itself.

Nonetheless, your rebuttal must be sufficiently expansive to allow the subsequent ASBO reviewer to make an in-depth evaluation of your interpretation, conclusion and implementation (or if not deemed necessary, non-implementation). Said another way, put yourself in the reviewers' position and keep in mind that the comments to which you are responding were not prepared by the current reviewer. What information would you need to understand fully your response/action plan?

Since many of the comments deal with accounting and auditing issues, your auditors should participate fully in the interpretation, implementation and presentation of the school system's response.

I would exhort you to act upon the review comments in a positive and professional manner and to reflect this approach in your responses. This, along with the CAFR, is how your school's professionalism is to be measured.

Conclusion

Throughout this article I have directed the responsibility for the professionalism of your school system's CAFR to you, the school's chief financial officer. I have emphasized how your professionalism is measured by the CAFR's professional presentation. It is incumbent upon you to set in place strong quality controls throughout the preparation and issuance process. Your leadership and oversight will ensure that your school's CAFR will achieve the excellence in financial reporting you strive to achieve through your participation in ASBO's Certificate of Excellence in Financial Reporting by Schools Program.□

Bernard F. Gatti, CPA, is a consultant to ASBO International, coordinating the ASBO International Certificate of Excellence program. He is a retired partner of KPMG Peat Marwick's Washington, DC office.

References

Government Finance Officers Association. (1988). *Governmental Accounting, Auditing and Financial Reporting*. Chicago, IL: Author.

Chapter Six

ACHIEVING EXCELLENCE WITH
FINANCIAL REPORTING OF GOVERNMENTS (F.R.O.G.)

When selecting a report-writer or report-generator for your GASB Statement 34 financial statements, you should choose one that can produce both current model reports and GASB Statement 34 reports. This ability will become important during the implementation of GASB Statement 34, since you will need to convert last year's current model financial statements to GASB Statement 34 financial statements. Financial Reporting of Governments (F.R.O.G.) report writing software was designed specifically to address the new financial reporting requirements that state and local governments must adhere to under the new reporting model. F.R.O.G. has incredible flexibility as well as the necessary ability to produce reports under both the current and new models. This flexibility is necessary during the transition period of implementation, since many governments will need to prepare financial reports under the current model for two to three years prior to GASB Statement 34 implementation. F.R.O.G. makes implementation easy, as it allows you to produce your GASB Statement 34 reports once the accrual entries are entered. The effectiveness of F.R.O.G. as an implementation tool has resulted in many school districts deciding to implement the new standard *early*.

F.R.O.G. was developed by the certified public accounting firm of Heinfeld, Meech & Co., P.C. Since its inception in 1986, this firm has specialized in auditing and preparing financial statements for governmental entities. Heinfeld, Meech & Co., P.C. has assisted its clients in obtaining more than 450 certificates of Excellence from ASBO International. F.R.O.G. has been utilized by the firm and its clients in preparing the reports necessary for these awards, including seven early GASB 34 implementations.

F.R.O.G. was developed as a result of Heinfeld, Meech & Co., P.C.'s cutting-edge leadership in governmental auditing and consulting. For over two years, F.R.O.G. has been used to prepare financial statements under both the new and old financial reporting models. After receiving feedback from the users of the program, a new version of F.R.O.G. has been developed to include virtually unlimited account code segments, data import and increased report generation flexibility. F.R.O.G. is a self-contained program, therefore there is no need to rely on complicating spreadsheet programs to prepare your financial statements. With all of these features, F.R.O.G. provides the flexibility, reliability and accuracy that results in quality that is unmatched by any other report writing software package designed exclusively for governments.

F.R.O.G. makes implementation easy due to its reliability and ease of use. F.R.O.G. does not replace the familiar as it stores the fund-based information in much the same fashion as your current general ledger. F.R.O.G. allows you to post government-wide journal entries to your fund-based financial data and produce presentation ready financial statements. Finally, F.R.O.G. has been battle tested as it has been used to prepare the financial statements for several entities that have decided to implement the new reporting model early. All of these entities issued Comprehensive Annual Financial Reports (CAFR) and F.R.O.G. was able to produce all of the financial statements contained within the reports. The financial statements presented in Appendices B & C (GASB 34 financial statements), were also prepared using F.R.O.G.

The following points highlight the basic features of the F.R.O.G. software.

- F.R.O.G. is a *self-contained*, database driven Windows-based program. So it is user friendly and familiar.

- F.R.O.G.'s toolbar allows quick access to the most frequently used features of the program.

- F.R.O.G.'s toolbar allows quick access to the most frequently used features of the program. This further facilitates and streamlines report preparation time.

- F.R.O.G. enables you to customize the account structure to suit your specific needs. This is accomplished when you initially setup your database structure. However, if you do not want to take the time to customize your account structure, you can copy one of the standard account code structures that come with the program.

- You determine the number of segments that you would like in your account structure. These segments can include, but are not limited to: *Fund, Department, Program, Function and Object.*

- Upon deciding on the number of segments you want, you can begin to set up the segment codes. This is when you would set up your fund, program, department, function and object codes.

- Once you have set up all of the codes needed for your segments, you are ready to take the next step of setting up your *account code structure*, by fund. This is the point where your F.R.O.G. software begins to look similar to the account code structure in a general ledger package.

- Once you have created the accounts for a particular fund, F.R.O.G. enables you to clone funds so that you may copy similar fund types (e.g., General, Special Revenue, Debt Service, etc.) and save time setting up fund account structures.

- Now you are ready to load the data from your general ledger using the quick data entry screen or data upload function.

- Once your general ledger data is in F.R.O.G you are able make adjustments to your fun financial information using the journal entr screen and your government-wide adjustment using the government-wide journal entry scree

- After all of your adjustments are made, you a now ready to print your reports. With a click a button you will have presentation-read financial statements. It is that easy and it is wonder why the number of users of F.R.O.(increase everyday.

To test out the many features of F.R.O.G. f yourself, visit the official F.R.O.G. website www.frogonline.net to download your free tr version today.

APPENDIX A

ASBO INTERNATIONAL ARTICLES

I.   GASB 34 Financial Statements are Easier with the Right Tools

II.   The Practical Value of ASBO International is Certificate of Excellence in Financial Reporting Program

III. CAFRs Valuable in Meeting GASB Requirements

IV.   ASBO International Recognizes 25 Years of Excellence in School System Financial Reporting

V.   Sharpen Your Pencils and Roll Up Your Sleeves: A Case Study in Implementing the GASB's New Reporting Model

VI.   Asphalt, Fleets, Brick, and Mortar

(This page intentionally left blank)

GASB 34 Financial Statements Are Easier With The Right Tools

By Gary Heinfeld, CPA, CGFM, C. Christopher Arvizu, CPA
and Michael L. Herrera, CPA, CGFM

After talking a lot about GASB Statement 34 over the past two years, the time has come to put together a GASB 34 financial report. This article describes our own experience with creating GASB 34 financial reports and outlines the proper tools and resources that will help you implement GASB Statement 34. An article in the October 1999 edition of *School Business Affairs* explains the provisions of GASB Statement 34. An article in the October 2000 edition of *School Business Affairs* explains a case study in implementing GASB's New Financial Reporting Model.

Experience

Heinfeld & Meech, P.C., an Arizona Certified Public Accounting firm, has specialized in school systems since its inception in 1986. We have audited and prepared financial statements for over 1,000 school systems. Since our inception, we have consistently assisted our clients in obtaining the coveted Association of School Business Officials Certificate of Excellence in Financial Reporting for their annually published Comprehensive Annual Financial Reports (CAFR), and last year alone we prepared 54 CAFR's. In addition, we have prepared several GASB 34 Implementation plans and have prepared GASB 34 financial statements for the following school systems:

- Kyrene Elementary School District (Phase 1 School, implemented one year early)
- Gilbert Unified School District (Phase 1 School, implemented one year early)
- Sunnyside Unified School District (Phase 1 School, implemented one year early)
- Tempe Elementary School District (Phase 2 School, implemented two years early)
- Wilson Elementary School District (Phase 2 School, implemented two years early)

We can't emphasize enough the importance of an early start to your implementation of GASB 34. Every school system should implement at least one year prior to their due date, providing you with the time to find and correct problems without the pressure of an upcoming deadline. Although implementing GASB Statement 34 will be challenging, the right tools will certainly make the process smoother for your school system.

Proper Tools and Resources

We believe that the following tools are mandatory to ensure a smooth process.

- Governmental Accounting Standards Board Statement No. 34, Basic Financial Statements – and Management's Discussion and Analysis-for State and Local Governments (GASB 34)
- Governmental Accounting Standards Board – Guide to Implementation of GASB Statement 34 on Basic Financial Statements – and Management's Discussion and Analysis – for State and Local Governments (GASB 34) – Questions and Answers (Please note: A second Questions and Answers will be released this year on GASB.)
- Association of School Business Officials International (ASBOI) Statement 34 Implementation Recommendations for School Districts
- Governmental Accounting Standards Board – What You Should Know About Your School District's Finances – A Guide to Financial Statements

- Association of School Business Officials International Certificate of Excellence (COE) in Financial Reporting (to be released in November 2001)
- A Financial Statement Report Writer that can produce current and GASB Statement 34 financial reports

As everybody should already have the first four of these items as reference material, our following discussion will focus upon ABSO's New COE Guide Book and financial statement report writers.

ASBO International's *New* COE Guide Book

The formation of ASBO's Certificate of Excellence in Financial Reporting Program in 1972 initiated a new era for school business officials seeking to present financial statements in a concise, readable format that exceeds the minimum reporting requirements. Currently over 400 school systems participate in ASBO's Certificate of Excellence program through submitting their Comprehensive Annual Financial Report to ASBO for review in accordance with the program's reporting requirements. An invaluable tool for school systems in their preparation of CAFR's, General Purpose Financial Statements, or GASB 34 Financial Statements is ASBO International's Certificate of Excellence Guide Book. The Guide Book outlines the sections of a CAFR under the new reporting model GASB Statement 34 and, more importantly, provides specific examples of financial statements and other applicable financial information included in actual CAFR's prepared by school systems. Also included in the appendix of the Guide Book are two complete fiscal year 2000 CAFR's of Kyrene Elementary School District in Tempe, Arizona. One presents the CAFR under the old reporting model and the other presents the CAFR under the new reporting model (GASB Statement 34). These two CAFR's provide a clear comparison between the two reporting models and are used as reference material throughout the Guide Book. The Guide Book is intended to be additional reference material for the preparations of a school system CAFR and should be used in conjunction with the other reference material listed above. In addition, you should consult with school system's independent auditor.

The COE Guide Book begins by providing the reader with background information and the general requirements of the program. One of the important functions of the COE program is the promotion of the benefits of CAFR preparation to its participants, especially those gained through the review process. Chapter one of the COE Guide Book discusses some of these benefits, including national recognition, enhanced presentation, uniformity and comparability, and most importantly, added fiscal credibility. This chapter also outlines the application and review processes. These processes are essential to the timely issuance of certificates by the program. The six-month timeline, the self-evaluation worksheet, and the ASBO Panel of Review are just a few of the items discussed in this section. Chapter one concludes with a brief discussion of the program's general requirements, including the differences between general-purpose financial statements and GASB Statement 34 financial statements, and a general outline of a CAFR's contents.

The "Introductory Section" is the first major section of the CAFR and is discussed in chapter two of the COE Guide Book. The primary focus of this chapter is the transmittal letter. With the implementation of GASB Statement 34, it is recommended that the content of transmittal letter be modified to prevent the duplication of information presented in the Management's Discussion and Analysis (MD&A). Two examples of transmittal letters are included, in addition to examples of a cover, the presentation of the Certificate of Excellence, a list of principal officials, and organizational charts. Detailed discussion and additional guidance on the required elements of the MD&A is included in ASBO's Statement 34 *Implementation Recommendations for School Districts.*

The Guide Book continues with chapter three's discussion of the "Financial Section" of the CAFR. This chapter provides not only a brief description of the financial section, but also a recommended outline of the MD&A, financial statements, combining statements, and schedules to be included in the financial section of the CAFR. Exhibits of this chapter include the following:

- Management's Discussion and Analysis (MD&A)
- Government wide statements
- Fund financial statements
- Reconciliations to the government-wide statements
- Budgetary comparison for major funds (RSI)
- Alternative statements and schedules

Additional examples of these statements as well as the remaining statements and schedules of the financial section are also contained in the complete example CAFR provided in the appendix.

Chapter four of the Guide Book presents a list of the required data and tables to be included in the "Statistical Section" of the CAFR. While most of the tables listed are referenced in the appendix, several additional tables and charts that further enhance the presentation of financial information in the CAFR are included in this chapter. Chapter four also provides examples of the two new government-wide statistical tables that present the fiscal year expenses and revenues on an accrual basis.

The Guide Book concludes in chapter five by providing some insight to common problems that the panel review process has identified in CAFR's. These common problems include areas such as overall appearance, typographical errors, consistency, completeness, and discrepancies with the self-evaluation worksheet. Many of these problems can be easily avoided; however, they are often overlooked during the preparation of the report due to the considerable amount of information that must be included in a CAFR.

As mentioned previously, the appendix to the Guide Book includes two complete CAFR's that should be used as reference throughout the CAFR preparation process. As both the old and new reporting models are included, the appendix will be an especially valuable resource during the year of implementation. The appendix to the Guide Book also includes several articles previously released in *ASBO Accents* that discuss the importance and value of the preparation of a Comprehensive Annual Financial Report and ASBO's encouragement of school systems to prepare CAFR's through its Certificate of Excellence in Financial Reporting program.

Financial Report Writer

A critical tool that is a must for the implementation of GASB Statement 34 is a report writer. We have all produced reports with various spreadsheet programs, which are great for single page reports; however, a database system is the way to go to ensure reliable reports for financial statements. When selecting a report writer, you should consider one that can produce current model reports as well as GASB Statement 34 reports. This ability will become important during the implementation of GASB Statement 34, as you will need to convert your last year's current model financial statements to GASB Statement 34 financial statements. For our preparation of

GASB 34 financial statements, we utilized the report writer F.R.O.G (Financial Reporting of Governments). F.R.O.G. has incredible flexibility as well as the necessary ability to produce reports under both the current and new models. This flexibility is absolutely necessary during the transition period of implementation, as many governments will need to prepare financial reports under the current model for two to three years prior to GASB Statement 34 implementation. F.R.O.G. makes implementation easy, as it allows you to produce your GASB Statement 34 reports once the accrual entries are inputted. The effectiveness of F.R.O.G. as an implementation tool has resulted in many of our clients' decision to implement the new standard *early*. The reliability of this software to produce presentation-ready financial statements under the old and new models has resulted in increased efficiencies for both our clients and our firm.

F.R.O.G.

Some important features of this software are outlined below:

- Windows-based navigation and data entry, including data import functionality
- Unlimited account code string in four segments including Fund, Function, Program and Object Code
- Compatibility with Microsoft Office Suite® that enables the user to export financial reports directly into Excel® for additional analysis and formatting
- The ability to post journal entries to both the Fund and Government-wide Financial Statements
- The ability to 'rollover' prior year data for current year comparative analysis such as will be required in the Management Discussion and Analysis under the new reporting model
- The ability to easily produce combining financial statements for non-major funds to be included in the CAFR

With FROG's ability to post journal entries to both the Fund and Government-wide Financial Statements, the school system does not need to make significant changes in its accounting records when implementing GASB Statement 34.

This software can produce either the Basic Financial Statements or a CAFR. You can produce old model financial statements until the required implementation date as well as "what if" financial statements in anticipation of the implementation of GASB Statement 34. The capabilities of data import, report exports, and comparative data rollover from year to year streamline the enormous process of CAFR report preparation. F.R.O.G. has enabled our firm to produce more CAFR's in a limited time frame that would have not been possible otherwise. Please call ASBOI for more information or visit www.frogonline.net to learn more about this invaluable tool.

Responsibility of School Systems/Auditors

In addition to the above tools, you need to have available experts in GASB Statement 34 and a clear assignation of responsibilities to either the school system or your auditor. Certainly, your auditor must be familiar with GASB 34. You should include this as a requirement during your Request for Proposal (RFP) process. If the school system prepares your GASB 34 financial statements, the auditor's responsibility is only to opine and issue its Independent Auditor Report. However, if the school system has the auditor prepare the financial statements, the following list provides an example of the division of responsibilities between the two parties. These responsibilities should also be listed in your RFP.

School System's Responsibilities for the Implementation of GASB Statement 34:

1. Drafts school system section of Management Discussion and Analysis (MD&A).
2. Provides documentation for full accrual adjustment.
3. Has capital asset inventory listing available to calculate depreciation.
4. Records gain/loss on disposition of capital items.
5. Determines the depreciation expense, estimates salvage value, estimates useful lives, and calculates accumulated depreciation.
6. Establishes policy on change in function activity. Determines the functional category of capital assets for charging of depreciation expense to each functional category.
7. Determines program revenues and identifies charges for service, operating grants and contributions, capital grants, and contributions.
8. Identifies special and extraordinary items.

Auditors' Responsibilities for Implementation of GASB Statement 34:

1. Draft the MD&A language required for the school system.
2. Add the government-wide financial statements.
3. Determine which funds to report as major funds.
4. Format the fund financial statement for major funds display.
5. Determine and qualify the differences between the current financial resources measurement-modified accrual basis of accounting and the economic resources measurement focus-accrual basis of accounting (such as calculating depreciation expense, accrued interest on general long-term debt, and the gain or loss on the sale of disposition of capital assets.)
6. Prepare the reconciliation between the fund financial statements and the Government-wide financial statements.
7. Revise the notes to the basic financial statement to focus on the school system's government activities, business-type activities, major funds, and aggregate non-major funds. Delete obsolete notes, add new notes, and change the terminology of the notes.
8. Revise and relocate the budgetary comparison information and certain note disclosures to require supplemental information (RSI).
9. Format the combining statements and schedules to display non-major funds only.
10. Determine which changes may be necessary for GASB 34's changes in fund definitions.
11. Determine the eliminations needed for internal balances and activities.
12. Calculate the amount of the net asset categories.
13. Change the layout of the annual financial report. GASB 34 dictates the placement of certain items, such as the MD & A, other RSI, and the financial statement reconciliations.
14. Change terminology throughout the report.

The school system must decide how much work to outsource.

The implementation of GASB Statement 34 may seem like an overwhelming challenge. However, early implementation will go a long way in easing the pressure of these upcoming deadlines for your school system. Any problems can be found in time for you to find the solution and implement the necessary corrections without the added stress of a looming deadline. Remember, it is never too early to start!

Bibliography

Association of School Business Officials International. (2000, September). *Statement 34 implementation recommendations for school districts.* Reston, VA: Author.

Government Accounting Standards Board. (1999, June). *Basic financial statements – and management's discussion and analysis – for state and local goverments (Statement No. 34).* Norwalk, CT: Author.

Governmental Accounting Standards Board. (2000, May). *Guide to implementation of GASB Statement No. 34 on basic financial statements – and management's discussion and analysis – for state and local governments: Questions and answers.* Norwalk, CT: Author.

Governmental Accounting Standards Board. (2000, November). *What you Should Know about your School District's Finances.* Norwalk, CT: Author

Gary Heinfeld, CPA, CGFM is the managing partner of Heinfeld and Meech, P.C., Independent Auditors and Consultants, in Phoenix and Tucson, Arizona. Gary is on the ASBO International Certificate of Excellence (COE) Committee; ASBO International Accounting, Auditing and Budgeting Committee; GASB – Advisory Committee for User-Guide for Public Schools; GASB – Advisory Committee for second Questions and Answers on GASB 34; Member of GFOA Special Review Committee for the Certificate of Achievement for Excellence in Financial Reporting; Panel Review Chairperson for ASBO International Certificate of Excellence Program; and ASBO International Eagle Awards Selection Panel member.

C. Christopher Arvizu, CPA is a manager in the Tucson office of Heinfeld and Meech, P.C.

Michael L. Herrera, CPA, CGFM is a senior at Heinfeld and Meech, P.C. and is in charge of F.R.O.G. support.

ASSOCIATION OF SCHOOL BUSINESS OFFICIALS INTERNATIONAL

School Business Affairs

September 1997

The Practical Value of ASBO International's Certificate of Excellence in Financial Reporting Program
By Richard P. Larkin

There is one point that needs to be made clear: there is a great deal more value in the achievement of ASBO International's Certificate of Excellence in Financial Reporting than the recognition by your peers in the financial management of our school systems. It can help achieve a higher bond rating, and is viewed positively by analysts and investors that bid on your bonds. Both can save your district hundreds of thousands of dollars in interest costs when you sell bonds to build schools.

During my 21 years at S&P's Municipal Bond Rating Department, I was frequently asked about the value of GFOA's Certificate of Achievement Program. This program, like ASBO's Excellence in Financial Reporting Program, honors those governmental units whose audited financial reports conformed to a strict model and format for reporting financial results of operations and statistical appendices that summarize key demographic and operating statistics of the unit. My answer was always the same—although S&P would view this award as a positive development, it was no guarantee of a higher rating. Not a glowing endorsement by any stretch of the imagination.

As an executive of a rating agency, I would shy away from any black-or-white definitive statements on rating judgments, because there could always be other factors or considerations that would render such a definitive statement of position or policy as wrong. Achievement of the Certificate of Excellence in Financial Reporting will not always result in a high rating. The obvious example is the case of Washington, DC. This city has won GFOA's financial reporting award for many years, but operates on the brink of fiscal bankruptcy and cannot stay current in meeting its regular financial obligations.

Having left Standard & Poor's last May, I can now afford to be more candid on how bond analysts view awards such as ASBO's Certificate of Excellence, or GFOA's Certificate of Achievement. I am singularly citing the view of bond analysts, not necessarily bond rating analysts. To explain this subtle, but important point, I'll provide a quick overview of how the financial markets for municipal bonds work and the role played by rating agencies and other industry bond analysts.

The Role of Bond Rating Agencies

The municipal bond market can be likened to a bank, which can make loans to cities and school districts for operating or capital cash needs. The major difference is that there is no central banker or department to which you apply for the loan. Bond amounts can range from the tens of millions to billions of dollars, which can exceed the lending capacity of a single lender. Therefore, the bond market solves that problem by allowing the formation of "syndicates" of lenders, which take portions of the loans.

Continuing the analogy of the bond market as a lending bank, you see there is still the need to perform the credit approval function. In the bank, you would make application to the lending officer, and fill out application forms that document your income and expenses, balance sheets or bank accounts, income and employment history and past borrowing and repayment history. In the bond market, however, there is no central credit approval department; that role is filled by the bond rating agencies (the major firms being Standard & Poor's, Fitch and Moody's Investors Service), municipal bond insurance companies and bond analysts in the municipal credit departments of the large- and middle-sized investment banking and brokerage houses.

Looking at the rating agencies, you'd see that they are perhaps the most influential evaluators of credit in the bond issue process. They would be the first to remind you, however, that they do not approve or disapprove your municipal bond loan. As independent credit analysts, the rating agencies do not buy or sell bonds, make loans or in any other way order or require an issuer to perform as a pre-requisite to sell bonds. They do not even make recommendations as to whether any rated bond issues are good or bad investments. Their sole purpose in life is to provide to potential lenders an independent evaluation of credit risk—the likelihood that there could be default or nonpayment of bonded debt.

Hy Grossman, the leading bond rater at Standard & Poor's, is fond of saying that if there were no such thing as bond raters, then the market would create such an entity. The bond raters have been in the business of publishing bond credit ratings since the 1900s, and are responsible for the development of today's methods and process for evaluating potential bond default risk. They provide the leading benchmarks for other bond analysts to compare their own evaluations of credit risk. Because of this central and important role, an increase or decrease in the bond rating by a major rating agency can greatly affect the interest cost on borrowed bond money.

A one-category downgrade of a bond rating from "AA" to "A", for example, could increase the interest rate on borrowed money by as much as .25 percent. While this does not seem like much on the surface, the difference on a typical $20-million bond issue would be an extra $500,000 of debt costs heaped onto taxpayers over a normal 20-year bond repayment.

Despite their influence and effect on the bond market, the raters clearly state that they do not approve or disapprove a loan, or set the bond issue's interest rates. Those decisions are made by investors, perhaps after consulting the current ratings agencies. In some cases, bonds can be, and are, sold without an investment grade (BBB/Baa) bond rating. And many smaller issuers sell their debt to local banks with no rating.

The Role of Municipal Bond Insurance Analysts

In the last 25 years, major developments have affected the importance and role of the bond raters in the municipal bond market. Starting in 1971, with the establishment of AMBAC, there has been the creation of municipal bond insurance companies. Their primary role is to provide insurance, or a guarantee, against the possibility of default on the municipal bonds that they insure. This additional source of bond repayment reduces the credit risk of default, and has the significant affect of lowering the interest cost on your funds borrowed in a bond issue. Bond ratings are important here as well, because since 1974, one or more of the bond rating agencies have been assigning "AAA" ratings, their highest rating, to bonds that carry municipal bond insurance. These high ratings are the reason why purchasing municipal bond insurance can lower your bond interest costs.

Bond insurance has grown in importance and influence to the point where, in 1996, fully half of all municipal bonds issued were guaranteed by a bond insurance policy. This growth has not been without consequence; because of the potential risk of downgrades of the bond insurance companies below "AAA" and the increase in the supply of insured bonds in investors' portfolios (which introduces more concentration of investment credit risk), the net interest costs associated with a "AAA" rated insured bond are comparable to a nonguaranteed bond rated "A+/A1."

The role of bond insurance, therefore, is significant. Each of the bond insurance companies monitor credit risk by reviewing credit ratings and evaluations by the major bond insurance companies. Each firm, however, employs its own corps of credit analysts, which use similar methods and criteria for evaluating credit risk as the bond raters. Many of the senior staff at all of the

insurers, for example, had prior bond rating experience at one of the Big Three bond rating companies. In recent years, relying more on the review and assessment by their own credit departments, bond insurance companies are more frequently granting bond insurance guarantees on bonds rated speculative and below investment grade by one or more of the major rating firms.

Perhaps the most visible example here was last year's Recovery Bond issue by bankrupt Orange County, CA, which was used to make repayment on debts in default resulting from speculative money management practices. MBIA, the largest of the major bond insurance companies, insured bonds issued by the county in both 1995 and 1996, which resulted in "AAA" ratings based on the insurance. Standard & Poor's, however, deemed the underlying bonds and risk taken on by MBIA as speculative and below investment grade. Although this has been a rare occurrence, it has happened more frequently in the last two years, indicating the growing independence of the bond insurers in making their underwriting decisions.

Finally, many of the portfolio managers of bond funds and large institutional investors maintain their own staffs of bond credit analysts who do their own research independently of the raters and bond insurers. Many analysts, in fact, do not treat insured bonds as unequivocally "AAA" quality, although they will count this credit enhancement as a positive in their bidding for bonds. This group is increasing its influence on the municipal bond market, and must be contended with as an influence equal to the raters and insurers. This group has the authority to bid on bonds in the face of low or noninvestment grade ratings, and is a driving force behind regulators' push for improved secondary market disclosure.

What Is Secondary Market Disclosure?

Simply put, disclosure is a set of guidelines about current financial information that bond issuers will need to supply if they desire unfettered market access. It is termed "secondary market" because of the lack of information when bonds are sold years after the initial offering. In the past, the minimum requirement was to have available an annual financial report for review by investors and analysts. Now, these same analysts are demanding the same information (tax rates, tax collection records, assessed value trends) that are routinely supplied to rating agencies. They have also recently demanded that issuers include a statement in their official statements, pledging to continue to make this information available years after the bond sale. Information repositories have been created to collect and store this information, financial reports and budgets in order to provide centralized access to interested parties.

The Value of CAFRs and Certificates of Excellence

Comprehensive Annual Financial Reports (CAFRs) not only provide these analysts with the operating financial results they need, but a great deal of other credit information as well. The financial statements and statistical data included in the CAFR provide, in one document, 90 percent of what is needed for credit evaluation—a one-stop compliance with

disclosure requirements. The value here for CAFRs is not necessarily interest savings, but assurance that there will be a market for your bonds; bond dealers may be restricted from buying or selling your bonds if disclosure has not been fulfilled and a credit review performed.

The value of a Certificate of Excellence is, of course, reduced rates of interest and debt service savings. Those savings, however, are not limited to a higher bond rating; interest rate savings can be passed on by investors in unrated debt as well—investors that have done their own in-house "rating" review. And superior disclosure can save thousands of dollar in insurance premiums paid at the time of the bond sale.

How Much Can I Save?

The following examples estimate the financial value of issuing CAFRs with the ASBO Certificate of Excellence. As indicated earlier, the award will not necessarily result in a higher rating but can contribute to a higher rating. And although it is not a formal part of agency rating criteria, the ability of an issuer to achieve the rare and coveted "Aaa/AAA" rating hinges on demonstrating superior financial management. From this point of view (it was my unwritten rule of thumb when I was chief rating officer for S&P), a Certificate of Excellence is almost a pre-requisite for "AAA" ratings.

Rating upgrades have been estimated to result in a lower interest rate, from 10 to 25 basis points, depending on the magnitude of the rating change (a basis point equals one one-hundredth of a percentage point, or .0001; 25 basis points, therefore, equals one-fourth of a percent). On a $20-million, 20-

year bond, this can add up to between $200,000 to $500,000 over the life of the bonds.

Savings are likely even without an upgrade. If analysts place a mere 5 basis point premium (or one-twentieth of a percent) on their bid as a result of the added confidence they get from an issuer that has achieved the award, this can total up to $100,000 over 20 years on that same bond issue.

And if a bond insurer places the same small value on your CAFR and Certificate, the five basis points can save you $15,000 to $24,000 on the premium for a $20 million bond issue, payable at the time of issuance.

As S&P's Grossman would tell you, if you've "applied a couple of times (for the Certificate of Excellence) and not quite achieved it......keep going and keep pushing." When you do finally receive the award, don't be shy—brag about the achievement. It is more than a prestigious honor—it can help you to tell the bond market to "show me the money"—interest savings, well earned.

Richard P. Larkin joined Fairmount Capital Advisors after a 21-year career at Standard & Poor's, leaving that firm as its chief rating officer for municipal ratings. He is a member of GFOA and NFMA (the National Federation of Municipal Analysts), which honored him with their Award for Excellence in 1996. Larkin is also a member of the National Advisory Council on State and Local Budgeting (NACSLB).

For more information on ASBO International's Certificate of Excellence in Financial Reporting Program, contact ASBO International at: 11401 North Shore Drive, Reston, VA 20190 / Phone: (703) 478-0405 / www.asbointl.org.

(This page intentionally left blank)

CAFRs Valuable in Meeting GASB Requirements
By Gary Heinfeld, CPA, CGFM

The Governmental Accounting Standard Board (GASB) believes Comprehensive Annual Financial Reports (CAFRs) should be prepared and published as the standard financial report. GASB's new reporting model in Exposure Draft assumes most governmental entities will issue a CAFR. If incomplete or summary financial data are presented, then information about major funds is required in separate columns in the financial statement or in a condensed format as notes to the financial statement. Therefore, it will be easier for school systems to meet the new GASB requirements by issuing a CAFR.

SEC Requirements

Effective July 1, 1995, the United States Securities and Exchange Commission (SEC) required most new issuers of municipal securities (including school districts) to file annual continuing disclosure documents to Nationally Recognized Municipal Securities Repositories. This continuing disclosure will help investors determine the appropriate price for bonds traded in the secondary market. In many cases, filing a CAFR may be all that is necessary to comply with the annual filing requirement. For school districts that have financial statements audited by an independent CPA, it would be cost-effective to have your audit include preparation of a CAFR, thus transferring much of the responsibility to the auditor.

CAFR Checklist

ASBO International's Certificate of Excellence in Financial Reporting (COE) Program utilizes a CAFR preparation checklist, the Self-Evaluation Worksheet to assist in the preparation and issuance of a CAFR. This worksheet is a set of guidelines that serves as a valuable tool for developing a CAFR. The guidelines promote uniformity by referencing specific standards established by GASB. School systems that submit their CAFRs to ASBO International and meet the guidelines of the COE Program receive the prestigious Certificate of Excellence in Financial Reporting Award.

One State's Perspective

With almost 60 percent (73 out of 124) of Arizona school systems participating and receiving the Certificate of Excellence Award, Arizona accounts for 18 percent of the applications received by ASBO International. Why do so many Arizona school systems prepare CAFRs and participate in the COE Program?

In Arizona, numerous board members, taxpayers, and citizen's groups have acknowledged that the CAFR provides meaningful information and they praise school systems for preparing these reports. Preparing a CAFR and receiving ASBO International's Certificate of Excellence Award "improved the trust level from the board, staff and community and improved community relations and relations with other districts. It gives credibility to the business office as a whole," said Sherry Celaya, business manager for Casa Grande Union High School District #82.

Jim DiCello, assistant superintendent for business at Paradise Valley Unified School District, said, "My district features the Certificate of Excellence Award in the annual report that goes out to all patrons of the school district. It gives them a comfort level about the financial operations."

"When Avondale Elementary School District receives the COE award, it gives a message to the governing board and the community that we are committed to providing the best possible financial management for our district," said Starr Burks, director of business services for the Avondale, AZ, school district.

In turn, bond rating agencies responded by upgrading the bond rating of many Arizona school districts that were issuing CAFRs. The insurance companies also lowered the cost of insuring bonds. A one-category upgrade or downgrade of a bond rating could change the interest rate on borrowed money by as much as .25 percent. This may not seem like much, but on a $20 million bond issue it totals about $500,000 in savings.

Keith Clark, RSBA, school business official in Lake Havasu Unified School District, said he knows participation in the COE program is of value to his school district. After meeting with the rating analysts for both Standard and Poors and Moody's Investor Services, he said, "Having been awarded the Certificate of Excellence was a major factor in our bond rating upgrade."

According to Jeff Siemer, business manager, of Wilson Elementary School District,

"Moody's has mentioned to me that the program is meaningful and does contribute to the bond rating."

Dicello also reported that the COE had an impact on their bond sales. "At our last bond sale, we had 15 firms bid on our bonds," he said. "Our bond consultant indicated they rarely see more than eight to ten bids."

Brian Mee, assistant superintendent business and technology, Murphy Elementary School District concurs with DiCello. "Receiving the award has many benefits. Bonding companies give school districts more favorable ratings. Insurance and other financial institutions look upon your school district as a better risk and the community sees your organization as being fiscally sound."

Measurable Benefits

The value of preparing a CAFR and participating in ASBO's COE Program can be measured in debt service savings as well as the honor and recognition that comes from receiving a prestigious national award. Everyone in the school district will benefit and be proud of the accomplishment of the school district.

Gary Heinfeld, CPA, CGFM, is the managing partner of Heinfeld & Meech, P.C., in Tucson, AZ

For more information on ASBO International's Certificate of Excellence in Financial Reporting Program, contact ASBO International at: 11401 North Shore Drive, Reston, VA 20190 / Phone: (703) 478-0405 / www.asbointl.org.

ASSOCIATION OF SCHOOL BUSINESS OFFICIALS INTERNATIONAL

ASBO ACCENTS

May 1997

ASBO International Recognizes 25 Years of Excellence in School System Financial Reporting

By Linda K. Prevatte

Over 25 years ago, ASBO members set out to create a program that would help school systems create an annual financial document that would do more than report the standard numbers for the year. The program, which was quick to win national recognition, was entitled Certificate of Excellence in Financial Reporting (COE) and it did its job better than anyone could have imagined—helping school systems develop comprehensive annual financial reports (CAFRs) that actually help educate the school board and the public about the status of a school system's finances. Moreover, the main goal of the COE program was to publicly acknowledge a superior CAFR by awarding a Certificate of Excellence to those school systems who meet the guidelines of the program.

These guidelines help a school system create a document that not only chronicles the numbers but also reveals the story behind the numbers. The CAFR becomes an all-purpose ledger of the system's finances. It also validates the credibility of the school system's operations, measures the integrity and technical competence of the business staff, assists in strengthening presentations for bond issuance statements and provides professional recognition opportunities.

First-time as well as long-term recipients of this prestigious award find participation in the COE program a valuable experience.

Financial Records of High Quality

School systems have various reasons for applying to the COE program. In the case of Little Silver Board of Education (NJ), a first-time applicant and recipient, the program was a constructive and enriching experience for both the school district and its school business administrator, Cindy S. Barr-Rague. As Barr-Rague states, "The school financial records were in such bad state when I came on board that it took nearly six months to correct and update the records. Once we reached that point, I thought it was an excellent opportunity to enlighten the school board and community that the financial records were in the best condition possible. That's why I submitted our CAFR to the COE program for the first-time in December 1995."

Seal of Approval

Beaverton School District 48 (OR) has applied to the COE program for 14 consecutive years. What is their motivation? In response, Janice M. Ebner, Beaverton's school finance coordinator states that her district's yearly Certificate of Excellence Award gives their CAFR a "seal of approval" respected by bond holders and rating agencies. "The award increases the value of our CAFR in the eyes of the reader. If we did not apply each year, the users of the CAFR could assume that we have been unable to maintain our high standards of financial reporting or that our operations are not running as well as they should be. It might be interpreted as a sign that we are doing a less credible job."

Enhances Credibility

Another reason for participation in the COE program is the effect the program has on the credibility of a school entity's CAFR. For Illinois Valley Community College, participation in the program validates the work of their business office. Five-year recipient, Dr. Francis J. Zeller, Dean of Business Services, explains, "We had a malcontent run for office and attack the credibility of our financial reporting. The audit was used to inform the public of our straight forward financial reporting. We explained that we had received the Certificate of Excellence in Financial Reporting Award, based upon proper reporting of 10 years of financial data. It's always an asset to the business office to be able to say that it has received ASBO's imprimatur, the Certificate of Excellence Award."

Strengthen Investor Confidence

Does the program really make a difference to a school system? According to Dade County Public Schools, FL, the fourth largest school district in the U.S., it can and it does! Dade's Rodolfo J. Rodriguez, CPA, Controller, believes it has a definitive impact upon debt issuance. Rodriguez says, "Our debt issuance (i.e., General Obligation Bonds and Certificates of Participation) rating and investor confidence has been strengthened as a result of our participation in the COE program." As a 12-time COE recipient, Rodriguez knows the value of the award.

Professional Recognition

Participation in the program leads to professional recognition, say the professionals interviewed in this article. Janice Ebner states, "The COE award validates the work I do as a CPA. It is public recognition for a job well done...to attain this standard brings a feeling of real satisfaction."

Illinois Valley Community College's Zeller believes, "The award makes our board, administrative team and the community aware of the exceptional functions performed by the business office team." Barr-Raque concurs with her colleagues: "This award is a great reflection of the district. I take great pride in being able to share this document with our citizens and feel it gives them comfort knowing the financial records are documented accurately." Moreover, Rodriguez adds, "The award provides an added level of assurance regarding our finances for our school board and citizens of Dade County. We strongly support the COE program and will certainly continue to participate because of the value it provides for the staff and the school system."

For more information on ASBO International's Certificate of Excellence in Financial Reporting Program, contact ASBO International at: 11401 North Shore Drive, Reston, VA 20190 / Phone: (703) 478-0405 / www.asbointl.org.

Sharpen Your Pencils and Roll Up Your Sleeves:
A Case Study in Implementing the GASB's New Financial Reporting Model

By Tim Green, CPA, Margie E. Williamson, CPA, and
William L. Endris, Jr.

The Vernon Parish (Louisiana) School Board (district) early implemented Governmental Accounting Standards Board Statement No. 34, *Basic Financial Statements—and Management's Discussion and Analysis—for State and Local Governments* (GASB 34), for the fiscal year ending June 30, 1999. This article explains that experience and provides a lesson plan for others facing the same assignment. An article in the October 1999 edition of *School Business Affairs* explains the provisions of GASB 34.

Summary of Experience

Implementing GASB 34 was not only mentally challenging, it also required a large, tedious accounting effort. GASB 34 (commonly referred to as the "new financial reporting model") requires that the governmentwide financial statements use the economic resources measurement focus and accrual basis of accounting. The district did not enter the adjustments from modified accrual to accrual in its accounting records. A large part of our implementation challenge concerned capital assets.

The resulting comprehensive annual financial report (CAFR) was more informative yet more daunting than it had previously been. The readers of the district's report will need time to understand it and to establish benchmarks for grading the district's performance from year to year and for comparing that performance with that of other districts. Both the management's discussion and analysis (MD&A) and the governmentwide financial statement are enlightening and a substantial enhancement to the financial report.

Implementing GASB 34 was a great team effort between the district's Department of Finance and its independent auditors, with assistance from the Office of the Louisiana Legislative Auditor. The endeavor was hard work but brought pride of accomplishment and fabulous media recognition. Special thanks go to the district's superintendent and board for their support. Our discussion of the issues we faced and the ways in which we resolved them is intended to be informative only, not directional. Each district will face myriad issues and may need to solve the ones we discuss differently from the way we did, depending on particular facts, circumstances, and materiality.

Background

The district is the sole public school system in rural Vernon Parish. It has a student population of 10,000, 19 school buildings, and a central office building. The district reports approximately 40 funds in its CAFR, but has no component units or proprietary funds. Allen, Green & Company, LLP, has been the district's auditors for the past 8 years. The CAFR was submitted to the ASBO International Certificate of Excellence in Financial Reporting Program in January 2000 with an unqualified audit opinion.

Reasons for Early Implementation

The district was not required to implement GASB 34 until fiscal year 2002. (An individual district's implementation date ranges from fiscal year 2001 to fiscal year 2003, depending on the amount of its revenues in fiscal year 1999 and depending on whether it is a component of another government.) However, the director of finance liked the auditors' suggestion of early implementation. There was appeal in giving back to the school business official profession by providing a report example and communicating to others the issues encountered, thus easing the burden for those who followed. Also, the district might receive favorable recognition for leadership in government accounting and financial reporting and good stewardship of public dollars.

Homework

The district's auditors were familiar with GASB 34, having testified at two of the GASB public hearings on the project. Also, a member of the audit firm had served on the American Institute of Certified Public Accountants (AICPA) Governmental Accounting and Auditing Committee during the last 5 years of debate on GASB 34. That background made implementation less daunting than it might have been for many preparers and auditors. Also, with that background, the district decided to outsource much of the initial implementation work to the auditors, with the district becoming substantially more involved in subsequent years.

Even with a strong background in the particulars of the new financial reporting model, much homework was needed. Our primary chores related to the MD&A, fund classifications, and converting accounting data from modified accrual to accrual.

Developing the district's MD&A involved overhauling the municipal MD&A illustrated in GASB 34 to fit a school district. Since the district's CAFR was issued, illustrative MD&As for school districts have been issued in the GASB staff's *Guide to Implementation of GASB Statement No. 34 on Basic Financial Statements—and Management's Discussion and Analysis— for State and Local Governments: Questions and Answers* (GASB 34 Q&A) and ASBO International's *Statement 34 Implementation Recommendations for School Districts*.

We had to evaluate the child nutrition and student activity funds in light of the new definitions included in GASB 34 for enterprise funds and agency funds, respectively. GASB 34 permits any activity that charges a fee to external users to be reported as an enterprise fund. It also requires an activity to be reported as an enterprise fund if the activity's principal revenue source meets any one of the following criteria:

- The revenue source is financed with debt that is secured solely by a pledge of the net revenues from fees and charges of the activity.
- Laws or regulations require that the activity's cost of providing services, including capital costs (such as depreciation or debt service), be recovered with fees and charges, rather than with taxes or similar revenues.
- The pricing policies of the activity establish fees and charges designed to recover its costs, including capital costs.

The district concluded that its child nutrition program did not meet the definition requiring reporting as an enterprise fund. That was because the amount of reimbursement the district receives from the federal government for each free or reduced meal served is set nationally and federal regulations generally prohibit the district from expending child nutrition funds for land and buildings. In addition, the program's fees and charges are not set to cover equipment, land, or building costs. The program was reported as a special revenue fund.

We also deliberated the more restrictive definition of agency funds. The issue was whether the district's student activity funds should be special revenue or agency funds. Are assets held strictly in a custodial or fiduciary capacity? Does the fund include assets that will be forwarded to another fund of the district? The district concluded that its student activity funds should continue to be reported as agency funds because of certain Louisiana statutory requirements. For example, budgeting is not required for agency funds, whereas all special revenue funds must be budgeted; a separate bank account for student activity funds is required; and the school principals are responsible for the custody and operating practices of the student activity funds. However, in some states, districts collect and disburse student activity funds at the central office and prepare budgets for the student activity funds, and if unused at year-end, the monies revert to the district's general fund. In those situations, the student activity funds may be more appropriately reported as special revenue funds.

We also had to determine the accounting differences between the current resources measurement focus–modified basis of accounting and the economic resources measurement focus–accrual basis of accounting for the activities reported in the government funds. Some differences were fairly obvious: capital outlay versus depreciation expense, principal payments on debt, and interest expense recognized when due versus accrued daily. Other differences were more subtle: revenue recognition when measurable and available versus when earned (or otherwise accruable), liability recognition when due and payable versus when incurred, and gain or loss on the sale of capital assets versus proceeds from the sale. GASB 34 provides examples of the accounting differences between the governmentwide financial statements and the government fund financial statements. The district also implemented GASB Statement No. 33, *Accounting and Financial Reporting for Nonexchange Transactions* (GASB 33). Beyond the specific examples provided in GASB 34 and GASB 33, we examined other significant revenue and expenditure items by asking ourselves, "Has the revenue been earned or the liability been incurred?" If the answer was yes, we researched whether an additional accrual would be needed for the governmentwide financial statements.

Test Results
Management's Discussion and Analysis
GASB 34, paragraph 11b, requires that the MD&A include certain comparisons of governmentwide financial information from the current year with that of the prior year. This might have been a problem because the district did not have that information for the prior year. However, paragraph 145 of GASB 34 provides that in the first period that GASB 34 is applied, governments are not required to restate prior periods for purposes of providing the comparative data for MD&A. Instead, GASB 34 requires a statement in the MD&A alerting the reader that a comparative analysis of governmentwide data will be provided in future years.

Initially, we were concerned about the overlap of information between the MD&A and the CAFR transmittal letter. In the first draft of the transmittal letter, the district included a sentence alerting readers that in instances of overlap, the details were included in the MD&A. However, as the district further developed its MD&A, it seemed the MD&A was more focused on the governmentwide financial statements, whereas the transmittal letter was directed more toward the fund financial statements. Therefore, the district removed the referencing sentence from the transmittal letter, concluding that the overlap did not merit mention. However, item 7 in the subsequently issued GASB 34 Q&A states that any overlap should be included in the MD&A and that, in areas where overlap could occur, the transmittal letter could refer to the MD&A. Accordingly, the district's future reports will address any overlap using the guidance in the GASB 34 Q&A.

Required Supplemental Information

GASB 34 makes the reporting of required supplemental information (RSI) a major element of a government's annual report through its requirement for MD&A and a provision that encourages RSI presentation of budgetary comparison information. Previously, districts rarely presented RSI in their annual reports. (See Table 1 for items that may be included in a district's RSI.) This addition raised questions regarding the auditor's responsibility for RSI. Section 558, "Required Supplemental Information," of the AICPA *Codification of Statements on Auditing Standards* provides auditors with RSI guidance. The auditor is not required to audit RSI but must perform certain limited procedures and may need to add information about those procedures and their results to the auditor's report. However, the auditor's *opinion* on the fair presentation of the financial statements in conformity with generally accepted accounting principles (GAAP) will not encompass the RSI or be affected by whether or how the RSI is presented unless the auditor has been engaged by the district to audit the RSI.

Major Funds

GASB 34 tweaks the traditional fund-based financial statements by replacing the fund type display for government and enterprise funds with columnar displays of the main operating fund (the general fund) and other major funds. GASB 34, paragraph 76, requires an individual government or enterprise fund to be reported as a major fund if (1) total assets, liabilities, revenues, or expenditures and expenses of that fund are at least 10% of the corresponding total for all funds of that category or type; *and* (2) the total assets, liabilities, revenues, or expenditures and expenses of that individual fund are at least 5% of the corresponding total for all government and enterprise funds combined. Both percentage criteria must be met for the same element.

The district was concerned that there might be a large number of major funds and about annually reformatting the report should the individual major funds change each year. The district's major funds turned out to be the typically largest funds for a district—the general, child nutrition, and Title I funds. In fact, the child nutrition and Title I funds teetered on the edge of meeting the major funds criteria; ultimately, they did not meet the criteria. However, we speculated that those two funds would probably be close to meeting the criteria each year. Rather than facing the potential of reformatting the report each year, and given that GASB 34 permits districts to report any government or enterprise funds as major, the district decided to display those two funds as major. No other fund came close to meeting the major funds criteria. In hindsight, we believe that many districts may have few major funds because the lion's share of many districts' revenues and expenditures are reported in the general fund. On occasion, capital projects and debt service funds may meet the criteria for reporting as major funds.

Capital Assets

For some districts, capital asset accounting may be the most burdensome part of implementing GASB 34. A companion article, "Asphalt, Fleets, Bricks, and Mortar," which describes the district's experience in implementing the new capital assets standards, is included elsewhere in this issue of *School Business Affairs*.

Accounting and Report Preparation

We were unpleasantly surprised with the large amount of time it took to develop the accounting information and change the report for GASB 34 requirements. Table 2 identifies some of the tasks we faced.

Except for enhancements to the capital asset records, the district made no significant changes in its accounting records when implementing GASB 34. Consistent with past years, the district maintained its accounting records during the year on a cash basis and made year-end adjustments in the general ledger to step up to the modified accrual basis of accounting. The adjustments needed to convert to the accrual basis of accounting for the governmentwide financial statements were made without general ledger entries. Those accrual-based adjustments were calculated after the financial results and balances for all funds had been consolidated, making it unnecessary to identify the effect of those adjustments on each of the district's 40 funds.

GASB 34 dictates the placement of several items, such as the MD&A, the budgetary comparison information, and the financial statement reconciliations. Beyond mandated placements, the district's goal was to make the report format as similar to that of the previous year as possible. We thought that presentation consistency would ease the transition for both the preparer and the users of the financial statements.

Incremental Cost

In evaluating the incremental cost of implementing GASB 34, districts should consider both the additional effort of district personnel and the cost of outsourcing. The effort for this district was less than it might have been because it outsourced two major parts of the implementation—the inventory of capital assets and report preparation. With those duties outsourced, Department of Finance personnel were able to fulfill their job duties, while also providing the information needed for the report preparation.

The district spent approximately $15,000 for a complete capital assets inventory. The new inventory not only served the purpose of GASB 34 but also provided long overdue improvements to the district's capital assets listing. The incremental cost to prepare and audit the report was approximately 25% more than the prior year's audit cost. We anticipate that the second year's cost for auditor services will be lower because the auditors will be less involved with report preparation.

Board and Media Reaction

We discussed the report for over an hour in a regular board meeting. Most board member questions related to the statement of activities. Questions arose because the loss shown in the fund financial statements for the child nutrition program was less than the net cost shown for that program in the governmentwide statement of activities. We explained the differences between the two measures, with depreciation expense in the governmentwide statement being the largest difference.

The report was the first issued in Louisiana that was prepared pursuant to GASB 34. The local, regional, and even statewide media coverage was very positive. The Louisiana legislative auditor confirmed the significance of the accomplishment. A second round of publicity occurred when a GASB press release praised the district for its courage in early implementation.

Plans for the 2000 CAFR

With the difficult first-year implementation complete and with the addition of another accounting position in the district's Department of Finance, the district will prepare the 2000 CAFR internally rather than outsource it to the auditors.

We believe that one item could be improved in the 2000 CAFR: the MD&A. Although the first MD&A included all the elements required by GASB 34, the district wishes to enhance the presentation.

The district plans to become engrossed in the details of the accounting and report preparation. With a thorough knowledge of those items, the district can assist other districts with their first GASB 34implementation.

Cheat Sheet

The benefits of homework have always been an axiom in education. This project is no exception. Obtain and read your research books. (See Table 3 for a list of research books and other sources of information.) You cannot accomplish this project with a 2-hour cram course; it will take some serious book cracking.

Start early. In our case, although the team had a good understanding of the new model, the project was a formidable challenge. Even with an early start, we experienced a small delay in issuing the district's report because of the extent of the effort.

A district should start planning for implementation 12 months before the beginning of the actual implementation year. This period will allow preparers and auditors to concur on the appropriate adjustments that will eventually be necessary to develop beginning-of-the-year account balances for the year of implementation. (Beginning balances for the governmentwide statement of net assets are needed to ensure that the statement of activities is properly stated in conformity with GAAP in the year of implementation.) Determining beginning balances while preparing and auditing the prior year's report will make the transition smoother and enhance the probability of accurate and verifiable beginning balances.

It is never too early to start work on necessary changes to the capital assets listing. (We discuss the tasks that may be needed in the companion article.) Early implementation enhances the probability of good media coverage. The goodwill that can be created by a positive article on good financial stewardship is priceless. The longer a district waits, the less newsworthy the accomplishment will be.

You don't need to change the way the accounting records are maintained. Our approach of making the step-up adjustments to the governmentwide financial statements outside of the accounting records was simple and effective. We plan to repeat this approach for the 2000 CAFR.

Bibliography

American Institute of Certified Public Accountants. (1999). *Codification of statements on auditing standards.* Jersey City, NJ: Author.

Association of School Business Officials International. (2000, September). *GASB Statement No. 34 implementation recommendations for school districts.* Reston, VA: Author.

Governmental Accounting Standards Board. (1998, December). *Accounting and financial reporting for nonexchange transactions* (Statement No. 33). Norwalk, CT: Author.

Governmental Accounting Standards Board. (1999, June). B*asic financial statements—and management's discussion and analysis—for state and local governments* (Statement No. 34). Norwalk, CT: Author.

Governmental Accounting Standards Board. (2000, March). *Recognition and measurement of certain liabilities and expenditures in governmental fund financial statements* (Interpretation No. 6). Norwalk, CT: Author.

Governmental Accounting Standards Board. (2000, April). *Recipient reporting for certain shared nonexchange revenues, an amendment of GASB Statement No. 33* (Statement No. 36). Norwalk, CT: Author.

Governmental Accounting Standards Board. (2000, May). *Guide to implementation of GASB Statement No. 34 on basic financial statements—and management's discussion and analysis—for state and local governments: Questions and answers.* Norwalk, CT: Author.

Wood, V. M. (1999). *Understanding and implementing GASB's new financial reporting model: A question and answer guide for preparers and auditors of state and local governmental financial statements.* New York: American Institute of Certified Public Accountants.

Tim Green, CPA, and Margie E. Williamson, CPA, are partners with Allen, Green & Company, LLP, independent auditors and consultants, in Monroe, Louisiana. Tim is a former chair of the AICPA Governmental Accounting and Auditing Committee. Margie is a member of the Society of Louisiana CPAs Governmental Accounting and Auditing Committee. Allen, Green & Company, LLP, audits more school districts in Louisiana than does any other firm.

William L. Endris, Jr., has been the director of finance for the Vernon Parish School Board in Leesville, Louisiana, for 15 of his 25-year tenure with the district.

Table 1
Annual Report Structure for School Districts

Required Supplementary Information	Management's Discussion & Analysis (MD&A)				Outside the Scope of the Audit
Required Reporting in Conformity with Generally Accepted Accounting Principles	Basic Financial Statements				Included in the Scope of the Audit
	Government-wide Financial Statements	Fund Financial Statements			
		Government Funds	Proprietary Funds	Fiduciary Funds	
	Notes to the Basic Financial Statements				
Required Supplementary Information	Budgetary Comparison Information Modified Approach Information (Infrastructure Assets) Pension Information (for Certain Plan Types)				Outside the Scope of the Audit

Table 2
Initial Homework Assignments

Study Governmental Accounting Standards Board Statement No. 34 (GASB 34) and other research books (see Table 3) and obtain training on GASB 34.

Determine whether the district qualifies as a special-purpose government engaged in a single program, thus allowing for fewer or modified financial statements. Although possible, it is extremely unlikely that a school district would be engaged in a single program (GASB 34, paragraphs 135–137).

Determine and quantify the differences between the current financial resources measurement–modified accrual basis of accounting and the economic resources measurement focus–accrual basis of accounting (such as calculating depreciation expense, accrued interest on general long-term debt, and the gain or loss on the sale or other disposition of capital assets).

Change the layout of the annual financial report. GASB 34 dictates the placement of certain items, such as the management's discussion and analysis (MD&A), other required supplemental information (RSI), and the financial statement reconciliations.

Draft the MD&A.

Add the governmentwide financial statements.

Determine which funds to report as major funds (GASB 34, paragraph 76).

Format the fund financial statements for major funds display.

Revise the notes to the basic financial statements to focus on the district's government activities, business-type activities, major funds, and aggregate nonmajor funds; delete obsolete notes; add new notes; and change the terminology in the notes.

Change the terminology throughout the report.

Revise and relocate the budgetary comparison information and certain note disclosures to RSI.
Format the combining statements and schedules to display nonmajor funds only.

Prepare the reconciliations between the fund financial statements and the governmentwide financial statements.

Revamp the capital asset inventory listing so that information is available to calculate depreciation.

Determine the assignment of capital assets to be able to charge depreciation expense to each functional category.

Determine the reporting of depreciation expense for capital assets used by multiple functions, including functional allocations if appropriate.

Determine which changes may be necessary for GASB 34's changes in fund definitions.

Determine the eliminations needed for internal balances and activities (GASB 34, paragraphs 58–62).

Differentiate program revenues and general revenues.

Analyze program revenues to identify charges for services, operating grants and contributions, and capital grants and contributions.

Identify special and extraordinary items.

Calculate the amounts of the net asset categories.

Table 3
Research Books and Sources of Additional Information

GASB Statement No. 33, *Accounting and Financial Reporting for Nonexchange Transactions*

GASB Statement No. 34, *Basic Financial Statements—and Management's Discussion and Analysis—for State and Local Governments*

GASB Statement No. 36, *Recipient Reporting for Certain Shared Nonexchange Revenues, an Amendment of GASB Statement No. 33*

GASB Interpretation No. 6, *Recognition and Measurement of Certain Liabilities and Expenditures in Governmental Fund Financial Statements*

Guide to Implementation of GASB Statement No. 34 on Basic Financial Statements—and Management's Discussion and Analysis—for State and Local Governments: Questions and Answers

ASBO International's *GASB Statement No. 34 Implementation Recommendations for School Districts*

Louisiana Legislative Auditor's web site (http://www.lla.state.la.us)
1. Two school district reports prepared pursuant to the new reporting model
2. Questions and answers on actual implementation experiences of a city and a school district

Vernon Parish School System's web site (http://www.vpsb.k12.la.us)
1. Fiscal year 1999 comprehensive annual financial report (CAFR)
2. Questions and answers on implementation experience of the district
3. Fiscal year 2000 CAFR (to be posted when available)
4. Annual report of district that includes only the minimum GASB 34 requirements

Asphalt, Fleets, Bricks, and Mortar

By Tim Green, CPA, Margie E. Williamson, CPA, and
William L. Endris, Jr.

Governmental Accounting Standards Board Statement No. 34, *Basic Financial Statements—and Management's Discussion and Analysis—for State and Local Governments* (GASB 34), generally requires school districts to capitalize and depreciate their capital assets in their financial statements. This article explains our experience in implementing those requirements for the Vernon Parish (Louisiana) School Board's (district's) June 30, 1999, comprehensive annual financial report (CAFR). A companion article, "Sharpen Your Pencils and Roll Up Your Sleeves: A Case Study in Implementing the GASB's New Financial Reporting Model," which describes other aspects of the district's early implementation of GASB 34, is included elsewhere in this issue of *School Business Affairs*.

Capital assets include land, land improvements, easements, buildings, building improvements, vehicles, machinery, equipment, works of art and historical treasures, infrastructure assets, and all other tangible or intangible assets that are used in operations and that have initial useful lives extending beyond a single reporting period.

GASB 34 (commonly referred to as the "new financial reporting model") requires the preparation of governmentwide financial statements using the economic resources measurement focus and the accrual basis of accounting. Unlike the present reporting of capital assets acquired through or associated with government funds, the new reporting model generally dictates that the consumption of those assets be reported through a charge in the governmentwide statement of activities for depreciation expense.

Our discussion of the issues we faced and the ways in which we resolved them is intended to be informative only, not directional. Each district will face myriad issues and may need to solve the ones we discuss differently from the way we did, depending on particular facts, circumstances, and materiality.

Outsourcing Physical Inventory

Early in its implementation process, the district concluded that its capital asset records had shortcomings. The district outsourced a complete inventory of capital assets at all of its 20 sites. The district decided to outsource the work because the vendor could complete the inventory within 30 days and had a database that could provide estimated historical cost for most of the district's capital assets. The vendor also had significant experience and a methodical inventory approach.

Acquisition Dates

The district's previous capital asset records did not include the dates that the assets had been acquired. Acquisition dates are needed to calculate depreciation expense and accumulated depreciation. Ultimately, the missing dates posed no significant problem. We realized that if, for example, a capital asset had a 6-year estimated useful life, it didn't matter whether the asset was purchased in 1985, 1989, or 1991; it would be fully depreciated. The acquisition date would be important only if the estimated time since the asset was acquired was less than the estimated useful life of the asset.

The daunting job of establishing acquisition dates quickly became a manageable task when we concluded that probably 75% of the district's capital assets were so old that they had been fully depreciated.

Depreciation Expense by Function

GASB 34 requires depreciation expense for capital assets that can be identified specifically with a function to be included in that function's direct expenses. In most cases, that means that depreciation expense will be recorded, for example, as a cost of regular instruction, special instruction, student transportation, the child nutrition program, or maintenance and operations. The vendor's capital asset inventory identified asset location but did not identify the functions for which the assets were used. The district had to add this information to the vendor's inventory report.

Depreciation Allocation

Another issue in assigning capital assets to functions is allocating depreciation expense for capital assets that benefit two or more functions. For example, the district's school buildings are used for the same several functions. We allocated school building depreciation based on percentages representing the relative square footage use of the buildings for instruction, the child nutrition program, and school administration. All of the depreciation expense for instruction was classified as regular instruction because only an immaterial portion of the time-use of the buildings was dedicated to special or other instruction. It is the only other instructional function the district reports in its CAFR. (If a district were to find that a building or other capital asset is used by "essentially all" of its functions, GASB 34, paragraph 44, permits the district not to allocate the depreciation among functions. Instead, it permits depreciation on that particular building or asset to be included as a separate line item or as part of a "general" function.)

Estimated Useful Lives

To determine estimated useful lives of its capital assets, the district used an Internal Revenue Service (IRS) publication that includes a fairly extensive list of assets and their estimated useful lives. After the district issued its CAFR, the GASB staff released its *Guide to Implementation of GASB Statement No. 34 on Basic Financial Statements—and Management's Discussion and Analysis—for State and Local Governments: Questions and Answers* (GASB 34 Q&A). The GASB 34 Q&A discourages the use of IRS established lives, stating in item 48 that "schedules of depreciable lives established by federal or state tax regulations are generally not intended to represent useful lives." Item 47 in the GASB 34 Q&A states, "Useful lives should be based upon the government's own experience and plans for the assets. Although comparison with other governments or other organizations may provide some guidance, property management practices, asset usage, and other variables (such as weather) may vary significantly between governments." Consequently, for the 2000 CAFR, we will review the previously assigned estimated useful lives using the guidance in the GASB 34 Q&A.

Salvage Value

Generally, the district uses its capital assets, except for vehicles, until they are completely worn out and either abandoned or used as parts. Therefore, salvage value was established for vehicles only. Recent experience indicated that the trade-in allowance for district vehicles was approximately 10% of their original purchase price. Accordingly, the district established a 10% salvage value for vehicles.

Depreciation Method
GASB 34, paragraph 161, permits governments to use any established depreciation method. The district adopted the straight-line method because of its ease of use. Also, the district had no compelling reason to use any other method.

Capital Asset Software
The district's new capital assets listing is an electronic spreadsheet that automatically calculates beginning and year-end accumulated depreciation and current year depreciation expense. The disadvantage of the spreadsheet is the ease of adding or deleting items without a record of the changes. Although this record served the district's purposes for the 1999 CAFR, we are concerned about the lack of control over future additions and deletions. The district has not yet addressed this control issue or decided whether to continue to use the spreadsheet.

Infrastructure Assets
Infrastructure assets are long-lived capital assets that are normally stationary in nature and can normally be preserved for a significantly greater number of years than most capital assets. Examples of infrastructure assets are roads, bridges, tunnels, drainage systems, water and sewer systems, dams, and lighting systems. Buildings are not considered infrastructure assets, except those that are an ancillary part of a network of infrastructure assets.

When the 1999 CAFR was prepared, we had not decided whether the district had general infrastructure assets that should be retroactively capitalized. We could address this issue later because GASB 34 permits a 4-year delay for the retroactive capitalization of those assets. (Note that GASB 34 also does not require very small governments to retroactively capitalize those assets.) The district has since concluded that it has no infrastructure assets.

Some asked whether football stadiums and tracks were infrastructure assets. We thought not and classified the tracks as exhaustible land improvements (which are subject to depreciation) and the football stadiums as buildings. We also classified surfaces for driveways and parking lots as exhaustible land improvements.

Summary
A district will likely have to give considerable attention to capital assets as it prepares to implement GASB 34. The present method of "rolling forward" the balances of capital asset amounts in the general fixed-asset account group by adding the current year's additions and deletions to prior-year balances will clearly not suffice for GASB 34. Specifically, districts may need more accurate records and additional capital asset data. Among other tasks, districts will also need to identify functional assignments and allocations for the assets and select a depreciation method.

Bibliography

American Institute of Certified Public Accountants. (1999). *Codification of statements on auditing standards.* Jersey City, NJ: Author.

Association of School Business Officials International. (2000, September). *Statement 34 implementation recommendations for school districts.* Reston, VA: Author.

Governmental Accounting Standards Board. (1999, June). *Basic financial statements—and management's discussion and analysis—for state and local governments (Statement No. 34).* Norwalk, CT: Author.

Governmental Accounting Standards Board. (2000, May). *Guide to implementation of GASB Statement No. 34 on basic financial statements—and management's discussion and analysis—for state and local governments: Questions and answers.* Norwalk, CT: Author.

Tim Green, CPA, and Margie E. Williamson, CPA, are partners with Allen, Green & Company, LLP, independent auditors and consultants, in Monroe, Louisiana. Tim is a former chair of the American Institute of Certified Public Accountants Governmental Accounting and Auditing Committee. Margie is a member of the Society of Louisiana CPAs Governmental Accounting and Auditing Committee. Allen, Green & Company, LLP, audits more school districts in Louisiana than does any other firm.

William L. Endris, Jr., has been the director of finance for the Vernon Parish School Board in Leesville, Louisiana, for 15 of his 25-year tenure with the district.

PREFACE TO APPENDICES B & C

APPENDICES B & C of this Book include two complete CAFR's of an Arizona School District. One presents the CAFR under the old reporting model and the other presents the CAFR under the new reporting model (GASB Statement 34). These two CAFR's provide a clear comparison between the two reporting models. The appendixes are intended to be additional reference material for the preparation of a school system's CAFR and should be used in conjunction with the other reference material.

APPENDIX B

ASBO INTERNATIONAL SCHOOL DISTRICT

COMPREHENSIVE ANNUAL FINANCIAL REPORT – OLD REPORTING MODEL

(This page intentionally left blank)

AVONDALE ELEMENTARY SCHOOL DISTRICT NO. 44

AVONDALE, ARIZONA

COMPREHENSIVE ANNUAL FINANCIAL REPORT
FOR THE FISCAL YEAR ENDED JUNE 30, 2001

Issued by:
Business & Finance Department

AVONDALE ELEMENTARY SCHOOL DISTRICT NO. 44

TABLE OF CONTENTS

AVONDALE ELEMENTARY SCHOOL DISTRICT NO. 44

TABLE OF CONTENTS (Cont'd)

AVONDALE ELEMENTARY SCHOOL DISTRICT NO. 44

TABLE OF CONTENTS (Concl'd)

INTRODUCTORY SECTION

(This page intentionally left blank)

"Serving the Communities
of Avondale and Goodyear"

Avondale
ELEMENTARY SCHOOL DISTRICT
NO. 44

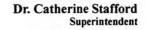

Dr. Catherine Stafford
Superintendent

Dr. Linda Ronnebaum
Assistant Superintendent

Julia E. Tribbett
Director of Business Operations

October 9, 2001

Governing Board
Avondale Elementary School District No. 44
235 West Western Avenue
Avondale, AZ 85323

The comprehensive annual financial report of Avondale Elementary School District No. 44 for the fiscal year ended June 30, 2001, is hereby submitted. Responsibility for both the accuracy of the data, and the completeness and fairness of the presentation, including all disclosures, rests with the District. To the best of our knowledge and belief, the enclosed data are accurate in all material respects and are reported in a manner designed to present fairly the financial position and results of operations of the various funds and account groups of the District. All disclosures necessary to enable the reader to gain an understanding of the District's financial activity have been included.

The comprehensive annual financial report is presented in three sections: introductory, financial and statistical. The introductory section includes this transmittal letter, the District's organization chart and a list of District officials and administrative staff. The financial section includes the general purpose financial statements and the combining and individual fund and account group financial statements and schedules, as well as the auditors' report on the financial statements and schedules. The statistical section includes selected financial and demographic information, generally presented on a multi-year basis. The District is required to undergo an annual single audit in conformity with the provisions of the Single Audit Act Amendments of 1996 and the U.S. Office of Management and Budget Circular A-133, *Audits of States, Local Governments, and Non-Profit Organizations*. The schedule of expenditures of federal awards required by the Single Audit Act is included in a separate report, along with the auditors' report on the internal control and compliance with applicable laws and regulations.

The financial reporting entity (the District) includes all the funds and account groups of the primary government (i.e., Avondale Elementary School District No. 44 as legally defined). The District's major operations include education, student transportation, construction and maintenance of District facilities and food services.

Avondale Elementary School District No. 44 is one of fifty-five public school districts located in Maricopa County, Arizona. It provides a program of public education from kindergarten through grade eight.

i

ECONOMIC CONDITION AND OUTLOOK

The Avondale Elementary School District No. 44 is located 17 miles west of downtown Phoenix. A portion of the City of Goodyear and the City of Avondale are included within the area served by the District. The District encompasses an area of approximately 30 square miles, and has set its vision as "Passion and Commitment for Educational Excellence".

The economy of the cities of Goodyear and Avondale and of Maricopa County, in general, is among the most positive in the State. Because of the District's close proximity to Phoenix, it is located in the direct path of the westward expansion of the City. Although agriculture has been the economic mainstay of the area for many years, commerce, light manufacturing, and residential development continue to expand and contribute to the District's growth and economic diversity. Some of the firms operating within the District's boundaries include Rubbermaid, Inc, Lockheed Martin, Cavco Industries, Inc, Arizona Public Services, Snyder of Hanover, and McLane Company, Inc,. The area is experiencing rapid expansion in retail service centers and commercial facilities. In recent years, new housing starts for both the cities of Goodyear and Avondale have steadily increased. These two cities are each governed by a mayor and a six-member council. Phoenix and the rest of Maricopa County have become one of the fastest growing regional markets in the United States. The number of manufacturing and wholesale businesses located in the metropolitan area is approaching 3,000. This growth has been stimulated by a combination of warm climate, a substantial, well-educated labor pool, a wide range of support industries, and a governmental climate that is supportive of economic growth and investment.

A few of the major firms represented in Phoenix include Honeywell/Allied Signal, General Electric, Goodyear, Motorola, American Express, McDonnell-Douglas, Western Electric, Digital Equipment, America West Airlines and Bank One. In addition, the metropolitan area provides excellent educational and training opportunities through seven community colleges, four private colleges and graduate schools, and one state university.

Maricopa County is located in the south-central portion of Arizona and encompasses an area of approximately 9,226 square miles. Its boundaries encompass the cities of Phoenix, Scottsdale, Mesa, Tempe, Glendale, Chandler, and such towns as Gilbert, Paradise Valley and Fountain Hills. The County's 1995 population was estimated at 2,528,700 or about 60 percent of the total population of the state. Maricopa County has a very wide range of economic sectors supporting its substantial growth. It has been estimated that 6,000 to 7,000 people are moving into Maricopa County every month. Maricopa County has, for some time, enjoyed an unemployment rate that was somewhat lower than the national average.

The service industry is the largest employment sector in the County, partly fueled by the $2+ billion per year tourist industry. The County has excellent accommodations, diverse cultural and recreational activities, and a favorable climate attracting millions to the area annually. Wholesale and retail trade is the second largest employment category, employing over a quarter million people. Retail sales have grown by about 50 percent in the past five or six years and, in 2000 exceeded $23 billion.

Manufacturing, consisting primarily of high technology companies is the third largest employment sector. Approximately 130,000 persons are working in the manufacturing industry. Other factors aiding economic growth include major expansions of the international airport serving the area, a favorable business climate and the presence of a well developed and expanding transportation infrastructure.

MAJOR INITIATIVES FOR THE YEAR AND FOR THE FUTURE

The District completed the construction of Wildflower School in March of 2000, financed through the bond sale of May 1998. The Arizona School Facilities Board now provides funds for new construction projects. Avondale Elementary District has one school, Desert Star, currently under construction with the opening scheduled for Fall of 2002. The State Facilities Board has approved three additional schools projected to open in the next five years. The District continues to increase and upgrade technology available to students and staff on all sites.

The Avondale Elementary School District is experiencing rapid growth. The secondary assessed value has grown at an average rate of 5.8% in the last 10 years and 13.9 in the last 5 years. This recognized growth has allowed the District to utilize its final bond sale proceeds from the voter authorized $14 million passed in May 1998.

FINANCIAL INFORMATION

Management of the District is responsible for establishing and maintaining internal control designed to ensure that the assets of the District are protected from loss, theft or misuse and to ensure that adequate accounting data are compiled to allow for the preparation of financial statements in conformity with generally accepted accounting principles. Internal control is designed to provide reasonable, but not absolute, assurance that these objectives are met. The concept of reasonable assurance recognizes that: (1) the cost of a control should not exceed the benefits likely to be derived; and (2) the valuation of costs and benefits requires estimates and judgments by management.

Single Audit. As a recipient of federal, state and county financial assistance, the District also is responsible for ensuring that adequate internal control is in place to ensure compliance with applicable laws and regulations related to those programs. Internal control is subject to periodic evaluation by management of the District.

As a part of the District's single audit, described earlier, tests are made to determine the adequacy of internal control, including that portion related to federal financial assistance programs, as well as to determine that the District has complied with applicable laws and regulations. The results of the District's single audit for the fiscal year ended June 30, 2001 provided no instances of material weaknesses in internal control or significant violations of applicable laws and regulations.

Budgeting Controls. In addition, the District maintains budgetary controls. The objective of these budgetary controls is to ensure compliance with legal provisions embodied in the annual expenditure budget approved by the District's governing board. Activities of the General Fund, Special Revenue Funds, Debt Service Fund and Capital Projects Funds are included in the annual expenditure budget. The level of budgetary control (that is, the level at which expenditures cannot exceed the appropriated amount) is established at the individual fund level for all funds. Although not adopted, an annual budget of revenue from all sources is prepared. The expenditure budget can be revised annually per Arizona Revised Statutes; however, the revenue budget cannot be revised. Therefore a deficit budgeted fund balance in some funds can occur when the expenditure budget is increased during a revision. The District also maintains an encumbrance accounting system as one technique of accomplishing budgetary control. Encumbered amounts lapse at year end. However, encumbrances generally are reappropriated as part of the following year's budget.

As demonstrated by the statements and schedules included in the financial section of this report, the District continues to meet its responsibility for sound financial management.

General Government Functions. The following schedule presents a summary of General Fund, Special Revenue Funds and Debt Service Fund revenues for the fiscal year ended June 30, 2001 and the amount and percentage of increases in relation to prior year revenues.

Revenues	Amount	Percent of Total	Increase from 1999-00	Percent of Increase
Other local	$ 1,328,018	7.9%	$ 261,205	24.5%
Property taxes	3,902,160	23.3	374,992	10.6
State aid and grants	8,928,865	53.3	847,604	10.5
Federal aid, grants and reimbursements	2,603,559	15.5	277,016	11.9
Total	$ 16,762,602	100.0%	$ 1,760,817	11.7%

The increase in other local revenues is due to increased county aid in the General Fund and an increase of interest income in the Debt Service Fund. The increase in property taxes revenue is due to an increase in the primary and secondary assessed valuations of District property. The increase in state aid and grants is due to increased state equalization revenue in the General Fund. The increase in federal aid and grants is due to increased revenues in the Title II - Eisenhower Grant, EHA Title VI-B Entitlement, Class Size Reduction, and Food Services Funds.

The following schedule presents a summary of General Fund, Special Revenue Funds and Debt Service Fund expenditures for the fiscal year ended June 30, 2001 and the percentage of increases and decreases in relation to prior year amounts.

Expenditures	Amount	Percent of Total	Increase/ (Decrease) from 1999-00	Percent of Increase/ (Decrease)
Current - Instruction	$ 8,742,386	52.2%	$ 1,071,692	14.0%
Support services – Students and Staff	1,344,685	8.0	177,097	15.2
Support services – Administration	1,455,641	8.7	105,253	7.8
Operation and maintenance of plant services	1,583,815	9.5	108,750	7.4
Student transportation services	460,365	2.7	34,359	8.1
Operation of non-instructional services	1,088,019	6.5	35,720	3.4
Capital Outlay	304,554	1.8	(106,958)	(26.0)
Debt Service	1,767,689	10.6	(263,420)	(13.0)
Total	$ 16,747,154	100.0%	$ 1,162,493	7.5%

The overall increase in current expenditures is due to the significant increase in average daily membership. Capital outlay expenditures decreased due to decreases in capital expenditures in the E-

Rate and Food Services Funds. Debt Service expenditures decreased due to the retirement of capital appreciation bonds in the previous year.

Significant Changes in Fund Equity. The General Fund equity decreased from the prior year by $326,735 to $291,694 as of June 30, 2001, due to utilization of beginning fund balance to lower the tax rate. The Special Revenue Funds equity increased $158,807 to 1,332,455 due to increased federal revenue in the Title II - Eisenhower Grant, EHA Title VI-B Entitlement, Class Size Reduction and Food Services Funds. The Debt Service Fund shows an increase in fund equity of $342,149, to $601,977 as of June 30, 2001, due to an increase in property tax revenue. The Capital Projects Funds show an increase in fund equity of $212,670 to $4,086,368 as of June 30, 2001, due to increased revenue in the New School Facilities and Building Renewal Funds.

Debt Administration. The State of Arizona now provides funds for construction and maintenance of school facilities to meet the minimum capital facilities standards. Due to this change in funding, a school district may issue Class A school construction bonds until December 31, 1999. Beginning January 1, 2000, school districts may issue Class B bonds to enhance facilities beyond the minimum standards established by the State. Districts may issue Class B bonds up to an amount not exceeding 5% of the secondary assessed valuation or $1500 per student, whichever is greater. In addition, the Class B bonds, together with outstanding Class A bonds previously issued, cannot exceed the constitutional debt limit of 15% of the secondary assessed valuation. The District currently has no Class B bonds outstanding.

At June 30, 2001, the District had a number of debt issues outstanding. As of June 30, 2001, the District's net general obligation and refunding bonded debt was $9,543,023, and debt per capita equaled $284.

Cash Management. Cash temporarily idle during the year was invested in interest-bearing accounts and time certificates of deposit. In addition, the County Treasurer pools money from all districts in the County and invests surplus cash; allocating the interest back to the districts based on the districts' average monthly balances with the County Treasurer. In 2000-01, interest earned on all funds was $282,081.

The District's investment policy is to minimize credit and market risks while maintaining a competitive yield on its portfolio. Accordingly, deposits were either insured by federal depository insurance or collateralized.

Risk Management. The District's administration is charged with the responsibility of supervising the protection of the District's assets by employing various risk management techniques and procedures to reduce, absorb, minimize or transfer risk. The District carries insurance for general liability, auto liability and workers' compensation. District property is insured for its replacement value. The administration is also responsible for directing the District's fringe benefits program which includes the administration of health, life and other benefits for all full-time and some part-time employees.

OTHER INFORMATION

Independent Audit. State statutes require an annual audit by independent certified public accountants. The accounting firm of Heinfeld & Meech, P.C., CPAs, was selected by the District. In addition to meeting the requirements set forth in state statutes, the audit also was designed to meet the requirements of the federal Single Audit Act and related OMB Circular A-133. The auditors' report on the general purpose financial statements and combining, individual fund and account group financial statements and schedules is included in the financial section of this report. The auditors' reports related specifically to internal control and compliance with laws and regulations are included in the Single Audit section of this report.

Awards. The Association of School Business Officials (ASBO) awarded a Certificate of Excellence in Financial Reporting to the District for its comprehensive annual financial report for the fiscal year ended June 30, 2000. This was the seventh year that the District received this prestigious award. In addition, the Government Finance Officers Association (GFOA) awarded a Certificate of Achievement in Financial Reporting to the District for its comprehensive annual financial report for the fiscal year ended June 30, 2000. In order to be awarded these certificates, the District published an easily readable and efficiently organized comprehensive annual financial report. This report satisfied both generally accepted accounting principles and applicable legal requirements.

These certificates are valid for a period of one year only. We believe that our current comprehensive annual financial report continues to meet the programs' requirements and we are submitting it to ASBO and GFOA to determine its eligibility for fiscal year 2000-01.

Acknowledgments. The preparation of the comprehensive annual financial report on a timely basis was made possible by the dedicated service of the entire staff of the finance department. Each member of the department has our sincere appreciation for the contributions made in the preparation of this report.

In closing, without the leadership and support of the governing board of the District, preparation of this report would not have been possible.

Sincerely,

Dr. Catherine Stafford
  Superintendent

Julia Tribbett
Director of Business Services

ASSOCIATION OF SCHOOL BUSINESS OFFICIALS

INTERNATIONAL

This Certificate of Excellence in Financial Reporting is presented to

AVONDALE ELEMENTARY SCHOOL DISTRICT NO. 44

For its Comprehensive Annual Financial Report (CAFR)
For the Fiscal Year Ended June 30, 2000

Upon recommendation of the Association's Panel of Review which has judged that the Report substantially conforms to principles and standards of ASBO's Certificate of Excellence Program

Linda White
President

Don A. Kusper
Executive Director

Certificate of Achievement for Excellence in Financial Reporting

Presented to

Avondale Elementary School District No. 44, Arizona

For its Comprehensive Annual
Financial Report
for the Fiscal Year Ended
June 30, 2000

A Certificate of Achievement for Excellence in Financial
Reporting is presented by the Government Finance Officers
Association of the United States and Canada to
government units and public employee retirement
systems whose comprehensive annual financial
reports (CAFRs) achieve the highest
standards in government accounting
and financial reporting.

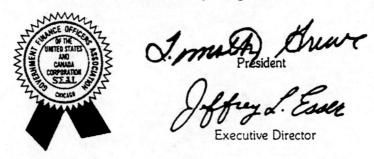

President

Executive Director

AVONDALE ELEMENTARY SCHOOL DISTRICT No. 44

- Governing Board
  - Superintendent
    - Assistant Superintendent
      - District Office Support Staff
        - Operations Director
          - Support Staff
        - Food Service Director
          - Support Staff
        - Business Director
          - Support Staff
        - Federal Programs & Bilingual Director
          - Support Staff
        - Special Services Director
          - Support Staff
      - Kinder/Elementary Principal
        - Teachers
        - Support Staff
      - Pioneer Principal
        - Teachers
        - Support Staff
      - Lattie Coor Principal
        - Teachers
        - Support Staff
      - Wildflower Principal
        - Teachers
        - Support Staff
      - AMS Principal
        - Teachers
        - Support Staff

AVONDALE ELEMENTARY SCHOOL DISTRICT NO. 44

LIST OF PRINCIPAL OFFICIALS

GOVERNING BOARD

Mark Gonzales
President

Tony Aguirre
Member

Juanita Rodriguez
Vice President

Stephen Warner
Member

Mollie Belcher
Member

ADMINISTRATIVE STAFF

Dr. Catherine Stafford, Superintendent

Dr. Linda Ronnebaum, Assistant Superintendent

Julia Tribbett, Director of Business Operations

FINANCIAL SECTION

(This page intentionally left blank)

OFFICIAL LETTERHEAD OF THE INDEPENDENT AUDITOR

INDEPENDENT AUDITORS' REPORT

Governing Board
Avondale Elementary School District No. 44

Illustrative examples of the Independent Auditors' Report are available from the American Institute of Certified Public Accountants (AICPA). These illustrative examples are provided by the AICPA in the organization's Guidance Related to OMB Circular A-133 *Audits of States, Local Governments, and Non-Profit Organizations* and can be found at the AICPA website at www.aicpa.org.

Certified Public Accountants

October 9, 2001

(This page intentionally left blank)

GENERAL PURPOSE FINANCIAL STATEMENTS

AVONDALE ELEMENTARY SCHOOL DISTRICT NO. 44
COMBINED BALANCE SHEET - ALL FUND TYPES AND ACCOUNT GROUPS
JUNE 30, 2001

		Governmental Fund Types		
	General	Special Revenue	Debt Service	Capital Projec
ASSETS AND OTHER DEBITS				
Assets:				
Cash and investments	$ 13,891	$ 1,276,298	$ 2,031,687	$ 4,186,3
Property taxes receivable	95,967		85,882	7,7
Due from governmental entities		218,621		
Due from other funds		91,455		
Prepaid items	284,763	47,336		
Inventory, at cost	81,523	18,031		
General fixed assets				
Other Debits:				
Amount available in Debt Service Fund				
Amount to be provided for retirement of general long term debt				
Total assets and other debits	$ 476,144	$ 1,651,741	$ 2,117,569	$ 4,194,
LIABILITIES, EQUITY AND OTHER CREDITS				
Liabilities:				
Accounts payable	$ 118,771	$ 21,548	$	$ 38,
Deposits held for others				
Due to other funds		91,455		
Due to student groups				
Compensated absences payable				
Deferred revenues	65,679	206,283	54,271	5,
Obligations under capital leases				
Construction contracts payable				64,
Bonds payable			1,200,000	
Bond interest payable			261,321	
Total liabilities	184,450	319,286	1,515,592	107
Equity and other credits:				
Investment in general fixed assets				
Fund balances (deficits) -				
Reserved for:				
Prepaid items	284,763	47,336		
Inventory	81,523	18,031		
Unreserved:				
Undesignated	(74,592)	1,267,088		
Designated for capital outlay				4,08
Designated for debt service			601,977	
Total equity and other credits	291,694	1,332,455	601,977	4,08
Total liabilities, equity and other credits	$ 476,144	$ 1,651,741	$ 2,117,569	$ 4,19

The notes to the financial statements are an integral part of this statement.

| Fiduciary Fund Type | Account Groups | | Totals |
Agency	General Fixed Assets	General Long Term Debt	(Memorandum Only)
$ 69,941	$	$	$ 7,578,207
			189,631
			218,621
			91,455
			332,099
			99,554
	26,919,055		26,919,055
		601,977	601,977
		10,583,119	10,583,119
$ 69,941	$ 26,919,055	$ 11,185,096	$ 46,613,718
$	$	$	$ 178,780
39,137			39,137
			91,455
30,804			30,804
		942,078	942,078
			331,484
		98,018	98,018
			64,092
		10,145,000	11,345,000
			261,321
69,941		11,185,096	13,382,169
	26,919,055		26,919,055
			332,099
			99,554
			1,192,496
			4,086,368
			601,977
	26,919,055		33,231,549
$ 69,941	$ 26,919,055	$ 11,185,096	$ 46,613,718

AVONDALE ELEMENTARY SCHOOL DISTRICT NO. 44
COMBINED STATEMENT OF REVENUES, EXPENDITURES AND CHANGES IN FUND BALANCES-
ALL GOVERNMENTAL FUND TYPES
YEAR ENDED JUNE 30, 2001

			Governmental Fund
	General	Special Revenue	Debt Service
Revenues:			
Other local	$ 771,454	$ 467,044	$ 89,520
Property taxes	1,983,196		1,918,964
State aid and grants	8,767,296	161,569	
Federal aid, grants and reimbursements		2,603,559	
Total revenues	11,521,946	3,232,172	2,008,484
Expenditures:			
Current -			
Instruction	7,520,140	1,222,246	
Support services - students and staff	942,404	402,281	
Support services - administration	1,342,284	113,357	
Operation and maintenance of plant services	1,579,999	3,816	
Student transportation services	455,613	4,752	
Operation of non-instructional services	16,005	1,072,014	
Capital outlay		304,554	
Debt service -			
Interest, premium and fiscal charges			567,689
Principal retirement			1,200,000
Total expenditures	11,856,445	3,123,020	1,767,689
Excess (deficiency) of revenues over expenditures	(334,499)	109,152	240,795
Other financing sources (uses):			
Operating transfers in		42,677	101,354
Operating transfers out		(42,677)	
Total other financing sources (uses)			101,354
Excess (deficiency) of revenues and other financing sources over expenditures and other financing uses	(334,499)	109,152	342,149
Fund balances, beginning of year, as restated	618,429	1,173,648	259,828
Increase (decrease) in reserve for inventory	(23,425)	2,319	
Increase in reserve for prepaid items	31,189	47,336	
Fund balances, end of year	$ 291,694	$ 1,332,455	$ 601,977

The notes to the financial statements are an integral part of this statement.

Types	Totals
Capital Projects	(Memorandum Only)

$ 564,504	$ 1,892,522
189,993	4,092,153
1,969,295	10,898,160
	2,603,559
2,723,792	19,486,394

	8,742,386
	1,344,685
	1,455,641
	1,583,815
	460,365
	1,088,019
2,325,813	2,630,367
12,923	580,612
71,032	1,271,032
2,409,768	19,156,922

314,024	329,472

	144,031
(101,354)	(144,031)
(101,354)	

212,670	329,472
3,873,698	5,925,603
	(21,106)
	78,525
$ 4,086,368	$ 6,312,494

| | General Fund | | |
	Budget	Non-GAAP Actual	Variance - Favorable (Unfavorable)
Revenues:			
Other local	$ 764,574	$ 771,454	$ 6,880
Property taxes	2,005,350	1,983,196	(22,154)
State aid and grants	8,573,567	8,767,296	193,729
Federal aid, grants and reimbursements			
Total revenues	11,343,491	11,521,946	178,455
Expenditures:			
Current -			
Instruction	7,720,577	7,447,849	272,728
Support services - students and staff	910,453	934,978	(24,525)
Support services - administration	1,392,694	1,332,509	60,185
Operation and maintenance of plant services	1,545,183	1,569,686	(24,503)
Student transportation services	462,611	451,487	11,124
Operation of non-instructional services	16,623	16,005	618
Capital outlay			
Debt service -			
Interest, premium and fiscal charges			
Principal retirement			
Total expenditures	12,048,141	11,752,514	295,627
Excess (deficiency) of revenues over expenditures	(704,650)	(230,568)	474,082
Other financing sources (uses):			
Operating transfers in			
Operating transfers out			
Total other financing sources (uses)			
Excess (deficiency) of revenues and other financing sources over expenditures and other financing uses	(704,650)	(230,568)	474,082
Fund balances, July 1, 2000, as restated	118,726	514,498	395,772
Increase (decrease) in reserve for inventory		(23,425)	(23,425)
Increase in reserve for prepaid items		31,189	31,189
Fund balances (deficits), June 30, 2001	$ (585,924)	$ 291,694	$ 877,618

The notes to the financial statements are an integral part of this statement.

	Special Revenue Funds			Debt Service Fund		
	Budget	Actual	Variance - Favorable (Unfavorable)	Budget	Actual	Variance - Favorable (Unfavorable)
	$ 357,345	$ 467,044	$ 109,699	$ 5,466	$ 89,520	$ 84,054
				1,929,119	1,918,964	(10,155)
	170,946	161,569	(9,377)			
	2,533,681	2,603,559	69,878			
	3,061,972	3,232,172	170,200	1,934,585	2,008,484	73,899
	1,302,752	1,222,246	80,506			
	547,436	402,281	145,155			
	190,422	113,357	77,065			
		3,816	(3,816)			
	34,000	4,752	29,248			
	1,320,376	1,072,014	248,362			
	25,896	304,554	(278,658)			
				658,560	567,689	90,871
				1,399,440	1,200,000	199,440
	3,420,882	3,123,020	297,862	2,058,000	1,767,689	290,311
	(358,910)	109,152	468,062	(123,415)	240,795	364,210
	15,621	42,677	27,056		101,354	101,354
	(34,497)	(42,677)	(8,180)			
	(18,876)		18,876		101,354	101,354
	(377,786)	109,152	486,938	(123,415)	342,149	465,564
	1,044,978	1,173,648	128,670	2,028,044	259,828	(1,768,216)
		2,319	2,319			
		47,336	47,336			
	$ 667,192	$ 1,332,455	$ 665,263	$ 1,904,629	$ 601,977	$ (1,302,652)

(Continued)

AVONDALE ELEMENTARY SCHOOL DISTRICT NO. 44
COMBINED STATEMENT OF REVENUES, EXPENDITURES AND CHANGES IN
FUND BALANCES - BUDGET AND ACTUAL - ALL GOVERNMENTAL FUND TYPES
YEAR ENDED JUNE 30, 2001
(Concluded)

	Capital Projects Funds		
	Budget	Actual	Variance - Favorable (Unfavorable)
Revenues:			
Other local	$ 83,516	$ 564,504	$ 480,988
Property taxes	197,624	189,993	(7,631)
State aid and grants	7,091,055	1,969,295	(5,121,760)
Federal aid, grants and reimbursements			
Total revenues	7,372,195	2,723,792	(4,648,403)
Expenditures:			
Current -			
Instruction			
Support services - students and staff			
Support services - administration			
Operation and maintenance of plant services			
Student transportation services			
Operation of non-instructional services			
Capital outlay	11,579,322	2,325,813	9,253,509
Debt service -			
Interest, premium and fiscal charges		12,923	(12,923)
Principal retirement		71,032	(71,032)
Total expenditures	11,579,322	2,409,768	9,169,554
Excess (deficiency) of revenues over expenditures	(4,207,127)	314,024	4,521,151
Other financing sources (uses):			
Operating transfers in			
Operating transfers out		(101,354)	(101,354)
Total other financing sources (uses)		(101,354)	(101,354)
Excess (deficiency) of revenues and other financing sources over expenditures and other financing uses	(4,207,127)	212,670	4,419,797
Fund balances, July 1, 2000, as restated	3,907,048	3,873,698	(33,350)
Increase (decrease) in reserve for inventory			
Increase in reserve for prepaid items			
Fund balances (deficits), June 30, 2001	$ (300,079)	$ 4,086,368	$ 4,386,447

The notes to the financial statements are an integral part of this statement.

NOTE 1 - SUMMARY OF SIGNIFICANT ACCOUNTING POLICIES

The financial statements of Avondale Elementary School District No. 44 have been prepared in conformity with generally accepted accounting principles (GAAP) as applied to government units. The Governmental Accounting Standards Board (GASB) is the accepted standard - setting body for establishing governmental accounting and financial reporting principles. The more significant of the District's accounting policies are described below.

A. Reporting Entity

The Governing Board is organized under Section 15 - 321 of the Arizona Revised Statutes (A.R.S.). Management of the District is independent of other State or local governments. The County Treasurer collects taxes for the District, but exercises no control over its expenditures.

The membership of the Governing Board consists of five members elected by the public. Under existing statutes, the Governing Board's duties and powers include, but are not limited to, the acquisition, maintenance and disposition of school property; the development and adoption of a school program; and the establishment, organization and operation of schools.

The Board also has broad financial responsibilities, including the approval of the annual budget, and the establishment of a system of accounting and budgetary controls.

In accordance with GASB Statement No. 14, the financial reporting entity consists of a primary government and its component units. The District is a primary government because it is a special-purpose government that has a separately elected governing body, is legally separate, and is fiscally independent of other state or local governments. Furthermore, there are no component units combined with the District for financial statement presentation purposes, and it is not included in any other governmental reporting entity. Consequently, the District's financial statements include only the funds and account groups of those organizational entities for which its elected governing board is financially accountable. The District's major operations include education, student transportation, construction and maintenance of District facilities and food services.

B. Fund Accounting

The District's accounts are maintained in accordance with the principles of fund accounting to ensure observance of limitations and restrictions on the resources available. The principles of fund accounting require that resources be classified for accounting and reporting purposes into funds or account groups in accordance with the activities or objectives specified for the resources. Each fund is considered a separate entity and its operations are accounted for in a separate set of self-balancing accounts that comprises its assets, liabilities, fund equity, revenues and expenditures.

NOTE 1 - SUMMARY OF SIGNIFICANT ACCOUNTING POLICIES (Cont'd)

An account group, on the other hand, is a financial reporting device designed to provide accountability for certain assets and liabilities that are not recorded in the funds because they do not directly affect net expendable available financial resources. Although accounts are separately maintained for each fund and account group, in the accompanying financial statements, funds that have similar characteristics have been combined into fund types, which are further classified into broad categories as follows.

Governmental Funds - account for the District's general government activities using the flow of current financial resources measurement focus and include the following fund types.

General Fund - The General Fund accounts for all resources used to finance District maintenance and operation except those required to be accounted for in other funds. It is described as the Maintenance and Operation Fund by Arizona Revised Statutes (A.R.S.).

Special Revenue Funds - The Special Revenue Funds account for the proceeds of specific revenue sources legally restricted to expenditures for specified purposes.

Debt Service Fund - The Debt Service Fund accounts for the accumulation of resources for, and the payment of, general long-term debt principal, interest and related costs.

Capital Projects Funds - The Capital Projects Funds account for resources to be used for the acquisition or construction of capital facilities, and acquisition of furniture, equipment, vehicles, and textbooks.

Fiduciary Funds - account for assets held by the District on behalf of others and include the following fund type.

Agency Funds - The Agency Funds include the Student Activities Fund and the Employee Withholding Fund. The Student Activities Fund accounts for monies raised by students to finance student clubs and organizations but held by the District as an agent. The Employee Withholding Fund accounts for unremitted payroll deductions temporarily held by the District as an agent.

Account Groups - are used to establish accounting control and accountability for certain District assets and liabilities that are not recorded in the funds and include the following two groups:

General Fixed Assets - The General Fixed Assets Account Group accounts for all fixed assets of the District.

General Long-Term Debt - The General Long-Term Debt Account Group accounts for all long-term obligations of the District.

NOTE 1 - SUMMARY OF SIGNIFICANT ACCOUNTING POLICIES (Cont'd)

C. Basis of Accounting/Measurement Focus

Basis of accounting relates to the timing of the measurements made, regardless of the measurement focus applied and determines when revenues and expenditures are recognized in the accounts and reported in the financial statements. The financial statements are presented on the modified accrual basis of accounting.

Revenues are recognized when they become both measurable and available for use during the year. Under the modified accrual basis of accounting, available means due within the current period and collected within the current period or soon enough thereafter to be used to pay liabilities of the current period. Such time thereafter shall not exceed 60 days. Significant revenues which have been accrued under the modified accrual basis of accounting include property taxes, State and County aid and investment income. Food services and miscellaneous revenues are not susceptible to accrual because generally they are not measurable until received in cash. Grants and similar items are recognized as revenue as soon as all eligibility requirements imposed by the provider have been met. Deferred revenues also arise when resources are received by the District before it has a legal claim to them, as when grant monies are received prior to meeting all eligibility requirements imposed by the provider.

Generally, expenditures are recognized when the related fund liability is incurred. Debt service resources are provided during the current year for payment of general long-term debt principal and interest due early in the following year and, therefore, the expenditures and related liabilities have been recognized in the Debt Service Fund.

Governmental Fund types are accounted for on a current financial resources measurement focus. Governmental Fund operating statements represent increases and decreases in net current assets. Their reported fund balances are considered a measure of available spendable resources.

D. Budgets and Budgetary Accounting

The District operates within the budget requirements for school districts as specified by State law and as required by the Arizona Department of Education and the Auditor General. The financial reports reflect the following budgetary standards.

- For the fiscal year beginning July 1, a proposed expenditure budget is presented by the Governing Board to the County School Superintendent and/or Superintendent of Public Instruction on or before July 5.

- The proposed expenditure budget is advertised in the local newspaper, together with a notice of public hearing.

NOTE 1 - SUMMARY OF SIGNIFICANT ACCOUNTING POLICIES (Cont'd)

- The Governing Board legally adopts the final expenditure budget prior to July 15, after a public hearing has been held.

- Once adopted, the expenditure budget can be revised only by the Governing Board for specific reasons set forth in the A.R.S. The budget was revised in fiscal year 2000-01, however the revision was insignificant. Budget amendments and budget transfers between District funds by management are not allowed without Governing Board approval.

- Although it is not adopted or published, a budget of revenue from all sources for the fiscal year is prepared by the District and transmitted to the County School Superintendent and the Superintendent of Public Instruction on or before September 15. The revenue budget cannot be revised.

- Property tax revenue of the General, Debt Service and Capital Projects Funds from an authorized levy is allocated to each of the funds to match or balance the budget.

- Budgets for the General, Special Revenue, Debt Service, and Capital Projects Funds are prepared on the modified accrual basis of accounting except as explained in Note 11.

- All appropriations, including encumbered appropriations, lapse at year end.

- The legal level of budgetary control (that is, the level at which expenditures cannot legally exceed the appropriated amount) is established at the individual fund level for all funds.

E. Encumbrances

Encumbrance accounting, under which purchase orders, contracts and other commitments for the expenditure of monies are recorded to reserve that portion of the applicable fund balance, is employed as an extension of formal budgetary control. Open encumbrances are not reported as reservations of fund balance at June 30, 2001, but liquidated and re-established at the beginning of the next fiscal year, since outstanding purchase orders are cancelled at year end.

F. Investments

A.R.S. authorize the District to invest public monies in the State Treasurer's Local Government Investment Pool, the County Treasurer's investment pool, interest-bearing savings accounts, certificates of deposit, and repurchase agreements in eligible depositories; bonds or other obligations of the U.S. government that are guaranteed as to principal and interest by the U.S. government; and bonds of the State of Arizona counties, cities, towns, school districts, and special districts as specified by statute.

NOTE 1 - SUMMARY OF SIGNIFICANT ACCOUNTING POLICIES (Cont'd)

The State Board of Deposit provides oversight for the State Treasurer's pools, and the Local Government Investment Pool Advisory Committee provides consultation and advice to the Treasurer. The fair value of a participant's position in the pool approximates the value of that participant's pool shares. No comparable oversight is provided for the County Treasurer's investment pool, and the structure of that pool does not provide for shares.

A.R.S. require the District to deposit certain cash with the County Treasurer. That cash is pooled for investment purposes, except for cash of the Debt Service and Bond Building Funds that may be invested separately. Interest earned from investments purchased with pooled monies is allocated to each of the District's funds based on their average monthly balances.

Nonparticipating interest-earning investment contracts are stated at cost. Money market investments and participating interest-earning investment contracts with a remaining maturity of one year or less at time of purchase are stated at amortized cost. All other investments are stated at fair value.

G. Investment Income

Investment income is included in other local revenue and is composed of interest and net changes in the fair value of applicable investments.

H. Inventory

Inventories of the General Fund consist of expendable supplies held for consumption. Inventories of the Food Services Fund consist of supplies held for sale. Inventories are recorded as an asset for informational purposes only and are offset by a reserve of fund balance. Inventories are stated at cost using the first in-first out method. The cost is recorded as an expenditure at the time individual inventory items are purchased.

The United States Department of Agriculture (USDA) commodity portion of the food services inventory consists of food donated by the USDA. It is valued at estimated market prices paid by the USDA.

I. Prepaid Items

Payments for services that will benefit periods beyond fiscal year end are recorded as prepaid items. Prepaid items are recorded as an asset for informational purposes only and are offset by a reserve of fund balance.

NOTE 1 - SUMMARY OF SIGNIFICANT ACCOUNTING POLICIES (Cont'd)

J. General Fixed Assets

All acquisitions of land, buildings and improvements with a cost in excess of $5,000 and vehicles, furniture, and equipment with a cost in excess of $1,000 are capitalized. Fixed assets capitalized in the General Fixed Assets Account Group are recorded at the time of purchase as expenditures in the funds from which the expenditures were made. Such assets are capitalized at historical cost, or estimated historical cost if actual historical cost is not available. Donated fixed assets are recorded at the fair market value on the date donated. Depreciation on general fixed assets is not recorded nor has interest been capitalized.

K. Property Tax Revenues

Property tax revenues are recognized as revenues in the year they are levied and collected or if they are collected within 60 days subsequent to year-end. Property taxes not collected within 60 days subsequent to fiscal year-end or collected in advance of year-end for which they are levied are reported as deferred revenues.

Property tax levies are obtained by applying tax rates against either the primary assessed valuation or the secondary assessed valuation. Primary and secondary valuation categories are composed of the exact same properties. However, the primary category limits the increase in property values to 10% from the previous year while there is no limit to the increase in property values for secondary valuation. Override and debt service tax rates are applied to secondary assessed valuation and all other tax rates are applied to the primary assessed valuation.

The County levies real property taxes on or before the third Monday in August, which become due and payable in two equal installments. The first installment is due on the first day of October and becomes delinquent after the first business day of November. The second installment is due on the first day of March of the next year and becomes delinquent after the first business day of May.

The County also levies various personal property taxes during the year, which are due the second Monday of the month following receipt of the tax notice, and become delinquent 30 days thereafter.

Pursuant A.R.S., a lien against assessed real and personal property attaches on the first day of January preceding assessment and levy, however according to case law, an enforceable legal claim to the asset does not arise.

NOTE 1 - SUMMARY OF SIGNIFICANT ACCOUNTING POLICIES (Concl'd)

L. Compensated Absences

The District's employee vacation and sick leave policies generally provide for granting vacation and sick leave with pay. Accrued sick leave is earned by all full-time employees working at least 10 months a year, at a rate of 1 day a month. All twelve-month employees earn vacation, at a rate of one week of vacation after one year of employment, two weeks after 3 years, 3 weeks after 8 years, and 4 weeks after 18 years. The liability for accumulated vacation and sick leave is recorded in the General Long Term Debt Account Group since the amount expected to be paid from current resources is insignificant. Expenditures for compensated absences are recorded when paid in the General and Special Revenue Funds.

M. Total Columns on Combined Statements

Total columns on the Combined Statements are captioned Memorandum Only to indicate that they are presented only to facilitate financial analysis. Data in these columns do not present financial position or results of operations in conformity with generally accepted accounting principles. Neither is such data comparable to a consolidation. Interfund eliminations have not been made in the aggregation of this data.

NOTE 2 - CASH AND INVESTMENTS

The captions and amounts of cash and investments on the balance sheet consist of the following.

	General Fund	Special Revenue Funds	Debt Service Fund	Capital Projects Funds	Agency Funds
Cash in bank	$	$	$	$	$69,941
Cash and investments held by the County Treasurer	13,891	1,276,298	2,031,687	4,186,390	
Total	$13,891	$1,276,298	$2,031,687	$4,186,390	$69,941

The District's deposits (bank balance) at June 30, 2001 were entirely covered by Federal depository insurance.

GASB Statement No. 31 requires certain investments to be reported at fair value rather than at cost. At June 30, 2001, the District's investments consisted of the following.

NOTE 2 - CASH AND INVESTMENTS (Concl'd)

	Fair Value
Cash and investments held by the County Treasurer	$ 7,508,266
Total	$ 7,508,266

The District's investment in the County Treasurer's investment pool represents a proportionate interest in the pool's portfolio; however, the District's portion is not identified with specific investments and is not subject to custodial credit risk.

NOTE 3 - PROPERTY TAXES RECEIVABLE

Property taxes receivable represent uncollected property taxes as determined from the records of the Maricopa County Treasurer's Office and at June 30, 2001, were as follows.

Year	General Fund	Debt Service Fund	Capital Projects Funds
2000-01	$ 84,219	$ 69,331	$ 6,829
Prior	11,748	16,551	953
Total	$ 95,967	$ 85,882	$ 7,782

That portion of property taxes receivable not collected within 60 days after fiscal year end, has been deferred, and consequently, is not included in current revenues. Property taxes receivable are net of allowances for uncollectibles.

NOTE 4 - CHANGES IN GENERAL FIXED ASSETS

A summary of the changes in general fixed assets follows.

	Balance July 1, 2000	Additions	Deletions	Balance June 30, 2001
Land and improvements	$ 467,950	$ 135,794	$	$ 603,744
Buildings and improvements	20,337,075	2,183,399		22,520,474
Vehicles, furniture and equipment	2,951,674	617,777	79,101	3,490,350
Construction in progress	1,222,622	849,979	1,768,114	304,487
Total	$24,979,321	$ 3,786,949	$ 1,847,215	$26,919,055

General fixed assets at June 30, 2001 of this report do not agree to the June 30, 2001 report prepared in compliance with GASB 34 due to the District's change in capitalization policy.

NOTE 5 - COMPENSATED ABSENCES

The liability for vested compensated absences, including related benefits, is recorded in the General Long-Term Debt Account Group. The amount expected to be paid from current resources is not significant. A summary of changes in liabilities for compensated absences in the General Long-Term Debt Account Group for the year ended June 30, 2001 follows.

Balance at July 1, 2000	$ 833,519
Net current year increase in liability for compensated absences	108,559
Balance at June 30, 2001	$ 942,078

NOTE 6 - OBLIGATIONS UNDER CAPITAL LEASES

The District has acquired copiers under the provisions of long-term lease agreements classified as capital leases. Accordingly, the principal amount of the assets, totaling $381,440, is capitalized in the General Fixed Assets Account Group. The leases provide bargain purchase options and transfer of title at the end of the lease terms. The future minimum lease payments under the capital leases together with the present value of the net minimum lease payments as of June 30, 2001 were as follows.

Year ending June 30:

2002	$ 71,780
2003	19,179
2004	9,501
2005	5,543
Total minimum lease payments	106,003
Less amount representing interest	7,985
Present value of net minimum capital lease payments	$ 98,018

A summary of the changes in capital lease obligations follows:

	Balance July 1, 2000	Increase	Reduction	Balance June 30, 2001
Capital lease obligations	$169,050	$	$ 71,032	$ 98,018
Total	$169,050	$	$ 71,032	$ 98,018

AVONDALE ELEMENTARY SCHOOL DISTRICT NO. 44
NOTES TO FINANCIAL STATEMENTS
JUNE 30, 2001

NOTE 7 - BONDS PAYABLE

Bonds payable at June 30, 2001, consisted of the outstanding general obligation and refunding bonds presented below. The bonds are both callable and noncallable with interest payable semiannually.

Description	Interest Rates	Maturity	Outstanding Principal July 1, 2000	Retirements	Outstanding Principal June 30, 2001
Refunding, Capital Appreciation Bonds, Series 1993	4.0-4.3%	7/1/00-02	$ 3,620,000	$1,150,000	$ 2,470,000
School Improvement Bonds of 1998, Series A, 1998	4.0-4.7%	7/1/00-13	4,500,000	150,000	4,350,000
School Improvement Bonds of 1998, Series B, 1999	4.0-5.25%	7/1/00-13	4,650,000	125,000	4,525,000
Total			$12,770,000		$11,345,000

Outstanding principal at June 30, 2001 includes amounts transferred to the Debt Service Fund to ret bonds payable on July 1, 2001.

Principal and interest payments on general obligation and refunding bonds at June 30, 2001, are summarized as follows.

Year	Principal	Interest	Total
2002	$ 1,200,000	$ 497,741	$ 1,697,741
2003	1,270,000	445,537	1,715,537
2004	650,000	404,257	1,054,257
2005	675,000	375,353	1,050,353
2006	700,000	344,588	1,044,588
Thereafter	6,850,000	1,414,111	8,264,111
Total	$ 11,345,000	$ 3,481,587	$14,826,587

NOTE 8 - STEWARDSHIP, COMPLIANCE AND ACCOUNTABILITY

Expenditures in Excess of Appropriations - The following funds had expenditures that exceeded appropriations for the year ended June 30, 2001:

Fund Type/Fund	Appropriations	Expenditures	Excess
Special Revenue:			
E - Rate	$ -0-	$ 296,568	$ 296,568

However, additional resources became available to cover expenditures of these funds.

Page 20

NOTE 9 - INTERFUND RECEIVABLES AND PAYABLES

At June 30, 2001, interfund receivables and payables were as follows:

Fund Type/Fund	Due from other funds	Due to other funds
Special Revenue Funds:		
Title I - Educationally Disadvantaged	$	$ 23,121
Title I - Migrant		28,035
Medicaid Reimbursement	91,455	
Title III - Goals 2000		40,299
Total	$ 91,455	$ 91,455

NOTE 10 - DUE FROM GOVERNMENTAL ENTITIES

The captions and amounts of due from governmental entities on the balance sheet consist of the following.

	Special Revenue Funds
Due form Federal government	$ 171,143
Due from State government	47,478
Total	$ 218,621

NOTE 11 - BUDGETARY BASIS OF ACCOUNTING

The adopted budget of the District is prepared on a basis consistent with generally accepted accounting principles with the following exception: 1) a portion of fiscal year 2000-01 insurance payments were charged against the fiscal year 1999-2000 budget. Consequently, the following adjustments are necessary to present actual expenditures and other financing sources (uses) on a budgetary basis in order to provide a meaningful comparison.

	General Fund	
	Total Expenditures	Fund Balance, July 1, 2000
Combined Statement of Revenues, Expenditures and Changes in Fund Balances - All Governmental Fund Types	$11,856,445	$ 618,429
Fiscal year 2000-01 insurance payments charged against fiscal year 1999-2000 budget	(103,931)	(103,931)
Combined Statement of Revenues, Expenditures and Changes in Fund Balances - Budget and Actual - All Governmental Fund Types	$11,752,514	$ 514,498

NOTE 12 - PRIOR PERIOD ADJUSTMENT

The July 1, 2000, fund balance of the Special Revenue and Capital Projects Funds do not agree to the prior year financial statements due to a correction of an error. In the prior year, expenditures were incorrectly classified in the School Opening Fund and this caused the fund to have a negative fund balance. Expenditures should have been made out of the Unrestricted Capital Fund.

	Special Revenue Funds	Capital Projects Funds
Fund balance, June 30, 2000, as previously reported	$ 1,136,921	$ 3,910,425
Correction of error	36,727	(36,727)
Fund balance, July 1, 2000 as restated	$ 1,173,648	$ 3,873,698

NOTE 13 - CONTINGENT LIABILITIES

Accumulated Sick Leave - Sick leave benefits provide for ordinary sick pay and are cumulative. Upon termination of employment, unvested sick leave benefits are forfeited. Unvested accumulated sick leave of District employees at June 30, 2001, totaled 2,997 days.

Compliance - The District participates in federally-funded and state-funded programs administered by various government agencies. The programs included in these financial statements may be subject to program compliance and/or financial monitoring by the granting agency or it representatives. The amount, if any, of expenditures which may be disallowed by the granting agencies cannot be determined at this time.

NOTE 14 - RISK MANAGEMENT

The District is exposed to various risks of loss related to torts; theft of, damage to and destruction of assets; errors and omissions; injuries to employees; and natural disasters. The District was unable to obtain general liability insurance at a cost considered to be economically justifiable. Therefore, the District joined the Arizona School Risk Retention Trust, Inc. (ASRRT), together with other districts in the State. ASRRT is a public entity risk pool currently operating as a common risk management and insurance program for 202 member school districts. The District pays an annual premium to ASRRT for its general coverage insurance. The Agreement provides that the ASRRT will be self-sustaining through member premiums and will reinsure through commercial companies for claims in excess of the following amounts for each category listed below.

NOTE 14 - RISK MANAGEMENT (Concl'd)

Insurance Category	Reinsurance
Property Insurance	$100,000,000 per occurrence
Automobile Physical Damage	$2,000,000 per occurrence as well as amounts in excess of Trust annual aggregate limit $100,000
General, Professional and Automobile Liability	$4.75 million or $4.5 million CSL per occurrence/aggregate in excess of $250,000 per occurrence
Excess General Public, Automobile And Professional Liability	$5,000,000 excess of $5,000,000 or $10,000,000 limit of liability
Excess General Public, Automobile And Professional Liability	$10,000,000 excess of $15,000,000 limit of liability
Crime Insurance	$500,000 Public Employee Dishonesty; $500,000 Forgery or Alteration; $150,000 Money and Securities; $500,000 Computer Fraud
Boiler and Machinery	$10,000,000 comprehensive form
Underground Storage Tank	$1,000,000 per release/$2,000,000 annual aggregate
Special Risk Insurance	$5,000,000 per occurrence, $100,000 death or dismemberment benefit each person/$500,000 aggregate
Non-Owned Aircraft Liability	$10,000,000 per occurrence, including passengers, with passenger liability limited to $1,000,000 per person

The District continues to carry commercial insurance for all other risks of loss, including workers compensation and employee health and accident insurance. Settled claims resulting from these risks have not exceeded commercial insurance coverage in any of the past three fiscal years.

NOTE 15 - RETIREMENT PLAN

Plan Description - The District contributes to a cost-sharing multiple-employer defined benefit pension plan administered by the Arizona State Retirement System. Benefits are established by state statute and generally provide retirement, death, long-term disability, survivor, and health insurance premium benefits. The System is governed by the Arizona State Retirement System Board according to the provisions of A.R.S. Title 38, Chapter 5, Article 2.

The System issues a comprehensive annual financial report that includes financial statements and required supplementary information. The most recent report may be obtained by writing the System, 3300 North Central Avenue, PO Box 33910, Phoenix, AZ 85067-3910 or by calling (602) 240-2000 or (800) 621-3778.

NOTE 15 - RETIREMENT PLAN (Concl'd)

Funding Policy -The Arizona State Legislature establishes and may amend active plan members' and the District's contribution rate. For the year ended June 30, 2001, active plan members and the District were each required by statute to contribute at the actuarially determined rate of 2.66 percent (2.17 percent retirement and 0.49 percent long term disability) of the members' annual covered payroll. The District's contributions to the System for the years ended June 30, 2001, 2000 and 1999 were $261,163, $231,143 and $282,002 respectively, which were equal to the required contributions for the year. The District provides no post-employment benefits.

NOTE 16 - CONSTRUCTION COMMITMENTS

As of June 30, 2001, the District is involved in the construction of Desert Star Elementary School. The estimated cost to complete the school is $6,907,484.

NOTE 17 - SUBSEQUENT EVENTS

Arizona voters passed Proposition 301, which increased the State sales tax rate from 5.0% to 5.6%. Approximately $264 million additional dollars raised through this increase in Arizona sales taxes is earmarked for a Classroom Site Fund for K-12 education. These funds are to be used for performance-based teacher compensation, increases in teachers' base salaries, and classroom enhancements such as reductions in class size, additional teachers and aides, teacher training and dropout prevention. In addition, these funds will be used to adjust the basic State aid formula that will include a 2% inflation factor for each of the next five years, as well as provide an additional school day each year for the next five years, for a total of 180 school days at the end of the five years. Preliminary estimates provided by the State indicate that the District will receive approximately $960,407 more in State aid funding in fiscal year 2001-02, due to this change in the law.

COMBINING, INDIVIDUAL FUND AND ACCOUNT GROUP
FINANCIAL STATEMENTS AND SCHEDULES

(This page intentionally left blank)

GENERAL FUND

The General Fund accounts for all resources used to finance District maintenance and operation except those required to be accounted for in other funds. It is described as the Maintenance and Operation Fund by Arizona Revised Statutes (A.R.S.).

	Budget	Non-GAAP Actual	Variance - Favorable (Unfavorable)
Regular education			
Instruction	$ 6,264,850	$ 6,065,153	$ 199,697
Support services - students and staff	760,925	778,888	(17,963)
Support services - administration	1,264,225	1,227,093	37,132
Operation and maintenance of plant services	1,545,183	1,569,686	(24,503)
Operation of non-instructional services	16,623	16,005	618
Total regular education	9,851,806	9,656,825	194,981
Special education			
Instruction	1,455,727	1,382,696	73,031
Support services - students and staff	149,528	156,090	(6,562)
Support services - administration	128,469	105,416	23,053
Student transportation services		17,152	(17,152)
Total special education	1,733,724	1,661,354	72,370
Student transportation services			
Student transportation services	462,611	434,335	28,276
Total student transportation services	462,611	434,335	28,276
Total expenditures	$ 12,048,141	$ 11,752,514	$ 295,627

(This page intentionally left blank)

SPECIAL REVENUE FUNDS

The following Special Revenue Funds are maintained by the District. Arizona Revised Statutes (A.R.S.) and the Uniform System of Financial Records (USFR) required the establishment of these funds for the specified activities.

Classroom Site - to account for the financial activity of the six-tenths of one percent increase in the state sales tax due to the passage of Proposition 301.

Title I – Educationally Disadvantaged - to account for financial assistance to local educational agencies for supplementary instructional programs for educationally disadvantaged students.

Title I - Migrant - to account for financial assistance to local educational agencies for supplementary instructional programs for migrant students.

Title II Eisenhower Grant - to account for financial assistance for supplementary math and science programs.

Technology Literacy Grant - to account for financial assistance for technology literacy programs.

Title IV - Safe & Drug Free Schools - to account for financial assistance for chemical abuse awareness programs funded by the Federal government.

Title VI - Innovative Education Program - to account for financial assistance for supplementary writing programs.

EHA Title VI-B Entitlement - to account for supplemental financial assistance to State and local educational agencies in providing a free, appropriate public education to disabled children.

Federal Preschool - to account for financial assistance for instructional programs for disabled preschool students

Emergency Immigrant Education - to account for financial assistance to local educational agencies for educational services and costs for immigrant children.

Medicaid Reimbursement - to account for financial assistance for Medicaid programs.

Title III - Goals 2000 - to account for financial assistance for the state and local education systemic improvement grants funded by the Federal government.

E-Rate – to account for Federal assistance administered by the Schools and Libraries Corporation (SLC) to provide discounts to schools and libraries on the cost of telecommunications (local and long-distance phone service), Internet access, and network wiring within buildings.

Class Size Reduction - to account for financial assistance received from the State for the preparation of individuals for employment.

Early Childhood - to account for financial assistance from the state for instructional programs for kindergarten through third grade students.

State Chemical Abuse - to account for financial assistance for chemical abuse awareness.

Gifted Education - to account for financial assistance received from the State for programs for gifted students.

Other State Projects - to account for financial assistance for other state projects.

School Plant - to account for proceeds from the sale or lease of school property.

Food Services - to account for the financial activity of the food services program. This program provides for regular and incidental meals, lunches and snacks in connection with school functions.

Civic Center - to account for monies received from the rental of school facilities for civic activities.

Community School - to account for revenues and expenditures for the purposes of academic and skill development for all citizens.

Extracurricular Activities Fees Tax Credit – to account for revenues and expenditures of monies collected in support of extracurricular activities to be taken as a tax credit by the taxpayer in accordance with A.R.S. 43-1089.01.

Gifts and Donations - to account for the revenues and expenditures of gifts, donations, bequests and private grants made to the District.

District Services – to account for the financial activity of providing goods and services to departments or schools within the District, or other districts on a cost reimbursement basis.

Fingerprinting - to account for the revenues and expenditures of fingerprinting new employees as mandated by the State.

School Opening - to account for revenues received for opening new schools.

Insurance Proceeds - to account for the monies received from insurance companies to be used for repair or replacement of lost, stolen or damaged property.

Textbooks - to account for monies received from students to replace or repair lost or damaged textbooks.

Indirect Costs - to account for monies transferred from Federal or State projects for administrative costs.

Unemployment Insurance - to account for unemployment insurance payments to the Department of Economic Security.

Insurance Refund - to account for insurance premium refunds.

Grants and Gifts to Teachers - to account for financial assistance for the funding of grants and gifts to teachers.

Intergovernmental Agreements - to account for the financial activities relating to agreements with other governments.

	Classroom Site	Title I - Educationally Disadvantaged	Title I - Migrant	Title II - Eisenhower Grant
ASSETS				
Cash and investments	$	$	$	$ 816
Due from governmental entities	47,478	6,838	28,338	
Due from other funds				
Prepaid items		22,895		
Inventory, at cost				
Total assets	$ 47,478	$ 29,733	$ 28,338	$ 816
LIABILITIES AND FUND EQUITY				
Liabilities:				
Accounts payable	$	$ 6,612	$ 303	$ 607
Due to other funds		23,121	28,035	
Deferred revenues	47,478			209
Total liabilities	47,478	29,733	28,338	816
Fund equity:				
Fund balances (deficits) -				
Reserved for:				
Prepaid items		22,895		
Inventory				
Unreserved:				
Undesignated		(22,895)		
Total fund equity				
Total liabilities and fund equity	$ 47,478	$ 29,733	$ 28,338	$ 816

Technology Literacy Grant	Title IV - Safe and Drug Free Schools	Title VI - Innovative Education Program	EHA Title VI-B Entitlement	Federal Preschool	Emergency Immigrant Education
$ 2,430	$ 16,515	$ 441	$ 74,559	$ 3,468	$ 22,349
			6,496		
$ 2,430	$ 16,515	$ 441	$ 81,055	$ 3,468	$ 22,349
$ 214	$ 611	$ 19	$ 4,453	$ 29	$ 977
2,216	15,904	422	76,602	3,439	21,372
2,430	16,515	441	81,055	3,468	22,349
			6,496		
			(6,496)		
$ 2,430	$ 16,515	$ 441	$ 81,055	$ 3,468	$ 22,349

(Continued)

	Medicaid Reimbursement	Title III - Goals 2000	E - Rate	Class Size Reduction
ASSETS				
Cash and investments	$ 8,695	$	$ 2,504	$ 11,141
Due from governmental entities		40,779		
Due from other funds	91,455			
Prepaid items				1,238
Inventory, at cost				
Total assets	$ 100,150	$ 40,779	$ 2,504	$ 12,379
LIABILITIES AND FUND EQUITY				
Liabilities:				
Accounts payable	$	$ 480	$	$ 545
Due to other funds		40,299		
Deferred revenues				11,834
Total liabilities		40,779		12,379
Fund equity:				
Fund balances (deficits) -				
Reserved for:				
Prepaid items				1,238
Inventory				
Unreserved:				
Undesignated	100,150		2,504	(1,238)
Total fund equity	100,150		2,504	
Total liabilities and fund equity	$ 100,150	$ 40,779	$ 2,504	$ 12,379

	Early Childhood	State Chemical Abuse	Gifted Education	Other State Projects	School Plant	Food Services
	$ 11,074	$ 5,466	$ 227	$ 11,238	$ 119,638	$ 94,718
						95,188
	3,094					13,613
						18,031
	$ 14,168	$ 5,466	$ 227	$ 11,238	$ 119,638	$ 221,550
	$ 4,292	$	$	$	$	$ 1,076
	9,876	5,466	227	11,238		
	14,168	5,466	227	11,238		1,076
	3,094					13,613
						18,031
	(3,094)				119,638	188,830
					119,638	220,474
	$ 14,168	$ 5,466	$ 227	$ 11,238	$ 119,638	$ 221,550

(Continued)

	Civic Center	Community School	Extracurricular Activities Fees Tax Credit	Gifts and Donations
ASSETS				
Cash and investments	$ 126,138	$ 2,999	$ 5,028	$ 7,642
Due from governmental entities				
Due from other funds				
Prepaid items				
Inventory, at cost				
Total assets	$ 126,138	$ 2,999	$ 5,028	$ 7,642
LIABILITIES AND FUND EQUITY				
Liabilities:				
Accounts payable	$ 263	$	$	$ 5
Due to other funds				
Deferred revenues				
Total liabilities	263			5
Fund equity:				
Fund balances (deficits) -				
Reserved for:				
Prepaid items				
Inventory				
Unreserved:				
Undesignated	125,875	2,999	5,028	7,637
Total fund equity	125,875	2,999	5,028	7,637
Total liabilities and fund equity	$ 126,138	$ 2,999	$ 5,028	$ 7,642

District Services		Fingerprinting		Insurance Proceeds		Textbooks		Indirect Costs		Unemployment Insurance	
$	63,121	$	1,391	$	37,778	$	6,556	$	72,168	$	543,337
$	63,121	$	1,391	$	37,778	$	6,556	$	72,168	$	543,337
$		$		$		$		$	49	$	188
									49		188
	63,121		1,391		37,778		6,556		72,119		543,149
	63,121		1,391		37,778		6,556		72,119		543,149
$	63,121	$	1,391	$	37,778	$	6,556	$	72,168	$	543,337

(Continued)

	Insurance Refund	Grants and Gifts to Teachers	Inter governmental Agreements	Totals
ASSETS				
Cash and investments	$ 9,859	$ 3,266	$ 11,736	$ 1,276,298
Due from governmental entities				218,621
Due from other funds				91,455
Prepaid items				47,336
Inventory, at cost				18,031
Total assets	$ 9,859	$ 3,266	$ 11,736	$ 1,651,741
LIABILITIES AND FUND EQUITY				
Liabilities:				
Accounts payable	$	$ 819	$ 6	$ 21,548
Due to other funds				91,455
Deferred revenues				206,283
Total liabilities		819	6	319,286
Fund equity:				
Fund balances (deficits) -				
Reserved for:				
Prepaid items				47,336
Inventory				18,031
Unreserved:				
Undesignated	9,859	2,447	11,730	1,267,088
Total fund equity	9,859	2,447	11,730	1,332,455
Total liabilities and fund equity	$ 9,859	$ 3,266	$ 11,736	$ 1,651,741

(This page intentionally left blank)

	Title I - Educationally Disadvantaged	Title I - Migrant	Title II - Eisenhower Grant
Revenues:			
Other local	$	$	$
State aid and grants			
Federal aid, grants and reimbursements	794,926	81,020	47,693
Total revenues	794,926	81,020	47,693
Expenditures:			
Current -			
Instruction	665,003	47,094	
Support services - students and staff	84,487	27,134	46,662
Support services - administration	50,648	2,784	
Operation and maintenance of plant services			
Student transportation services			
Operation of non-instructional services		2,344	
Capital outlay			
Total expenditures	800,138	79,356	46,662
Excess (deficiency) of revenues over expenditures	(5,212)	1,664	1,031
Other financing sources (uses):			
Operating transfers in			
Operating transfers out	(17,683)	(1,664)	(1,031)
Total other financing sources (uses)	(17,683)	(1,664)	(1,031)
Excess (deficiency) of revenues and other financing sources over expenditures and other financing uses	(22,895)		
Fund balances, beginning of year, as restated			
Increase in reserve for inventory			
Increase in reserve for prepaid items	22,895		
Fund balances, end of year	$	$	$

Technology Literacy Grant	Title IV - Safe and Drug Free Schools	Title VI - Innovative Education Program	EHA Title VI-B Entitlement	Federal Preschool	Emergency Immigrant Education
$	$	$	$	$	$
12,985	14,439	19,665	276,119	22,208	21,437
12,985	14,439	19,665	276,119	22,208	21,437
	2,904	19,265	178,477	21,728	13,442
2,531	11,286		97,899		5,201
			150		
10,454					2,302
12,985	14,190	19,265	276,526	21,728	20,945
	249	400	(407)	480	492
	(249)	(400)	(6,089)	(480)	(492)
	(249)	(400)	(6,089)	(480)	(492)
			(6,496)		
			6,496		
$	$	$	$	$	$

(Continued)

	Medicaid Reimbursement	Title III - Goals 2000	E - Rate
Revenues:			
Other local	$	$	$
State aid and grants			
Federal aid, grants and reimbursements	35,703	68,135	299,072
Total revenues	35,703	68,135	299,072
Expenditures:			
Current -			
Instruction			17,127
Support services - students and staff		66,784	
Support services - administration			11,081
Operation and maintenance of plant services			3,816
Student transportation services	2,127		
Operation of non-instructional services			
Capital outlay			264,544
Total expenditures	2,127	66,784	296,568
Excess (deficiency) of revenues over expenditures	33,576	1,351	2,504
Other financing sources (uses):			
Operating transfers in			
Operating transfers out		(1,351)	
Total other financing sources (uses)		(1,351)	
Excess (deficiency) of revenues and other financing sources over expenditures and other financing uses	33,576		2,504
Fund balances, beginning of year, as restated	66,574		
Increase in reserve for inventory			
Increase in reserve for prepaid items			
Fund balances, end of year	$ 100,150	$	$ 2,504

	Class Size Reduction	Early Childhood	State Chemical Abuse	Gifted Education	School Plant	Food Services
	$	$	$	$	$ 12,192	$ 284,668
		147,969	8,301	5,299		
	93,647					816,510
	93,647	147,969	8,301	5,299	12,192	1,101,178
	92,833	136,807		987		
		11,981	8,301	2,610		
		2,275				1,063,078
				1,702		25,552
	92,833	151,063	8,301	5,299		1,088,630
	814	(3,094)			12,192	12,548
	(2,052)					(11,186)
	(2,052)					(11,186)
	(1,238)	(3,094)			12,192	1,362
					107,446	203,180
						2,319
	1,238	3,094				13,613
	$	$	$	$	$ 119,638	$ 220,474

(Continued)

	Civic Center	Community School	Extracurricular Activities Fees Tax Credit
Revenues:			
Other local	$ 70,900	$ 553	$ 9,798
State aid and grants			
Federal aid, grants and reimbursements			
Total revenues	70,900	553	9,798
Expenditures:			
Current -			
Instruction			11,586
Support services - students and staff	10,558		
Support services - administration			
Operation and maintenance of plant services			
Student transportation services	2,625		
Operation of non-instructional services	4,100		
Capital outlay			
Total expenditures	17,283		11,586
Excess (deficiency) of revenues over expenditures	53,617	553	(1,788)
Other financing sources (uses):			
Operating transfers in			
Operating transfers out			
Total other financing sources (uses)			
Excess (deficiency) of revenues and other financing sources over expenditures and other financing uses	53,617	553	(1,788)
Fund balances, beginning of year, as restated	72,258	2,446	6,816
Increase in reserve for inventory			
Increase in reserve for prepaid items			
Fund balances, end of year	$ 125,875	$ 2,999	$ 5,028

	Gifts and Donations	District Services	Fingerprinting	Insurance Proceeds	Textbooks	Indirect Costs
	$ 8,556	$ 3,616	$ 2,097	$ 4,538	$ 1,615	$ 3,571
	8,556	3,616	2,097	4,538	1,615	3,571
	2,403				3,914	
	3,963			357		
			730			38,508
	217					
	6,583		730	357	3,914	38,508
	1,973	3,616	1,367	4,181	(2,299)	(34,937)
						42,677
						42,677
	1,973	3,616	1,367	4,181	(2,299)	7,740
	5,664	59,505	24	33,597	8,855	64,379
	$ 7,637	$ 63,121	$ 1,391	$ 37,778	$ 6,556	$ 72,119

(Continued)

AVONDALE ELEMENTARY SCHOOL DISTRICT NO. 44
COMBINING STATEMENT OF REVENUES, EXPENDITURES AND CHANGES IN FUND BALANCES-
ALL SPECIAL REVENUE FUNDS
YEAR ENDED JUNE 30, 2001
(Concluded)

	Unemployment Insurance	Insurance Refund	Grants and Gifts to Teachers
Revenues:			
Other local	$ 31,414	$ 565	$ 7,990
State aid and grants			
Federal aid, grants and reimbursements			
Total revenues	31,414	565	7,990
Expenditures:			
Current -			
Instruction			8,676
Support services - students and staff			
Support services - administration	9,456		
Operation and maintenance of plant services			
Student transportation services			
Operation of non-instructional services			
Capital outlay			
Total expenditures	9,456		8,676
Excess (deficiency) of revenues over expenditures	21,958	565	(686)
Other financing sources (uses):			
Operating transfers in			
Operating transfers out			
Total other financing sources (uses)			
Excess (deficiency) of revenues and other financing sources over expenditures and other financing uses	21,958	565	(686)
Fund balances, beginning of year, as restated	521,191	9,294	3,133
Increase in reserve for inventory			
Increase in reserve for prepaid items			
Fund balances, end of year	$ 543,149	$ 9,859	$ 2,447

Inter governmental Agreements	Totals
$ 24,971	$ 467,044
	161,569
	2,603,559
24,971	3,232,172
	1,222,246
22,527	402,281
	113,357
	3,816
	4,752
	1,072,014
	304,554
22,527	3,123,020
2,444	109,152
	42,677
	(42,677)
2,444	109,152
9,286	1,173,648
	2,319
	47,336
$ 11,730	$ 1,332,455

AVONDALE ELEMENTARY SCHOOL DISTRICT NO. 44
COMBINING STATEMENT OF REVENUES, EXPENDITURES AND CHANGES IN
FUND BALANCES - BUDGET AND ACTUAL - ALL SPECIAL REVENUE FUNDS
YEAR ENDED JUNE 30, 2001

	Title I - Educationally Disadvantaged		
	Budget	Actual	Variance - Favorable (Unfavorable)
Revenues:			
Other local	$	$	$
State aid and grants			
Federal aid, grants and reimbursements	863,237	794,926	(68,311)
Total revenues	863,237	794,926	(68,311)
Expenditures:			
Current -			
Instruction	682,822	665,003	17,819
Support services - students and staff	98,995	84,487	14,508
Support services - administration	62,820	50,648	12,172
Operation and maintenance of plant services			
Student transportation services			
Operation of non-instructional services			
Capital outlay			
Total expenditures	844,637	800,138	44,499
Excess (deficiency) of revenues over expenditures	18,600	(5,212)	(23,812)
Other financing sources (uses):			
Operating transfers in			
Operating transfers out	(18,600)	(17,683)	917
Total other financing sources (uses)	(18,600)	(17,683)	917
Excess (deficiency) of revenues and other financing sources over expenditures and other financing uses		(22,895)	(22,895)
Fund balances (deficits), July 1, 2000, as restated			
Increase in reserve for inventory			
Increase in reserve for prepaid items		22,895	22,895
Fund balances (deficits), June 30, 2001	$	$	$

Title I - Migrant			Title II - Eisenhower Grant		
Budget	Actual	Variance - Favorable (Unfavorable)	Budget	Actual	Variance - Favorable (Unfavorable)
$	$	$	$	$	$
82,196	81,020	(1,176)	47,802	47,693	(109)
82,196	81,020	(1,176)	47,802	47,693	(109)
45,818	47,094	(1,276)			
28,306	27,134	1,172	46,769	46,662	107
3,204	2,784	420			
3,191	2,344	847			
80,519	79,356	1,163	46,769	46,662	107
1,677	1,664	(13)	1,033	1,031	(2)
(1,677)	(1,664)	13	(1,033)	(1,031)	2
(1,677)	(1,664)	13	(1,033)	(1,031)	2
$	$	$	$	$	$

(Continued)

| | Technology Literacy Grant | | |
	Budget	Actual	Variance - Favorable (Unfavorable)
Revenues:			
Other local	$	$	$
State aid and grants			
Federal aid, grants and reimbursements	13,088	12,985	(103)
Total revenues	13,088	12,985	(103)
Expenditures:			
Current -			
Instruction			
Support services - students and staff	2,692	2,531	161
Support services - administration			
Operation and maintenance of plant services			
Student transportation services			
Operation of non-instructional services			
Capital outlay	10,396	10,454	(58)
Total expenditures	13,088	12,985	103
Excess (deficiency) of revenues over expenditures			
Other financing sources (uses):			
Operating transfers in			
Operating transfers out			
Total other financing sources (uses)			
Excess (deficiency) of revenues and other financing sources over expenditures and other financing uses			
Fund balances (deficits), July 1, 2000, as restated			
Increase in reserve for inventory			
Increase in reserve for prepaid items			
Fund balances (deficits), June 30, 2001	$	$	$

Title IV - Safe and Drug Free Schools			Title VI - Innovative Education Program		
Budget	Actual	Variance - Favorable (Unfavorable)	Budget	Actual	Variance - Favorable (Unfavorable)
$	$	$	$	$	$
29,198	14,439	(14,759)	20,087	19,665	(422)
29,198	14,439	(14,759)	20,087	19,665	(422)
5,274	2,904	2,370	19,687	19,265	422
23,644	11,286	12,358			
28,918	14,190	14,728	19,687	19,265	422
280	249	(31)	400	400	
(280)	(249)	31	(400)	(400)	
(280)	(249)	31	(400)	(400)	
$	$	$	$	$	$

(Continued)

AVONDALE ELEMENTARY SCHOOL DISTRICT NO. 44
COMBINING STATEMENT OF REVENUES, EXPENDITURES AND CHANGES IN
FUND BALANCES - BUDGET AND ACTUAL - ALL SPECIAL REVENUE FUNDS
YEAR ENDED JUNE 30, 2001
(Continued)

| | EHA Title VI-B Entitlement | | |
	Budget	Actual	Variance - Favorable (Unfavorable)
Revenues:	$	$	$
Other local			
State aid and grants			
Federal aid, grants and reimbursements	352,621	276,119	(76,502)
Total revenues	352,621	276,119	(76,502)
Expenditures:			
Current -			
Instruction	222,081	178,477	43,604
Support services - students and staff	120,650	97,899	22,751
Support services - administration	2,398	150	2,248
Operation and maintenance of plant services			
Student transportation services			
Operation of non-instructional services			
Capital outlay			
Total expenditures	345,129	276,526	68,603
Excess (deficiency) of revenues over expenditures	7,492	(407)	(7,899)
Other financing sources (uses):			
Operating transfers in			
Operating transfers out	(7,492)	(6,089)	1,403
Total other financing sources (uses)	(7,492)	(6,089)	1,403
Excess (deficiency) of revenues and other financing sources over expenditures and other financing uses		(6,496)	(6,496)
Fund balances (deficits), July 1, 2000, as restated			
Increase in reserve for inventory			
Increase in reserve for prepaid items		6,496	6,496
Fund balances (deficits), June 30, 2001	$	$	$

	Federal Preschool			Emergency Immigrant Education	
Budget	Actual	Variance - Favorable (Unfavorable)	Budget	Actual	Variance - Favorable (Unfavorable)
$	$	$	$	$	$
25,574	22,208	(3,366)	43,911	21,437	(22,474)
25,574	22,208	(3,366)	43,911	21,437	(22,474)
25,024	21,728	3,296	13,379	13,442	(63)
			16,113	5,201	10,912
			13,768	2,302	11,466
25,024	21,728	3,296	43,260	20,945	22,315
550	480	(70)	651	492	(159)
(550)	(480)	70	(651)	(492)	159
(550)	(480)	70	(651)	(492)	159
$	$	$	$	$	$

(Continued)

| | Medicaid Reimbursement | | |
	Budget	Actual	Variance - Favorable (Unfavorable)
Revenues:			
Other local	$	$	$
State aid and grants			
Federal aid, grants and reimbursements	34,000	35,703	1,703
Total revenues	34,000	35,703	1,703
Expenditures:			
Current -			
Instruction			
Support services - students and staff			
Support services - administration			
Operation and maintenance of plant services			
Student transportation services	34,000	2,127	31,873
Operation of non-instructional services			
Capital outlay			
Total expenditures	34,000	2,127	31,873
Excess (deficiency) of revenues over expenditures		33,576	33,576
Other financing sources (uses):			
Operating transfers in			
Operating transfers out			
Total other financing sources (uses)			
Excess (deficiency) of revenues and other financing sources over expenditures and other financing uses		33,576	33,576
Fund balances (deficits), July 1, 2000, as restated		66,574	66,574
Increase in reserve for inventory			
Increase in reserve for prepaid items			
Fund balances (deficits), June 30, 2001	$	$ 100,150	$ 100,150

*The E - Rate Fund was included in the District's budget, however, the budget was -0-.

	Title III - Goals 2000				E - Rate		
	Budget	Actual	Variance - Favorable (Unfavorable)		Budget*	Actual	Variance - Favorable (Unfavorable)
	$	$	$		$	$	$
	72,838	68,135	(4,703)			299,072	299,072
	72,838	68,135	(4,703)			299,072	299,072
	36		36		17,127		(17,127)
	71,263	66,784	4,479				
					11,081		(11,081)
					3,816		(3,816)
					264,544		(264,544)
	71,299	66,784	4,515			296,568	(296,568)
	1,539	1,351	(188)			2,504	2,504
	(1,539)	(1,351)	188				
	(1,539)	(1,351)	188				
						2,504	2,504
	$	$	$		$	$ 2,504	$ 2,504

(Continued)

AVONDALE ELEMENTARY SCHOOL DISTRICT NO. 44
COMBINING STATEMENT OF REVENUES, EXPENDITURES AND CHANGES IN
FUND BALANCES - BUDGET AND ACTUAL - ALL SPECIAL REVENUE FUNDS
YEAR ENDED JUNE 30, 2001
(Continued)

| | Class Size Reduction | | |
	Budget	Actual	Variance - Favorable (Unfavorable)
Revenues:			
Other local	$	$	$
State aid and grants			
Federal aid, grants and reimbursements	105,381	93,647	(11,734)
Total revenues	105,381	93,647	(11,734)
Expenditures:			
Current -			
Instruction	103,106	92,833	10,273
Support services - students and staff			
Support services - administration			
Operation and maintenance of plant services			
Student transportation services			
Operation of non-instructional services			
Capital outlay			
Total expenditures	103,106	92,833	10,273
Excess (deficiency) of revenues over expenditures	2,275	814	(1,461)
Other financing sources (uses):			
Operating transfers in			
Operating transfers out	(2,275)	(2,052)	223
Total other financing sources (uses)	(2,275)	(2,052)	223
Excess (deficiency) of revenues and other financing sources over expenditures and other financing uses		(1,238)	(1,238)
Fund balances (deficits), July 1, 2000, as restated			
Increase in reserve for inventory			
Increase in reserve for prepaid items		1,238	1,238
Fund balances (deficits), June 30, 2001	$	$	$

	Early Childhood			State Chemical Abuse	
Budget	Actual	Variance - Favorable (Unfavorable)	Budget	Actual	Variance - Favorable (Unfavorable)
$	$	$	$	$	$
155,489	147,969	(7,520)	10,158	8,301	(1,857)
155,489	147,969	(7,520)	10,158	8,301	(1,857)
141,325	136,807	4,518			
11,979	11,981	(2)	10,158	8,301	1,857
2,185	2,275	(90)			
155,489	151,063	4,426	10,158	8,301	1,857
	(3,094)	(3,094)			
	(3,094)	(3,094)			
	3,094	3,094			
$	$	$	$	$	$

(Continued)

| | Gifted Education | | |
	Budget	Actual	Variance - Favorable (Unfavorable)
Revenues:			
Other local	$	$	$
State aid and grants	5,299	5,299	
Federal aid, grants and reimbursements			
Total revenues	5,299	5,299	
Expenditures:			
Current -			
Instruction	1,100	987	113
Support services - students and staff	2,467	2,610	(143)
Support services - administration			
Operation and maintenance of plant services			
Student transportation services			
Operation of non-instructional services			
Capital outlay	1,732	1,702	30
Total expenditures	5,299	5,299	
Excess (deficiency) of revenues over expenditures			
Other financing sources (uses):			
Operating transfers in			
Operating transfers out			
Total other financing sources (uses)			
Excess (deficiency) of revenues and other financing sources over expenditures and other financing uses			
Fund balances (deficits), July 1, 2000, as restated			
Increase in reserve for inventory			
Increase in reserve for prepaid items			
Fund balances (deficits), June 30, 2001	$	$	$

School Plant			Food Services		
Budget	Actual	Variance - Favorable (Unfavorable)	Budget	Actual	Variance - Favorable (Unfavorable)
$	$ 12,192	$ 12,192	$ 258,844	$ 284,668	$ 25,824
			843,748	816,510	(27,238)
	12,192	12,192	1,102,592	1,101,178	(1,414)
			1,280,000	1,063,078	216,922
				25,552	(25,552)
			1,280,000	1,088,630	191,370
	12,192	12,192	(177,408)	12,548	189,956
				(11,186)	(11,186)
				(11,186)	(11,186)
	12,192	12,192	(177,408)	1,362	178,770
107,447	107,446	(1)	177,408	203,180	25,772
				2,319	2,319
				13,613	13,613
$ 107,447	$ 119,638	$ 12,191	$	$ 220,474	$ 220,474

(Continued)

AVONDALE ELEMENTARY SCHOOL DISTRICT NO. 44
COMBINING STATEMENT OF REVENUES, EXPENDITURES AND CHANGES IN
FUND BALANCES - BUDGET AND ACTUAL - ALL SPECIAL REVENUE FUNDS
YEAR ENDED JUNE 30, 2001
(Continued)

	Civic Center		
	Budget	Actual	Variance - Favorable (Unfavorable)
Revenues:			
Other local	$	$ 70,900	$ 70,900
State aid and grants			
Federal aid, grants and reimbursements			
Total revenues		70,900	70,900
Expenditures:			
Current -			
Instruction			
Support services - students and staff	55,000	10,558	44,442
Support services - administration			
Operation and maintenance of plant services			
Student transportation services		2,625	(2,625)
Operation of non-instructional services		4,100	(4,100)
Capital outlay			
Total expenditures	55,000	17,283	37,717
Excess (deficiency) of revenues over expenditures	(55,000)	53,617	108,617
Other financing sources (uses):			
Operating transfers in			
Operating transfers out			
Total other financing sources (uses)			
Excess (deficiency) of revenues and other financing sources over expenditures and other financing uses	(55,000)	53,617	108,617
Fund balances (deficits), July 1, 2000, as restated	72,258	72,258	
Increase in reserve for inventory			
Increase in reserve for prepaid items			
Fund balances (deficits), June 30, 2001	$ 17,258	$ 125,875	$ 108,617

| Community School | | | | Extracurricular Activities Fees Tax Credit | | |
Budget	Actual	Variance - Favorable (Unfavorable)		Budget	Actual	Variance - Favorable (Unfavorable)
$ 2,554	$ 553	$ (2,001)		$ 8,184	$ 9,798	$ 1,614
2,554	553	(2,001)		8,184	9,798	1,614
5,000		5,000		16,100	11,586	4,514
5,000		5,000		16,100	11,586	4,514
(2,446)	553	2,999		(7,916)	(1,788)	6,128
(2,446)	553	2,999		(7,916)	(1,788)	6,128
2,446	2,446			6,816	6,816	
$	$ 2,999	$ 2,999		$ (1,100)	$ 5,028	$ 6,128

(Continued)

AVONDALE ELEMENTARY SCHOOL DISTRICT NO. 44
COMBINING STATEMENT OF REVENUES, EXPENDITURES AND CHANGES IN
FUND BALANCES - BUDGET AND ACTUAL - ALL SPECIAL REVENUE FUNDS
YEAR ENDED JUNE 30, 2001
(Continued)

	Gifts and Donations		
	Budget	Actual	Variance - Favorable (Unfavorable)
Revenues:			
Other local	$ 29,336	$ 8,556	$ (20,780)
State aid and grants			
Federal aid, grants and reimbursements			
Total revenues	29,336	8,556	(20,780)
Expenditures:			
Current -			
Instruction		2,403	(2,403)
Support services - students and staff		3,963	(3,963)
Support services - administration			
Operation and maintenance of plant services			
Student transportation services			
Operation of non-instructional services	35,000	217	34,783
Capital outlay			
Total expenditures	35,000	6,583	28,417
Excess (deficiency) of revenues over expenditures	(5,664)	1,973	7,637
Other financing sources (uses):			
Operating transfers in			
Operating transfers out			
Total other financing sources (uses)			
Excess (deficiency) of revenues and other financing sources over expenditures and other financing uses	(5,664)	1,973	7,637
Fund balances (deficits), July 1, 2000, as restated	5,664	5,664	
Increase in reserve for inventory			
Increase in reserve for prepaid items			
Fund balances (deficits), June 30, 2001	$	$ 7,637	$ 7,637

	District Services				Fingerprinting			
	Budget	Actual	Variance - Favorable (Unfavorable)		Budget	Actual	Variance - Favorable (Unfavorable)
	$	$ 3,616	$ 3,616		$ 976	$ 2,097	$ 1,121
		3,616	3,616		976	2,097	1,121
	16,000		16,000		5,000	730	4,270
	16,000		16,000		5,000	730	4,270
	(16,000)	3,616	19,616		(4,024)	1,367	5,391
	(16,000)	3,616	19,616		(4,024)	1,367	5,391
	59,905	59,505	(400)		24	24	
	$ 43,905	$ 63,121	$ 19,216		$ (4,000)	$ 1,391	$ 5,391

(Continued)

AVONDALE ELEMENTARY SCHOOL DISTRICT NO. 44
COMBINING STATEMENT OF REVENUES, EXPENDITURES AND CHANGES IN
FUND BALANCES - BUDGET AND ACTUAL - ALL SPECIAL REVENUE FUNDS
YEAR ENDED JUNE 30, 2001
(Continued)

| | School Opening | | |
	Budget	Actual	Variance - Favorable (Unfavorable)
Revenues:			
Other local	$ 36,727	$	$ (36,727)
State aid and grants			
Federal aid, grants and reimbursements			
Total revenues	36,727		(36,727)
Expenditures:			
Current -			
Instruction			
Support services - students and staff			
Support services - administration			
Operation and maintenance of plant services			
Student transportation services			
Operation of non-instructional services			
Capital outlay			
Total expenditures			
Excess (deficiency) of revenues over expenditures	36,727		(36,727)
Other financing sources (uses):			
Operating transfers in			
Operating transfers out			
Total other financing sources (uses)			
Excess (deficiency) of revenues and other financing sources over expenditures and other financing uses	36,727		(36,727)
Fund balances (deficits), July 1, 2000, as restated	(36,727)		36,727
Increase in reserve for inventory			
Increase in reserve for prepaid items			
Fund balances (deficits), June 30, 2001	$	$	$

Insurance Proceeds			Textbooks		
Budget	Actual	Variance - Favorable (Unfavorable)	Budget	Actual	Variance - Favorable (Unfavorable)
$	$ 4,538	$ 4,538	$ 6,145	$ 1,615	$ (4,530)
	4,538	4,538	6,145	1,615	(4,530)
			15,000	3,914	11,086
30,000	357	29,643			
30,000	357	29,643	15,000	3,914	11,086
(30,000)	4,181	34,181	(8,855)	(2,299)	6,556
(30,000)	4,181	34,181	(8,855)	(2,299)	6,556
33,597	33,597		8,855	8,855	
$ 3,597	$ 37,778	$ 34,181	$	$ 6,556	$ 6,556

(Continued)

AVONDALE ELEMENTARY SCHOOL DISTRICT NO. 44
COMBINING STATEMENT OF REVENUES, EXPENDITURES AND CHANGES IN
FUND BALANCES - BUDGET AND ACTUAL - ALL SPECIAL REVENUE FUNDS
YEAR ENDED JUNE 30, 2001
(Continued)

| | Indirect Costs | | |
	Budget	Actual	Variance - Favorable (Unfavorable)
Revenues:			
Other local	$	$ 3,571	$ 3,571
State aid and grants			
Federal aid, grants and reimbursements			
Total revenues		3,571	3,571
Expenditures:			
Current -			
Instruction			
Support services - students and staff			
Support services - administration	80,000	38,508	41,492
Operation and maintenance of plant services			
Student transportation services			
Operation of non-instructional services			
Capital outlay			
Total expenditures	80,000	38,508	41,492
Excess (deficiency) of revenues over expenditures	(80,000)	(34,937)	45,063
Other financing sources (uses):			
Operating transfers in	15,621	42,677	27,056
Operating transfers out			
Total other financing sources (uses)	15,621	42,677	27,056
Excess (deficiency) of revenues and other financing sources over expenditures and other financing uses	(64,379)	7,740	72,119
Fund balances (deficits), July 1, 2000, as restated	64,379	64,379	
Increase in reserve for inventory			
Increase in reserve for prepaid items			
Fund balances (deficits), June 30, 2001	$	$ 72,119	$ 72,119

Unemployment Insurance			Insurance Refund		
		Variance - Favorable			Variance - Favorable
Budget	Actual	(Unfavorable)	Budget	Actual	(Unfavorable)
$	$ 31,414	$ 31,414	$	$ 565	$ 565
	31,414	31,414		565	565
20,000	9,456	10,544	1,000		1,000
20,000	9,456	10,544	1,000		1,000
(20,000)	21,958	41,958	(1,000)	565	1,565
(20,000)	21,958	41,958	(1,000)	565	1,565
521,191	521,191		9,294	9,294	
$ 501,191	$ 543,149	$ 41,958	$ 8,294	$ 9,859	$ 1,565

(Continued)

AVONDALE ELEMENTARY SCHOOL DISTRICT NO. 44
COMBINING STATEMENT OF REVENUES, EXPENDITURES AND CHANGES IN
FUND BALANCES - BUDGET AND ACTUAL - ALL SPECIAL REVENUE FUNDS
YEAR ENDED JUNE 30, 2001
(Concluded)

	Grants and Gifts to Teachers		
	Budget	Actual	Variance - Favorable (Unfavorable)
Revenues:			
Other local	$ 8,866	$ 7,990	$ (876)
State aid and grants			
Federal aid, grants and reimbursements			
Total revenues	8,866	7,990	(876)
Expenditures:			
Current -			
Instruction	12,000	8,676	3,324
Support services - students and staff			
Support services - administration			
Operation and maintenance of plant services			
Student transportation services			
Operation of non-instructional services			
Capital outlay			
Total expenditures	12,000	8,676	3,324
Excess (deficiency) of revenues over expenditures	(3,134)	(686)	2,448
Other financing sources (uses):			
Operating transfers in			
Operating transfers out			
Total other financing sources (uses)			
Excess (deficiency) of revenues and other financing sources over expenditures and other financing uses	(3,134)	(686)	2,448
Fund balances (deficits), July 1, 2000, as restated	3,134	3,133	(1)
Increase in reserve for inventory			
Increase in reserve for prepaid items			
Fund balances (deficits), June 30, 2001	$	$ 2,447	$ 2,447

	Inter governmental Agreements				Totals		
	Budget	Actual	Variance - Favorable (Unfavorable)		Budget	Actual	Variance - Favorable (Unfavorable)
	$ 5,713	$ 24,971	$ 19,258		$ 357,345	$ 467,044	$ 109,699
					170,946	161,569	(9,377)
					2,533,681	2,603,559	69,878
	5,713	24,971	19,258		3,061,972	3,232,172	170,200
					1,302,752	1,222,246	80,506
	24,400	22,527	1,873		547,436	402,281	145,155
					190,422	113,357	77,065
						3,816	(3,816)
					34,000	4,752	29,248
					1,320,376	1,072,014	248,362
					25,896	304,554	(278,658)
	24,400	22,527	1,873		3,420,882	3,123,020	297,862
	(18,687)	2,444	21,131		(358,910)	109,152	468,062
					15,621	42,677	27,056
					(34,497)	(42,677)	(8,180)
					(18,876)		18,876
	(18,687)	2,444	21,131		(377,786)	109,152	486,938
	9,287	9,286	(1)		1,044,978	1,173,648	128,670
						2,319	2,319
						47,336	47,336
	$ (9,400)	$ 11,730	$ 21,130		$ 667,192	$ 1,332,455	$ 665,263

(This page intentionally left blank)

CAPITAL PROJECTS FUNDS

Unrestricted Capital Fund - to account for transactions relating to the acquisition of capital items by purchase or lease as prescribed by A.R.S.

Adjacent Ways Fund - to account for transactions relating to special assessments to finance the improvement of public streets, alleys, etc. adjacent to school property, in accordance with A.R.S. Section 15-995.

Soft Capital Fund - to account for transactions relating to the acquisition of capital items that are capital materials and equipment needed to assist students in mastering Arizona's Academic Standards.

Bond Building Fund - to account for monies received from District bond issues to finance the acquisition of sites or to construct school buildings

Gifts and Donations Fund - to account for gifts and donations to be expended for capital projects.

Capital Equity Fund - to account for monies received from the State for capital improvements.

Deficiencies Correction Fund - to account for monies received from the School Facilities Board that are used to correct deficiencies in square footage and in quality of facilities and equipment.

New School Facilities - to account for monies received from the School Facilities Board that are used to purchase land, to construct new school buildings, and related architectural and engineering fees.

Building Renewal Fund - to account for monies received from the School Facilities Board that are used for infrastructure or for major upgrades, repairs, or renovate areas, systems, or buildings that will maintain or extend their useful life.

AVONDALE ELEMENTARY SCHOOL DISTRICT NO. 44
COMBINING BALANCE SHEET - ALL CAPITAL PROJECTS FUNDS
JUNE 30, 2001

	Unrestricted Capital	Adjacent Ways	Soft Capital	Bond Building
ASSETS				
Cash and investments	$ 143,002	$ 100,426	$ 302,792	$ 2,160,636
Property taxes receivable		104	7,678	
Total assets	$ 143,002	$ 100,530	$ 310,470	$ 2,160,636
LIABILITIES AND FUND EQUITY				
Liabilities:				
Accounts payable	$ 10,874	$	$ 2,265	$
Deferred revenues		104	5,147	
Construction contracts payable				
Total liabilities	10,874	104	7,412	
Fund equity:				
Fund balances -				
Unreserved:				
Designated for capital outlay	132,128	100,426	303,058	2,160,636
Total fund equity	132,128	100,426	303,058	2,160,636
Total liabilities and fund equity	$ 143,002	$ 100,530	$ 310,470	$ 2,160,636

	Gifts and Donations		Capital Equity		Deficiencies Correction		New School Facilities		Building Renewal		Totals
$	461,249	$	339	$	3,619	$	522,549	$	491,778	$	4,186,390
											7,782
$	461,249	$	339	$	3,619	$	522,549	$	491,778	$	4,194,172
$	25,322	$		$		$		$		$	38,461
											5,251
							4,731		59,361		64,092
	25,322						4,731		59,361		107,804
	435,927		339		3,619		517,818		432,417		4,086,368
	435,927		339		3,619		517,818		432,417		4,086,368
$	461,249	$	339	$	3,619	$	522,549	$	491,778	$	4,194,172

	Unrestricted Capital	Adjacent Ways	Soft Capital
Revenues:			
Other local	$ 40,318	$ 4,994	$ 59,238
Property taxes	227	24,584	165,182
State aid and grants	154,823	10	745,256
Total revenues	195,368	29,588	969,676
Expenditures:			
Capital outlay	473,168	6,634	657,911
Debt service -			
Interest, premium and fiscal charges	12,923		
Principal retirement	71,032		
Total expenditures	557,123	6,634	657,911
Excess (deficiency) of revenues over expenditures	(361,755)	22,954	311,765
Operating transfers out			
Total other financing sources (uses)			
Excess (deficiency) of revenues and other financing sources over expenditures and other financing uses	(361,755)	22,954	311,765
Fund balances (deficits), beginning of year, as restated	493,883	77,472	(8,707)
Fund balances, end of year	$ 132,128	$ 100,426	$ 303,058

Bond Building	Gifts and Donations	Capital Equity	Deficiencies Correction	New School Facilities	Building Renewal
$ 101,354	$ 358,270	$ 329	$	$	$ 1
			253,281	515,785	300,140
101,354	358,270	329	253,281	515,785	300,141
380,030	25,322	23,200	249,662	305,788	204,098
380,030	25,322	23,200	249,662	305,788	204,098
(278,676)	332,948	(22,871)	3,619	209,997	96,043
(101,354)					
(101,354)					
(380,030)	332,948	(22,871)	3,619	209,997	96,043
2,540,666	102,979	23,210		307,821	336,374
$ 2,160,636	$ 435,927	$ 339	$ 3,619	$ 517,818	$ 432,417

(Continued)

	Totals
Revenues:	
Other local	$ 564,504
Property taxes	189,993
State aid and grants	1,969,295
Total revenues	2,723,792
Expenditures:	
Capital outlay	2,325,813
Debt service -	
Interest, premium and fiscal charges	12,923
Principal retirement	71,032
Total expenditures	2,409,768
Excess (deficiency) of revenues over expenditures	314,024
Operating transfers out	(101,354)
Total other financing sources (uses)	(101,354)
Excess (deficiency) of revenues and other financing sources over expenditures and other financing uses	212,670
Fund balances (deficits), beginning of year, as restated	3,873,698
Fund balances, end of year	$ 4,086,368

(This page intentionally left blank)

AVONDALE ELEMENTARY SCHOOL DISTRICT NO. 44
COMBINING STATEMENT OF REVENUES, EXPENDITURES AND CHANGES IN
FUND BALANCES - BUDGET AND ACTUAL - ALL CAPITAL PROJECTS FUNDS
YEAR ENDED JUNE 30, 2001

| | Unrestricted Capital | | |
	Budget	Actual	Variance - Favorable (Unfavorable)
Revenues:			
Other local	$ 25,000	$ 40,318	$ 15,318
Property taxes		227	227
State aid and grants	46,784	154,823	108,039
Total revenues	71,784	195,368	123,584
Expenditures:			
Capital outlay	666,126	473,168	192,958
Debt service -			
Interest, premium and fiscal charges		12,923	(12,923)
Principal retirement		71,032	(71,032)
Total expenditures	666,126	557,123	109,003
Excess (deficiency) of revenues over expenditures	(594,342)	(361,755)	232,587
Other financing sources (uses):			
Operating transfers out			
Total other financing sources (uses)			
Excess (deficiency) of revenues and other financing sources over expenditures and other financing uses	(594,342)	(361,755)	232,587
Fund balances (deficits), July 1, 2000, as restated	530,610	493,883	(36,727)
Fund balances (deficits), June 30, 2001	$ (63,732)	$ 132,128	$ 195,860

	Adjacent Ways				Soft Capital		
	Budget	Actual	Variance - Favorable (Unfavorable)		Budget	Actual	Variance - Favorable (Unfavorable)
$	5,094	$ 4,994	$ (100)	$	51,632	$ 59,238	$ 7,606
	30,434	24,584	(5,850)		167,190	165,182	(2,008)
		10	10		511,057	745,256	234,199
	35,528	29,588	(5,940)		729,879	969,676	239,797
	113,000	6,634	106,366		707,121	657,911	49,210
	113,000	6,634	106,366		707,121	657,911	49,210
	(77,472)	22,954	100,426		22,758	311,765	289,007
	(77,472)	22,954	100,426		22,758	311,765	289,007
	77,472	77,472			(12,084)	(8,707)	3,377
$		$ 100,426	$ 100,426	$	10,674	$ 303,058	$ 292,384

(Continued)

AVONDALE ELEMENTARY SCHOOL DISTRICT NO. 44
COMBINING STATEMENT OF REVENUES, EXPENDITURES AND CHANGES IN
FUND BALANCES - BUDGET AND ACTUAL - ALL CAPITAL PROJECTS FUNDS
YEAR ENDED JUNE 30, 2001
(Continued)

| | Bond Building | | |
	Budget	Actual	Variance - Favorable (Unfavorable)
Revenues:			
Other local	$	$ 101,354	$ 101,354
Property taxes			
State aid and grants	5,959,334		(5,959,334)
Total revenues	5,959,334	101,354	(5,857,980)
Expenditures:			
Capital outlay	8,500,000	380,030	8,119,970
Debt service -			
Interest, premium and fiscal charges			
Principal retirement			
Total expenditures	8,500,000	380,030	8,119,970
Excess (deficiency) of revenues over expenditures	(2,540,666)	(278,676)	2,261,990
Other financing sources (uses):			
Operating transfers out		(101,354)	(101,354)
Total other financing sources (uses)		(101,354)	(101,354)
Excess (deficiency) of revenues and other financing sources over expenditures and other financing uses	(2,540,666)	(380,030)	2,160,636
Fund balances (deficits), July 1, 2000, as restated	2,540,666	2,540,666	
Fund balances (deficits), June 30, 2001	$	$ 2,160,636	$ 2,160,636

	Gifts and Donations			Capital Equity		
	Budget	Actual	Variance - Favorable (Unfavorable)	Budget	Actual	Variance - Favorable (Unfavorable)
	$	$ 358,270	$ 358,270	$ 1,790	$ 329	$ (1,461)
		358,270	358,270	1,790	329	(1,461)
	100,000	25,322	74,678	25,000	23,200	1,800
	100,000	25,322	74,678	25,000	23,200	1,800
	(100,000)	332,948	432,948	(23,210)	(22,871)	339
	(100,000)	332,948	432,948	(23,210)	(22,871)	339
	102,979	102,979		23,210	23,210	
	$ 2,979	$ 435,927	$ 432,948	$	$ 339	$ 339

(Continued)

| | Deficiencies Correction | | |
	Budget	Actual	Variance - Favorable (Unfavorable)
Revenues:			
Other local	$	$	$
Property taxes			
State aid and grants		253,281	253,281
Total revenues		253,281	253,281
Expenditures:			
Capital outlay	250,000	249,662	338
Debt service -			
Interest, premium and fiscal charges			
Principal retirement			
Total expenditures	250,000	249,662	338
Excess (deficiency) of revenues over expenditures	(250,000)	3,619	253,619
Other financing sources (uses):			
Operating transfers out			
Total other financing sources (uses)			
Excess (deficiency) of revenues and other financing sources over expenditures and other financing uses	(250,000)	3,619	253,619
Fund balances (deficits), July 1, 2000, as restated			
Fund balances (deficits), June 30, 2001	$ (250,000)	$ 3,619	$ 253,619

	New School Facilities				Building Renewal		
	Budget	Actual	Variance - Favorable (Unfavorable)		Budget	Actual	Variance - Favorable (Unfavorable)
	$	$	$		$	$ 1	$ 1
	442,179	515,785	73,606		131,701	300,140	168,439
	442,179	515,785	73,606		131,701	300,141	168,440
	750,000	305,788	444,212		468,075	204,098	263,977
	750,000	305,788	444,212		468,075	204,098	263,977
	(307,821)	209,997	517,818		(336,374)	96,043	432,417
	(307,821)	209,997	517,818		(336,374)	96,043	432,417
	307,821	307,821			336,374	336,374	
	$	$ 517,818	$ 517,818		$	$ 432,417	$ 432,417

(Continued)

		Totals	
	Budget	Actual	Variance - Favorable (Unfavorable)
Revenues:			
Other local	$ 83,516	$ 564,504	$ 480,988
Property taxes	197,624	189,993	(7,631)
State aid and grants	7,091,055	1,969,295	(5,121,760)
Total revenues	7,372,195	2,723,792	(4,648,403)
Expenditures:			
Capital outlay	11,579,322	2,325,813	9,253,509
Debt service -			
Interest, premium and fiscal charges		12,923	(12,923)
Principal retirement		71,032	(71,032)
Total expenditures	11,579,322	2,409,768	9,169,554
Excess (deficiency) of revenues over expenditures	(4,207,127)	314,024	4,521,151
Other financing sources (uses):			
Operating transfers out		(101,354)	(101,354)
Total other financing sources (uses)		(101,354)	(101,354)
Excess (deficiency) of revenues and other financing sources over expenditures and other financing uses	(4,207,127)	212,670	4,419,797
Fund balances (deficits), July 1, 2000, as restated	3,907,048	3,873,698	(33,350)
Fund balances (deficits), June 30, 2001	$ (300,079)	$ 4,086,368	$ 4,386,447

AGENCY FUNDS

Student Activities Fund - to account for monies raised by students to finance student clubs and organizations but held by the District as an agent.

Employee Withholding Fund - to account for unremitted payroll deductions temporarily held by the District as an agent.

AVONDALE ELEMENTARY SCHOOL DISTRICT NO. 44
COMBINING BALANCE SHEET - ALL AGENCY FUNDS
JUNE 30, 2001

	Student Activities	Employee Withholding	Total
ASSETS			
Cash and investments	$ 30,804	$ 39,137	$ 69,941
Total assets	$ 30,804	$ 39,137	$ 69,941
LIABILITIES			
Deposits held for others	$	$ 39,137	$ 39,137
Due to student groups	30,804		30,804
Total liabilities	$ 30,804	$ 39,137	$ 69,941

AVONDALE ELEMENTARY SCHOOL DISTRICT NO. 44
COMBINING STATEMENT OF CHANGES IN ASSETS AND LIABILITIES - AGENCY FUNDS
YEAR ENDED JUNE 30, 2001

	Balance July 1, 2000	Additions	Deductions	Balance June 30, 2001
STUDENT ACTIVITIES FUND				
Assets				
Cash and investments	$ 23,892	$ 195,750	$ 188,838	$ 30,804
Total assets	$ 23,892	$ 195,750	$ 188,838	$ 30,804
Liabilities				
Due to student groups	$ 23,892	$ 195,750	$ 188,838	$ 30,804
Total liabilities	$ 23,892	$ 195,750	$ 188,838	$ 30,804
EMPLOYEE WITHHOLDING FUND				
Assets				
Cash and investments	$ 28,448	$ 753,691	$ 743,002	$ 39,137
Total assets	$ 28,448	$ 753,691	$ 743,002	$ 39,137
Liabilities				
Deposits held for others	$ 28,448	$ 753,691	$ 743,002	$ 39,137
Total liabilities	$ 28,448	$ 753,691	$ 743,002	$ 39,137
TOTAL AGENCY FUNDS				
Assets				
Cash and investments	$ 52,340	$ 949,441	$ 931,840	$ 69,941
Total assets	$ 52,340	$ 949,441	$ 931,840	$ 69,941
Liabilities				
Deposits held for others	$ 28,448	$ 753,691	$ 743,002	$ 39,137
Due to student groups	23,892	195,750	188,838	30,804
Total liabilities	$ 52,340	$ 949,441	$ 931,840	$ 69,941

(This page intentionally left blank)

GENERAL FIXED ASSETS ACCOUNT GROUP

General Fixed Assets is a balanced account group used to establish control and accountability for the costs of all real property and moveable equipment owned by the District. The investment in General Fixed Assets is carried until the disposition of the property and ownership is relinquished. Depreciation on fixed assets is not recorded.

General Fixed Assets

Land and improvements	$ 603,744
Buildings and improvements	22,520,474
Vehicles, furniture and equipment	3,490,350
Construction in progress	304,487
Total	$ 26,919,055

Investment in General Fixed Assets

Investment in property acquired prior to July 1, 1993	$ 15,836,111
Investment in property acquired after July 1, 1993:	
Special Revenue Funds	
Capital Projects Funds	11,082,944
Total	$ 26,919,055

		Asset Classification			
Function and Activity	**Land and Improvements**	**Buildings and Improvements**	**Vehicles, Furniture and Equipment**	**Construction in Progress**	**Total**
District complex	$ 603,744	$ 22,520,474	$ 3,490,350	$ 304,487	$ 26,919,05

Function and Activity	**General Fixed Assets July 1, 2000**	**Additions**	**Deletions**	**General Fixed Assets June 30, 2001**
District complex	$ 24,979,321	$ 3,786,949	$ 1,847,215	$ 26,919,055

STATISTICAL SECTION

AVONDALE ELEMENTARY SCHOOL DISTRICT NO. 44
GENERAL SCHOOL SYSTEM EXPENDITURES BY FUNCTION*
LAST 10 FISCAL YEARS
(UNAUDITED)

Fiscal Year	Instruction & Suppport Services - Student & Staff	Support Services - Administration	Operation & Maintenance of Plant Services	Student Transportation Services	Operation of Non-instructional Services	Capital Outlay	Debt Service	Total
2000-01	$ 10,087,071	$ 1,455,641	$ 1,583,815	$ 460,365	$ 1,088,019	$ 304,554	$ 1,767,689	$ 16,747,15
1999-00	8,838,282	1,350,388	1,475,065	426,006	1,052,299	411,512	2,031,109	15,584,66
1998-99 **	8,340,427	1,411,422	1,443,340	415,185	1,016,181	370,167	1,565,996	14,562,71
1997-98	8,358,524	581,542	1,276,229	363,183	972,503	24,798	1,309,163	12,885,94
1996-97	7,981,868	567,969	1,420,716	339,412	925,872	75,233	1,216,583	12,527,65
1995-96	7,904,668	541,311	1,339,203	327,601	928,929	92,227	1,232,121	12,366,06
1994-95	8,007,782	555,053	1,391,550	310,228	886,939	41,599	1,306,187	12,499,33
1993-94	7,446,225	531,566	1,305,905	297,744	811,039	54,556	1,216,631	11,663,66
1992-93	7,148,905	525,147	1,380,377	284,509	729,127	33,409	1,314,596	11,416,07
1991-92	6,759,874	568,914	1,400,004	255,067	700,185	43,254	1,376,043	11,103,3

* Funds included are General, Special Revenue and Debt Service. The source of this information is District records.
** New functional categories were adopted in fiscal year 1998-99.

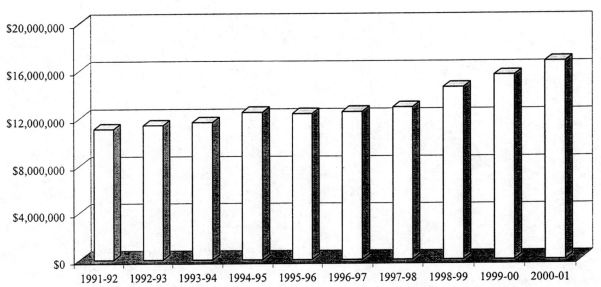

Total Expenditures

AVONDALE ELEMENTARY SCHOOL DISTRICT NO. 44
GENERAL SCHOOL SYSTEM REVENUES BY SOURCE*
LAST 10 FISCAL YEARS
(UNAUDITED)

Fiscal Year	Investment Income	Other Local County Aid & Grants	Food Services Sales	Other	Property Taxes	State Aid and Grants	Federal Aid, Grants & Reimbursements	Total
2000-01	$ 145,955	$ 770,360	$ 280,712	$ 130,991	$ 3,902,160	$ 8,928,865	$ 2,603,559	$ 16,762,602
1999-00	91,632	642,906	236,955	95,320	3,527,168	8,081,261	2,326,543	15,001,785
1998-99	176,912	628,778	197,910	108,782	3,115,881	8,199,740	2,259,837	14,687,840
1997-98	120,647	608,499	210,488	228,274	2,575,581	7,585,880	1,899,521	13,228,890
1996-97	128,050	578,004	176,995	148,905	2,566,489	7,207,526	1,865,949	12,671,918
1995-96	95,530	604,450	171,646	105,093	2,456,107	7,100,635	1,878,858	12,412,319
1994-95	72,463	636,833	143,687	75,710	2,496,286	7,155,204	1,845,949	12,426,132
1993-94	70,113	623,092	139,752	47,990	2,447,334	6,450,721	1,879,580	11,658,582
1992-93	142,406	619,509	137,629	45,424	2,208,711	6,345,265	1,482,078	10,981,022
1991-92	206,983	766,363	143,570	21,515	2,390,533	6,232,903	1,391,580	11,153,447

* Funds included are General, Special Revenue and Debt Service. The source of this information is District records.

Total Revenues

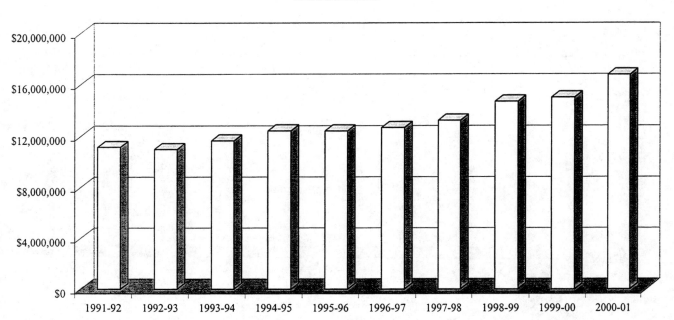

AVONDALE ELEMENTARY SCHOOL DISTRICT NO. 44
PROPERTY TAX LEVIES AND COLLECTIONS*
LAST 10 FISCAL YEARS
(UNAUDITED)

Fiscal Year	Real Property Tax Levy	Collected to June 30th End of Tax Fiscal Year		Collected to June 30, 2001	
		Amount	Percent of Levy	Amount	Percent of Levy
2000-01	$ 3,935,515	$ 3,702,921	94.09 %	$ 3,702,921	94.09 %
1999-00	3,541,198	3,332,627	94.11	3,524,359	99.52
1998-99	3,152,012	2,975,814	94.41	3,116,562	98.88
1997-98	2,687,195	2,502,551	93.13	2,680,353	99.75
1996-97	2,454,434	2,345,150	95.55	2,443,401	99.55
1995-96	2,640,143	2,490,713	94.34	2,622,155	99.32
1994-95	2,562,802	2,370,099	92.48	2,510,283	97.95
1993-94	2,475,482	2,318,899	93.67	2,396,469	96.81
1992-93	2,442,469	2,293,549	93.90	2,374,998	97.24
1991-92	2,735,908	2,460,336	89.93	2,669,451	97.57

* Unsecured personal property taxes are not included in this schedule because the dates of the monthly rolls vary each year. On the average, 93% of unsecured property taxes are collected within 90 days after the due date.

Amounts collected are on a cash basis.

The source of this information is the Maricopa Treasurer's records.

Property Taxes Collected to End of Fiscal Year

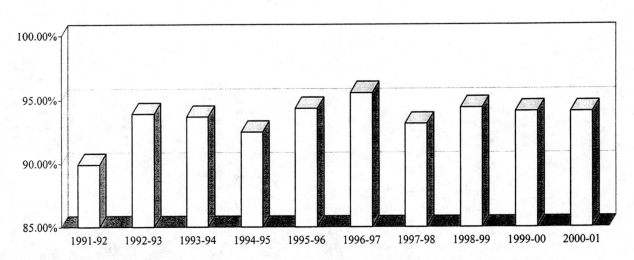

AVONDALE ELEMENTARY SCHOOL DISTRICT NO. 44
ASSESSED AND ESTIMATED ACTUAL VALUE OF TAXABLE PROPERTY*
LAST 10 YEARS
(UNAUDITED)

Fiscal Year	Net Secondary Assessed Value	Estimated Actual Value	Ratio of Net Assessed to Estimated Actual Value
2000-01	$ 100,418,449	$ 796,149,091	12.61 %
1999-00	82,226,968	536,882,332	15.32
1998-99	74,734,634	489,494,533	15.27
1997-98	65,889,795	443,319,384	14.86
1996-97	58,793,130	387,631,683	15.17
1995-96	56,570,881	361,821,939	15.64
1994-95	55,530,078	372,714,972	14.90
1993-94	59,670,064	342,268,831	17.43
1992-93	63,406,929	359,195,883	17.65
1991-92	66,584,190	376,186,369	17.70

* The source of this information is State and County Abstract of the Assessment Roll, Arizona Department of Revenue.

Ratio of Net Assessed to Estimated Actual Value

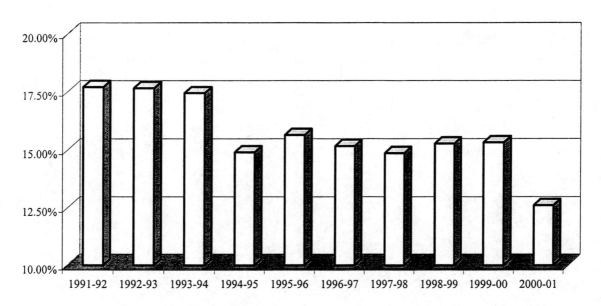

AVONDALE ELEMENTARY SCHOOL DISTRICT NO. 44
COMPARATIVE TAX RATES*
(PER $100 OF ASSESSED VALUE)
(UNAUDITED)

	2000-2001		1999-2000	
	Valuation	**Rate**	**Valuation**	**Rate**
Primary	$ 93,445,436		$ 76,594,232	
Maintenance & Operation		$ 2.3341		$ 2.6466
Adjacent Ways		0.0330		0.0021
Soft Capital		0.1955		0.2127
		$ 2.5626		$ 2.8614
Secondary	$ 100,418,449		$ 82,226,968	
Bond Interest & Redemption		$ 1.9292		$ 2.0986
		$ 1.9292		$ 2.0986

* The source of this information is District records.

2000-01 Tax Rates

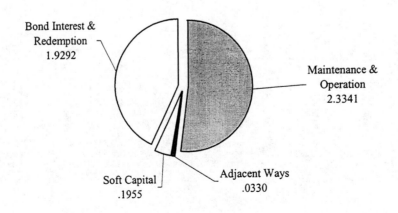

Bond Interest & Redemption 1.9292

Maintenance & Operation 2.3341

Soft Capital .1955

Adjacent Ways .0330

AVONDALE ELEMENTARY SCHOOL DISTRICT NO. 44
PROPERTY TAX RATES - DIRECT AND OVERLAPPING GOVERNMENTS*
(PER $100 OF ASSESSED VALUE)
LAST 10 FISCAL YEARS
(UNAUDITED)

| | | Maricopa County | | | | | | | |
Fiscal Year	State of Arizona	County-wide	Community College District	Flood Control District	Central AZ Water Conservation District	City of Avondale	City of Goodyear	Agua Fria Union High School District No. 216	Avondale Elementary School District No. 44
2000-01	0.00	1.27	1.11	0.23	0.13	1.28	1.95	3.88	4.49
1999-00	0.00	1.30	1.13	0.29	0.14	1.64	2.10	4.49	4.96
1998-99	0.00	1.28	1.11	0.33	0.14	1.78	2.09	4.63	4.82
1997-98	0.00	1.26	1.13	0.34	0.14	1.35	2.11	4.15	4.53
1996-97	0.00	1.78	1.05	0.34	0.14	1.58	2.13	4.14	4.56
1995-96	0.47	1.83	1.11	0.33	0.14	1.35	2.09	4.53	5.18
1994-95	0.47	1.77	0.89	0.36	0.14	1.32	2.10	4.59	5.24
1993-94	0.47	1.79	0.85	0.39	0.14	0.64	2.14	3.78	4.66
1992-93	0.47	1.74	0.85	0.39	0.14	0.60	2.04	4.35	4.30
1991-92	0.47	1.69	0.84	0.44	0.14	0.56	2.09	3.58	4.79

* The combined tax rate includes the tax rate for debt service payments, which is based on the secondary assessed valuation of the entity, and the tax rate for all other purposes such as maintenance and operation and capital outlay, which is based on the primary assessed valuation of the municipality.

The source of this information is the Maricopa County Treasurer's records.

AVONDALE ELEMENTARY SCHOOL DISTRICT NO. 44
RATIO OF NET GENERAL BONDED DEBT
TO ASSESSED VALUE AND NET BONDED DEBT PER CAPITA*
LAST 10 FISCAL YEARS
(UNAUDITED)

Fiscal Year	Population	Net Secondary Assessed Value	Net Bonded Debt	Ratio of Net General Bonded Debt to Assessed Value	Net Bonded Debt Per Capita
2000-01	33,600	$ 100,418,449	$ 9,543,023	9.50 %	$ 284
1999-00	32,000	82,226,968	11,085,172	13.48	346
1998-99	28,650	74,734,634	8,287,346	11.09	289
1997-98	26,020	65,889,795	8,818,003	13.38	339
1996-97	25,111	58,793,130	5,394,438	9.18	215
1995-96	24,000	56,570,881	6,419,378	11.35	267
1994-95	23,040	55,530,078	7,378,199	13.29	320
1993-94	22,839	59,670,064	8,160,016	13.68	357
1992-93	21,505	63,406,929	8,419,619	13.28	392
1991-92	18,837	66,584,190	9,705,816	14.58	515

* The source of this information is District records.

Net Bonded Debt

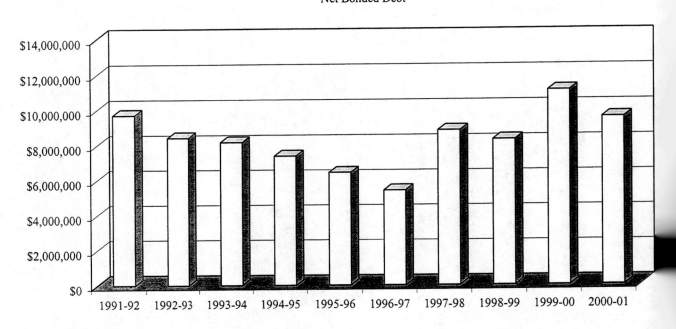

District General Obligation and Refunding Bonds:

Net secondary assessed value		$ 100,418,449
Debt limit - 15% of net assessed value		$ 15,062,767
Amount of debt applicable to debt limit:		
General Obligation and Refunding Bonds Outstanding (Class A)	$ 10,145,000	
Less:		
Assets in Debt Service Fund available for payment of principal	601,977	
Total amount of debt applicable to debt limit		9,543,023
Legal debt margin		$ 5,519,744

---

* The source of this information is District records.

The State of Arizona now provides funds for construction and maintenance of school facilities
to meet the minimum capital facilities standards. Due to this change in funding, a school district was
able to issue Class A school construction bonds until December 31, 1999. Beginning January 1, 2000,
school districts may issue Class B bonds to enhance facilities beyond the minimum standards
established by the State. Districts may issue Class B bonds up to an amount not exceeding 5% of the
secondary assessed valuation or $1500 per student, whichever is greater. In addition, the Class B bonds,
together with outstanding Class A bonds previously issued, cannot exceed the constitutional debt limit of
15% of the secondary assessed valuation. The District currently has no Class B bonds outstanding.

AVONDALE ELEMENTARY SCHOOL DISTRICT NO. 44
COMPUTATION OF DIRECT AND OVERLAPPING DEBT*
JUNE 30, 2001
(UNAUDITED)

Jurisdiction		Net Assessed Value		Net Debt Outstanding	Percentage Applicable to School District		Amount Applicable to School District
Overlapping:							
Maricopa County	$	21,138,917,389	$	79,595,000	0.43 %	$	342,2:
Community College District		21,138,917,389		269,990,000	0.43		1,160,9
City of Avondale		104,461,872		12,884,000	28.07		3,616,5
City of Goodyear		136,713,813		12,200,000	50.40		6,148,8
Wildflower Ranch Community Facilities District		3,598,387		650,000	89.88		584,2
Community Facilities General District No.1 of the City of Goodyear		20,429,623		2,850,000	25.61		729,8
Community Facilities Utilities District No.1 of the City of Goodyear		37,279,466		8,515,000	14.07		1,198,0
Agua Fria Union High School District No. 216		247,777,298		25,750,000	40.09		10,323,1
Total Overlapping:							24,103,8
Direct:							
Avondale Elementary School District No. 44		100,418,449		9,543,023	100.00		9,543,0
Total Direct and Overlapping General Obligation Bonded Debt						$	33,646,9

* The source of this information is District records and the State and County Abstract of the Assessment Roll, Arizona Department of Revenue.

Direct and Overlapping Debt Applicable to School District

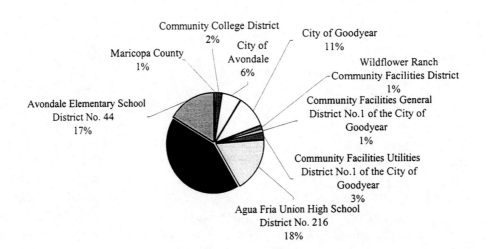

AVONDALE ELEMENTARY SCHOOL DISTRICT NO. 44
RATIO OF ANNUAL DEBT SERVICE FOR
GENERAL BONDED DEBT TO TOTAL GENERAL EXPENDITURES*
LAST 10 FISCAL YEARS
(UNAUDITED)

Fiscal Year	Principal	Interest and Fiscal Charges	Total Debt Service	Total Expenditures*	Ratio of Debt Service To Total Expenditures
2000-01	$ 1,200,000	$ 567,689	$ 1,767,689	$ 16,747,154	10.56 %
1999-00	1,425,000	606,109	2,031,109	15,584,661	13.03
1998-99	170,000	1,395,996	1,565,996	14,562,718	10.75
1997-98	1,115,000	194,163	1,309,163	12,885,942	10.16
1996-97	975,000	241,583	1,216,583	12,527,653	9.71
1995-96	925,000	307,121	1,232,121	12,366,060	9.96
1994-95	935,000	371,187	1,306,187	12,499,338	10.45
1993-94	860,000	356,631	1,216,631	11,663,666	10.43
1992-93	655,000	659,596	1,314,596	11,416,070	11.52
1991-92	550,000	826,043	1,376,043	11,103,341	12.39

* Funds included are General, Special Revenue and Debt Service. The source of this information is District records.

Ratio of Debt Service to Total Expenditures

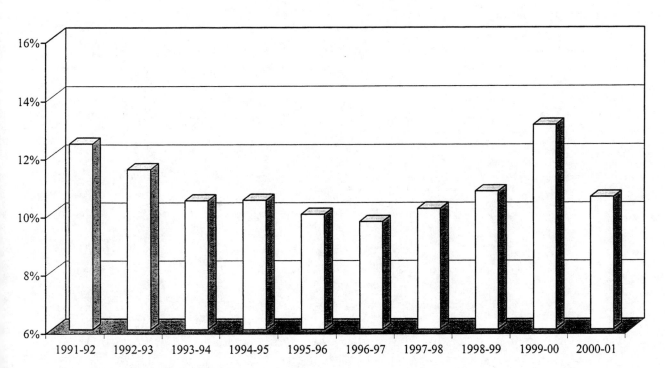

AVONDALE ELEMENTARY SCHOOL DISTRICT NO. 44
COUNTY-WIDE DEMOGRAPHIC STATISTICS*
LAST 10 YEARS
(UNAUDITED)

Calendar Year	Population as of July 1	Per Capita Income	Average Daily School Membership (through Grade 12)	College and University Enrollment	Unemployment Rate (June)
2000	3,072,149	$ **	539,430	**	2.6 %
1999	2,913,500	28,205	519,261	151,139	3.0
1998	2,806,100	27,254	499,949	149,247	2.7
1997	2,720,600	24,601	474,820	141,414	3.0
1996	2,634,600	23,435	428,541	152,373	3.6
1995	2,528,700	22,274	418,226	151,102	3.4
1994	2,355,900	21,364	378,283	153,898	4.7
1993	2,291,200	20,195	364,281	147,189	5.0
1992	2,233,700	19,367	351,280	140,479	6.4
1991	2,180,000	18,551	338,384	135,519	4.9

* Information is County-wide, since it is not available at District level. The source of this information is the Arizona Economic Indicators.

** Information is not available.

AVONDALE ELEMENTARY SCHOOL DISTRICT NO. 44
COUNTY-WIDE BUILDING PERMITS, BANK DEPOSITS AND RETAIL SALES*
LAST 10 YEARS
(UNAUDITED)

Calendar Year	Value of Building Permits Issued	New Housing Units Authorized	Bank Deposits	Retail Sales
2000	$ 4,774,188,000	42,205	$ 27,336,883,000	$ 25,881,116,287
1999	6,555,264,000	36,997	25,213,758,000	23,704,579,962
1998	8,488,426,000	47,801	24,940,253,000	21,504,574,000
1997	7,111,311,000	42,568	20,568,058,000	19,900,822,680
1996	6,793,533,000	39,626	17,806,183,000	18,547,512,000
1995	5,637,579,000	37,091	21,171,950,000	18,001,702,137
1994	3,877,559,000	26,733	20,017,167,000	15,446,000,000
1993	3,529,540,000	24,147	19,485,966,000	13,384,000,000
1992	3,228,423,000	20,489	19,358,015,000	12,756,889,000
1991	2,501,786,000	15,140	19,448,091,000	13,407,000,000

* Information is County-wide, since it is not available at the District level. The source of this information is the Arizona Department of Revenue and the Arizona Bankers Association.

AVONDALE ELEMENTARY SCHOOL DISTRICT NO. 44
NET SECONDARY ASSESSED VALUATION BY PROPERTY CLASSIFICATION*
JUNE 30, 2001
(UNAUDITED)

Legal Class	Description	Net Secondary Assessed Valuation	Percent of Total
2	Mining and Utilities	$ 7,519,761	7.49 %
3	Commercial & Industrial	51,049,180	50.84
4	Agricultural & Vacant	11,338,868	11.29
5	Residential (Owner Occupied)	22,664,170	22.57
6	Residential (Rented)	7,402,253	7.37
7	Railroad, Private Car, Airline Flight Properties	328,357	0.32
8	Properties (Governmental)	115,860	0.12
	Total	$ 100,418,449	100.00 %

* The source of this information is the State and County Abstract of the Assessment Roll, Arizona Department of Revenue.

Net Secondary Assessed Valuation By Property Classification

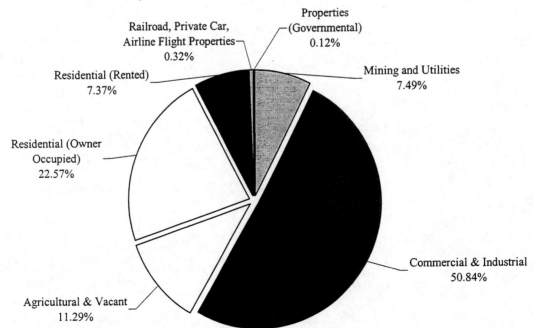

AVONDALE ELEMENTARY SCHOOL DISTRICT NO. 44
PRINCIPAL TAXPAYERS*
JUNE 30, 2001
(UNAUDITED)

Taxpayer		Actual Assessed Valuation	As Percent of District's Net Assessed Valuation
Arizona Public Service Company	$	5,126,703	4.79 %
Loral Corporation		3,981,490	3.72
Wigwam Outlet Stores		3,478,452	3.25
McLane Company		2,964,711	2.77
U.S. West Corporation		2,622,218	2.45
Rubbermaid, Inc.		2,311,833	2.16
SunCor Development Co.		2,236,912	2.09
Wal-Mart Stores, Inc.		1,519,816	1.42
Goodyear Hotel Partners		1,369,975	1.28
Unidynamics Phoenix, Inc.		1,102,402	1.03
	$	26,714,512	24.96 %

* The source of this information is the Maricopa County Assessors' records.

2000-01 Principal Taxpayers

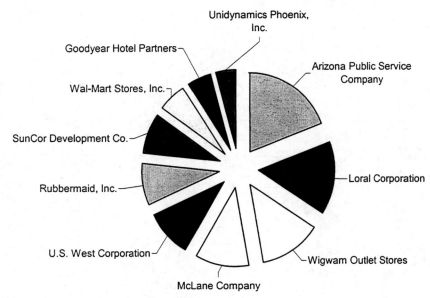

AVONDALE ELEMENTARY SCHOOL DISTRICT NO. 44
AVERAGE DAILY MEMBERSHIP (ADM)*
LAST 10 FISCAL YEARS
(UNAUDITED)

Fiscal Year	Total ADM
2000-01	3,168
1999-00	2,849
1998-99	2,823
1997-98	2,748
1996-97	2,699
1995-96	2,593
1994-95	2,585
1993-94	2,560
1992-93	2,524
1991-92	2,474

* The source of this information is District records.

Average Daily Membership

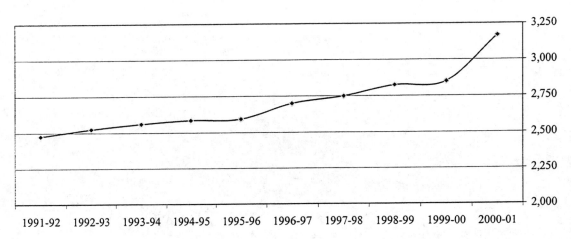

Date established	1894	
Area	30	square miles
Population	33,600	
Number of schools:		
Elementary	5	
Middle Schools	1	
Employees:		
Certified	190	
Classified	191	
Teacher/Student Ratio	1 : 18	
Student Count	3,168	

---

* The source of this information is District records.

(This page intentionally left blank)

APPENDIX C

ASBO INTERNATIONAL SCHOOL DISTRICT

COMPREHENSIVE ANNUAL FINANCIAL REPORT - NEW REPORTING MODEL

(This page intentionally left blank)

AVONDALE ELEMENTARY SCHOOL DISTRICT NO. 44

AVONDALE, ARIZONA

COMPREHENSIVE ANNUAL FINANCIAL REPORT
FOR THE FISCAL YEAR ENDED JUNE 30, 2001

Issued by:
Business & Finance Department

AVONDALE ELEMENTARY SCHOOL DISTRICT NO. 44

TABLE OF CONTENTS

AVONDALE ELEMENTARY SCHOOL DISTRICT NO. 44

TABLE OF CONTENTS (Cont'd)

AVONDALE ELEMENTARY SCHOOL DISTRICT NO. 44

TABLE OF CONTENTS (Concl'd)

INTRODUCTORY SECTION

(This page intentionally left blank)

Dr. Catherine Stafford
Superintendent

Dr. Linda Ronnebaum
Assistant Superintendent

Julia E. Tribbett
Director of Business Operations

"Serving the Communities
of Avondale and Goodyear"

ELEMENTARY SCHOOL DISTRICT
NO. 44

October 9, 2001

Governing Board
Avondale Elementary School District No. 44
235 West Western Avenue
Avondale, Arizona 85323

State law requires that school districts receiving over $300,000 of federal monies publish a complete set of financial statements presented in conformity with accounting principles generally accepted in the United States of America and audited in accordance with auditing standards generally accepted in the United States of America by a certified public accounting firm licensed in the State of Arizona. Pursuant to that requirement, we hereby issue the Comprehensive Annual Financial Report of the Avondale Elementary School District No. 44 for the fiscal year ended June 30, 2001.

This report consists of management's representations concerning the finances of the Avondale Elementary School District No. 44. Consequently, management assumes full responsibility for the completeness and reliability of all of the information presented in this report. To provide a reasonable basis for making these representations, management of the Avondale Elementary School District No. 44 has established a comprehensive internal control framework that is designed both to protect the District's assets from loss, theft, or misuse and to compile sufficient reliable information for the preparation of the Avondale Elementary School District No. 44's financial statements in conformity with accounting principles generally accepted in the United States of America. Because the cost of internal controls should not outweigh their benefits, the Avondale Elementary School District No. 44's comprehensive framework of internal controls has been designed to provide reasonable rather than absolute assurance that the financial statements will be free from material misstatement. As management, we assert that, to the best of our knowledge and belief, this financial report is complete and reliable in all material respects.

The Avondale Elementary School District No. 44's financial statements have been audited by Heinfeld & Meech, P.C., a certified public accounting firm. The goal of the independent audit was to provide reasonable assurance that the financial statements of the Avondale Elementary School District No. 44 for the fiscal year ended June 30, 2001, are free of material misstatement. The independent audit involved examining, on a test basis, evidence supporting the amounts and disclosures in the financial statements; assessing the accounting principles used and significant estimates made by management; and evaluating the overall financial statement presentation. The independent auditor concluded, based upon the audit, that there was a reasonable basis for rendering an unqualified opinion that the Avondale Elementary School District No. 44's financial statements for the fiscal year ended June 30, 2001, are fairly presented in conformity with accounting principles generally accepted in the United States of America. The independent auditors' report is presented as the first component of the financial section of this report.

The independent audit of the financial statements of the Avondale Elementary School District No. 44 was part of a broader, federally mandated "Single Audit" designed to meet the special needs of federal grantor agencies. The standards governing Single Audit engagements require the independent auditor to report not only on the fair presentation of the financial statements, but also on the audited District's internal controls and compliance with legal requirements, with special emphasis on internal controls and legal requirements involving the administration of federal awards. These reports are available in a separately issued Single Audit Reporting Package.

Accounting principles generally accepted in the United States of America require that management provide a narrative introduction, overview, and analysis to accompany the basic financial statements in the form of Management's Discussion and Analysis (MD&A). This letter of transmittal is designed to complement the MD&A and should be read in conjunction with it. The Avondale Elementary School District No. 44's MD&A can be found immediately following the report of the independent auditors.

PROFILE OF THE DISTRICT

The Avondale Elementary School District No. 44 is one of fifty-five public school districts located in Maricopa County, Arizona. It provides a program of public education from kindergarten through grade eight.

The District's Governing Board is organized under Section 15-321 of the Arizona Revised Statutes (A.R.S.). Management of the District is independent of other state or local governments. The County Treasurer collects taxes for the District, but exercises no control over its expenditures.

The membership of the Governing Board consists of five members elected by the public. Under existing statutes, the Governing Board's duties and powers include, but are not limited to, the acquisition, maintenance and disposition of school property; the development and adoption of a school program; and the establishment, organization and operation of schools. The Board also has broad financial responsibilities, including the approval of the annual budget, and the establishment of a system of accounting and budgetary controls.

The financial reporting entity consists of a primary government and its component units. The District is a primary government because it is a special-purpose government that has a separately elected governing body, is legally separate, and is fiscally independent of other state or local governments. Furthermore, there are no component units combined with the District for financial statement presentation purposes, and the District is not included in any other governmental reporting entity. Consequently, the District's financial statements include the funds of those organizational entities for which its elected governing board is financially accountable. The District's major operations include education, pupil transportation, construction and maintenance of District facilities, and food services.

The Avondale Elementary School District No. 44 is located 17 miles west of downtown Phoenix. A portion of the City of Goodyear and the City of Avondale are included within the area served by the District. The District encompasses an area of approximately 30 square miles, and has set its vision as "Passion and Commitment for Educational Excellence".

The annual expenditure budget serves as the foundation for the District's financial planning and control. The objective of these budgetary controls is to ensure compliance with legal provisions embodied in the annual expenditure budget approved by the District's Governing Board. The District's proposed expenditure budget is presented to the Governing Board for review prior to July 5. The Governing Board is required to hold a public hearing on the proposed budget and to adopt the final budget by no later than July 15. The expenditure budget is prepared by fund for all Governmental Funds, and includes function and object code detail for the General and some Capital Projects Funds. The level of budgetary control (that is, the level at which expenditures cannot exceed the appropriated amount) is established at the individual fund level for all funds. Although not adopted, an annual budget of revenue from all sources is prepared. The expenditure budget can be revised annually in accordance with Arizona Revised Statutes, however the revenue budget cannot be revised. Therefore a deficit budgeted fund balance can occur when the expenditure budget is increased during a revision.

Budget-to-actual comparisons are provided in this report for the General Fund. This comparison is presented as required supplementary information. For other Governmental Funds, this comparison is presented in the Combining and Individual Fund Financial Statements and Schedules section of this report.

FACTORS AFFECTING FINANCIAL CONDITION

The information presented in the financial statements is perhaps best understood when it is considered from the broader perspective of the specific environment within which the District operates.

Local Economy. The economy of the cities of Goodyear and Avondale and of Maricopa County, in general, is among the most positive in the State. Because of the District's close proximity to Phoenix, it is located in the direct path of the westward expansion of the City. Although agriculture has been the economic mainstay of the area for many years, commerce, light manufacturing, and residential development continue to expand and contribute to the District's growth and economic diversity. Some of the firms operating within the District's boundaries include Rubbermaid, Inc, Lockheed Martin, Cavco Industries, Inc, Arizona Public Services, Snyder of Hanover, and McLane Company, Inc,. The area is experiencing rapid expansion in retail service centers and commercial facilities. In recent years, new housing starts for both the cities of Goodyear and Avondale have steadily increased. These two cities are each governed by a mayor and a six-member council. Phoenix and the rest of Maricopa County have become one of the fastest growing regional markets in the United States. The number of manufacturing and wholesale businesses located in the metropolitan area is approaching 3,000. This growth has been stimulated by a combination of warm climate, a substantial, well-educated labor pool, a wide range of support industries, and a governmental climate that is supportive of economic growth and investment.

A few of the major firms represented in Phoenix include Honeywell/Allied Signal, General Electric, Goodyear, Motorola, American Express, McDonnell-Douglas, Western Electric, Digital Equipment, America West Airlines and Bank One. In addition, the metropolitan area provides excellent educational and training opportunities through seven community colleges, four private colleges and graduate schools, and one state university.

Maricopa County is located in the south-central portion of Arizona and encompasses an area of approximately 9,226 square miles. Its boundaries encompass the cities of Phoenix, Scottsdale, Mesa, Tempe, Glendale, Chandler, and such towns as Gilbert, Paradise Valley and Fountain Hills. The County's 1995 population was estimated at 2,528,700 or about 60 percent of the total population of the state. Maricopa County has a very wide range of economic sectors supporting its substantial growth. It has been estimated that 6,000 to 7,000 people are moving into Maricopa County every month. Maricopa County has, for some time, enjoyed an unemployment rate that was somewhat lower than the national average.

The service industry is the largest employment sector in the County, partly fueled by the $2+ billion per year tourist industry. The County has excellent accommodations, diverse cultural and recreational activities, and a favorable climate attracting millions to the area annually. Wholesale and retail trade is the second largest employment category, employing over a quarter million people. Retail sales have grown by about 50 percent in the past five or six years and, in 2000 exceeded $23 billion.

Manufacturing, consisting primarily of high technology companies is the third largest employment sector. Approximately 130,000 persons are working in the manufacturing industry.

Other factors aiding economic growth include major expansions of the international airport serving the area, a favorable business climate and the presence of a well developed and expanding transportation infrastructure.

The District completed the construction of Wildflower School in March of 2000, financed through the bond sale of May 1998. The Arizona School Facilities Board now provides funds for new construction projects. Avondale Elementary District has one school, Desert Star, currently under construction with the opening scheduled for Fall of 2002. The State Facilities Board has approved three additional schools projected to open in the next five years. The District continues to increase and upgrade technology available to students and staff on all sites.

The mission of 1) Support Learning, 2) Make a Difference, 3) Release the Potential and 4) Enjoy the Experience ... One child at a time, will continue to guide the strategic planning for the operations budget in the future.

Long-term Financial Planning. The Avondale Elementary School District is experiencing rapid growth. The secondary assessed value has grown at an average rate of 5.8% in the last 10 years and 13.9 in the last 5 years. This recognized growth has allowed the District to utilize its final bond sale proceeds from the voter authorized $14 million passed in May 1998.

Cash Management. Cash temporarily idle during the year was invested in interest-bearing accounts and time certificates of deposit. In addition, the County Treasurer pools money from all districts in the County and invests surplus cash; allocating the interest back to the districts based on the districts' average balances with the County Treasurer. The District's investment policy is to minimize credit and market risks while maintaining a competitive yield on its portfolio.

Risk Management. The District's administration is charged with the responsibility of supervising the protection of the District's assets by employing various risk management techniques and procedures to reduce, absorb, minimize or transfer risk. The District carries insurance for general liability, auto liability and workers' compensation. District property is insured for its replacement value. The administration is also responsible for directing the District's fringe benefits program which includes the administration of health, life and other benefits for all full-time and some part-time employees.

Pension Plan. The District contributes to a cost-sharing multiple-employer defined benefit pension plan administered by the Arizona State Retirement System. Benefits are established by state statute and generally provide retirement, death, long-term disability, survivor, and health insurance premium benefits. The District's contribution to the System for the year ended June 30, 2001 was equal to the required contribution for the year.

AWARDS AND ACKNOWLEDGMENT

Awards. The Association of School Business Officials (ASBO) awarded a Certificate of Excellence in Financial Reporting to the District for its comprehensive annual financial report for the fiscal year ended June 30, 2000. This was the seventh consecutive year that the District has received this prestigious award. In addition, the Government Finance Officers Association (GFOA) awarded a Certificate of Achievement in Financial Reporting to the District for its comprehensive annual financial report for the fiscal year ended June 30, 2000. In order to be awarded these certificates, the District published an easily readable and efficiently organized comprehensive annual financial report. This report satisfied both accounting principles generally accepted in the United States of America and applicable legal requirements.

These certificates are valid for a period of one year only. We believe that our current comprehensive annual financial report continues to meet the programs' requirements and we are submitting it to ASBO and GFOA to determine its eligibility for the fiscal year 2000-2001 certificates.

Acknowledgments. The preparation of the comprehensive annual financial report on a timely basis was made possible by the dedicated service of the entire staff of the business and finance department. Each member of the department has our sincere appreciation for the contributions made in the preparation of this report.

In closing, without the leadership and support of the Governing Board of the District, preparation of this report would not have been possible.

Respectfully submitted,

Dr. Catherine Stafford
   Superintendent

Julia E. Tribbett
   Director of Business Operations

ASSOCIATION OF SCHOOL BUSINESS OFFICIALS

INTERNATIONAL

This Certificate of Excellence in Financial Reporting is presented to

AVONDALE ELEMENTARY SCHOOL DISTRICT NO. 44

For its Comprehensive Annual Financial Report (CAFR)
For the Fiscal Year Ended June 30, 2000

Upon recommendation of the Association's Panel of Review which has judged that the Report
substantially conforms to principles and standards of ASBO's Certificate of Excellence Program

Linda White
President

Don A. Kuper
Executive Director

Certificate of Achievement for Excellence in Financial Reporting

Presented to

Avondale Elementary School District No. 44, Arizona

For its Comprehensive Annual
Financial Report
for the Fiscal Year Ended
June 30, 2000

A Certificate of Achievement for Excellence in Financial
Reporting is presented by the Government Finance Officers
Association of the United States and Canada to
government units and public employee retirement
systems whose comprehensive annual financial
reports (CAFRs) achieve the highest
standards in government accounting
and financial reporting.

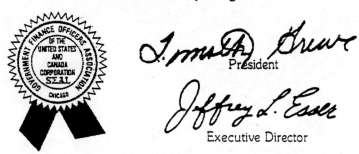

President

Executive Director

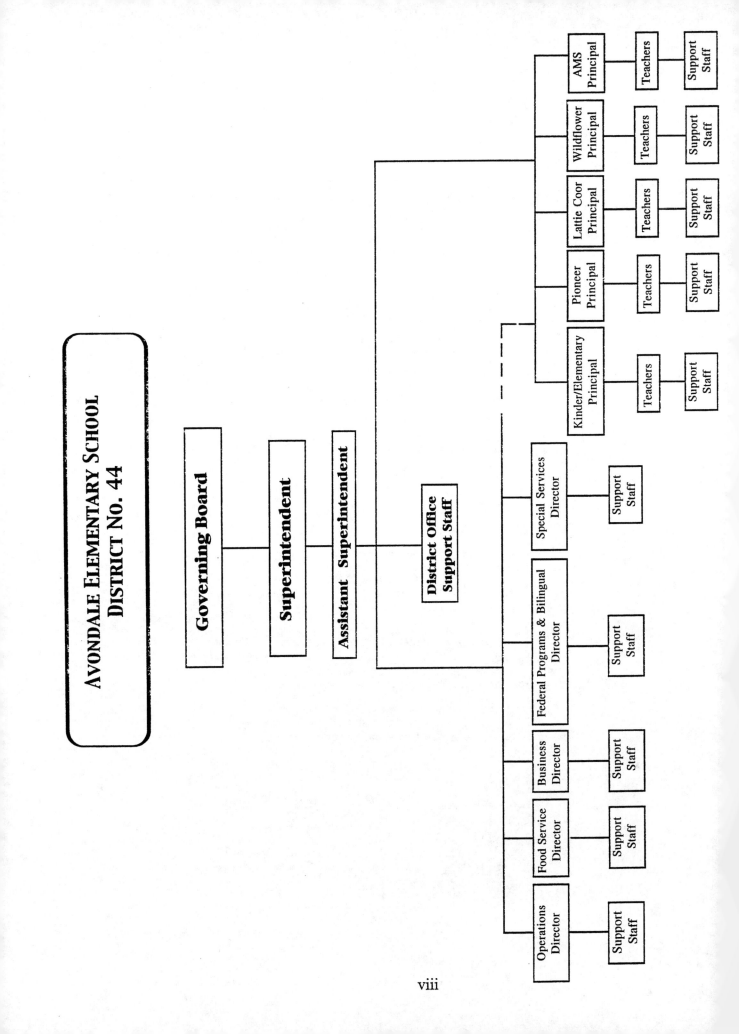

AVONDALE ELEMENTARY SCHOOL DISTRICT No. 44

Governing Board

Superintendent

Assistant Superintendent

District Office Support Staff

Operations Director — Support Staff

Food Service Director — Support Staff

Business Director — Support Staff

Federal Programs & Bilingual Director — Support Staff

Special Services Director — Support Staff

Kinder/Elementary Principal — Teachers — Support Staff

Pioneer Principal — Teachers — Support Staff

Lattie Coor Principal — Teachers — Support Staff

Wildflower Principal — Teachers — Support Staff

AMS Principal — Teachers — Support Staff

AVONDALE ELEMENTARY SCHOOL DISTRICT NO. 41

LIST OF PRINCIPAL OFFICIALS

GOVERNING BOARD

Mark Gonzales
President

Tony Aguirre
Member

Juanita Rodriguez
Vice President

Stephen Warner
Member

Mollie Belcher
Member

ADMINISTRATIVE STAFF

Dr. Catherine Stafford, Superintendent

Dr. Linda Ronnebaum, Assistant Superintendent

Julia E. Tribbett, Director of Business Operations

(This page intentionally left blank)

FINANCIAL SECTION

(This page intentionally left blank)

OFFICIAL LETTERHEAD OF THE INDEPENDENT AUDITOR

INDEPENDENT AUDITOR'S REPORT

As of the release date of this publication, the American Institute of Certified Public Accountants (AICPA) had not yet determined the appropriate form of the independent auditor's report for audits of financial statements prepared in conformity with Governmental Accounting Standards Board's Statement No. 34, *Basic Financial Statements – and Management's Discussion and Analysis – for State and Local Governments*. The AICPA will provide authoritative guidance on the topic, including illustrative examples, in future editions of the audit guide *Audits of State and Local Governmental Units*.

Certified Public Accountants

October 9, 2001

(This page intentionally left blank)

MANAGEMENT'S DISCUSSION AND ANALYSIS (MD&A)

(This page intentionally left blank)

As management of the Avondale Elementary School District No. 44 (District), we offer readers of the District's financial statements this narrative overview and analysis of the financial activities of the District for the fiscal year ended June 30, 2001. We encourage readers to consider the information presented here in conjunction with additional information that we have furnished in our letter of transmittal, which can be found on pages i to v of this report.

FINANCIAL HIGHLIGHTS

- The District's total net assets of governmental activities increased $2.5 million which represents a 19.7 percent increase from fiscal year 2000 as a result of current year funding used for capital additions and debt service.

- General revenues accounted for $15.9 million in revenue, or 81.9 percent of all fiscal year 2001 revenues. Program specific revenues in the form of charges for services and grants and contributions accounted for $3.5 million or 18.1 percent of total fiscal year 2001 revenues.

- The District had approximately $17 million in expenses related to governmental activities; of which $3.5 million of these expenses were offset by program specific charges for services or grants and contributions. General revenues of $15.9 million were adequate to provide for the remaining costs of these programs.

- Among major funds, the General Fund had $11.5 million in fiscal year 2001 revenues, which primarily consisted of state aid and property taxes, and $11.9 million in expenditures. The General Fund's fund balance decrease from $618,429 as of June 30, 2000 to $291,694 as of June 30, 2001 was primarily due utilization of excess beginning fund balance to lower our tax rate.

- The District's total debt decreased by $1.5 million during the current fiscal year. The key factor in this decrease was the retirement of $1.4 million in general obligation bonds.

OVERVIEW OF FINANCIAL STATEMENTS

This discussion and analysis is intended to serve as an introduction to the District's basic financial statements. The District's basic financial statements comprise three components: 1) government-wide financial statements, 2) fund financial statements, and 3) notes to the financial statements. This report also contains other supplementary information in addition to the basic financial statements themselves.

Government-wide financial statements. The *government-wide financial statements* are designed to provide readers with a broad overview of the District's finances, in a manner similar to a private-sector business.

OVERVIEW OF FINANCIAL STATEMENTS (Cont'd)

The *statement of net assets* presents information on all of the District's assets and liabilities, with the difference between the two reported as *net assets*. Over time, increases or decreases in net assets may serve as a useful indicator of whether the financial position of the District is improving or deteriorating.

The *statement of activities* presents information showing how the District's net assets changed during the most recent fiscal year. All changes in net assets are reported as soon as the underlying event giving rise to the change occurs, *regardless of the timing of related cash flows*. Thus, revenues and expenses are reported in this statement for some items that will only result in cash flows in future fiscal periods (e.g., uncollected taxes and earned but unused compensated absences).

The government-wide financial statements outline functions of the District that are principally supported by property taxes and intergovernmental revenues (*governmental activities*). The governmental activities of the District include instruction, support services, operation and maintenance of plant, student transportation, and operation of non-instructional services.

The government-wide financial statements can be found on pages 18-19 of this report.

Fund financial statements. A *fund* is a grouping of related accounts that is used to maintain control over resources that have been segregated for specific activities or objectives. The District uses fund accounting to ensure and demonstrate compliance with finance-related legal requirements. All of the funds of the District can be divided into two categories: governmental funds and fiduciary funds.

Governmental funds. Governmental funds are used to account for essentially the same functions reported as *governmental activities* in the government-wide financial statements. However, unlike the government-wide financial statements, governmental fund financial statements focus on *near-term inflows of spendable resources,* as well as on *balances of spendable resources* available at the end of the fiscal year. Such information may be useful in evaluating the District's near-term financing requirements.

Because the focus of governmental funds is narrower than that of the government-wide financial statements, it is useful to compare the information presented for *governmental funds* with similar information presented for *governmental activities* in the government-wide financial statements. By doing so, readers may better understand the long-term impact of the District's near-term financing decisions. Both the governmental fund balance sheet and the governmental fund statement of revenues, expenditures, and changes in fund balances provide a reconciliation to facilitate this comparison between *governmental funds* and *governmental activities*. These reconciliations are on pages 23 and 26, respectively.

OVERVIEW OF FINANCIAL STATEMENTS (Concl'd)

In accordance with Arizona Revised Statutes (A.R.S.), the District maintains forty-five individual governmental funds. Information is presented separately in the governmental fund balance sheet and in the governmental fund statement of revenues, expenditures, and changes in fund balances for the General, Debt Service and Bond Building Funds, all of which are considered to be major funds. Data from the other forty-two governmental funds are combined into a single, aggregated presentation. Individual fund data for each of these non-major governmental funds is provided in the form of combining statements beginning on page 54 in this report.

The basic governmental fund financial statements can be found on pages 22 - 26 of this report.

Fiduciary funds. Fiduciary funds are used to account for resources held for the benefit of parties outside the District. Fiduciary funds are *not* reflected in the government-wide financial statements because the resources of those funds are *not* available to support the District's own programs. The accrual basis of accounting is used for fiduciary funds.

The basic fiduciary fund financial statement can be found on page 27 of this report.

Notes to the financial statements. The notes provide additional information that is essential to a full understanding of the data provided in the government-wide and fund financial statements. The notes to the financial statements can be found on pages 28 - 44 of this report.

Other information. In addition to the basic financial statements and accompanying notes, this report also presents certain *required supplementary information* concerning the District's budget process. The District adopts an annual expenditure budget for all governmental funds. A budgetary comparison statement has been provided for the General Fund as required supplementary information. The required supplementary information can be found on page 47 of this report.

The combining statements referred to earlier in connection with non-major governmental funds are presented immediately following the major budgetary comparisons. Combining and individual fund statements and schedules can be found on pages 54 - 116 of this report.

GOVERNMENT-WIDE FINANCIAL ANALYSIS

Net assets may serve over time as a useful indicator of a government's financial position. In the case of the District, assets exceeded liabilities by $14,902,823 as of June 30, 2001.

By far the largest portion of the District's net assets (57.4 percent) reflects its investment in capital assets (e.g., land and improvements, buildings and improvements, vehicles, furniture and equipment and construction in progress), less any related debt used to acquire those assets that is still outstanding. The District uses these capital assets to provide services to its students; consequently, these assets are *not* available for future spending. Although the District's investment in its capital assets is reported net of related debt, it should be noted that the resources needed to repay this debt must be provided from other sources, since the capital assets themselves cannot be used to liquidate these liabilities.

The District's financial position is the product of several financial transactions including the net results of activities, the acquisition and payment of debt, the acquisition and disposal of capital assets, and the depreciation of capital assets.

The following table presents a summary of the District's net assets for the fiscal year ended June 30, 2001.

	Amount
Current assets	$ 8,348,171
Capital assets, net	19,650,224
Total assets	27,998,395
Current liabilities	2,318,423
Long-term debt outstanding	10,777,149
Total liabilities	13,095,572
Net assets:	
Invested in capital assets, net of related debt	8,552,181
Restricted	4,747,867
Unrestricted	1,602,775
Total net assets	$ 14,902,823

The following are significant current year transactions that have had an impact on the Statement of Net Assets.

- The principal retirement of $1,425,000 of bonds.

- The addition of $1.6 million in capital assets through the construction of a new school, and other school improvements, and purchases of furniture, equipment and vehicles.

GOVERNMENT-WIDE FINANCIAL ANALYSIS (Cont'd)

Changes in net assets. The District's total revenues for the fiscal year ended June 30, 2001, were $19.4 million. The total cost of all programs and services was $17 million. The following table presents a summary of the changes in net assets for the fiscal year ended June 30, 2001.

	Amount
Revenues:	
Program revenues:	
Charges for services	$ 400,265
Operating grants and contributions	2,484,379
Capital grants and contributions	638,128
General revenues:	
Property taxes	4,046,440
Investment income	284,876
County aid	850,003
State aid	10,736,591
Total revenues	19,440,682
Expenses:	
Instruction	9,909,450
Support services - students and staff	1,403,453
Support services – administration	1,531,860
Operation and maintenance of plant services	1,661,091
Student transportation services	717,784
Operation of non-instructional services	1,180,000
Interest on long-term debt	580,612
Total expenses	16,984,250
Increase in net assets	$ 2,456,432

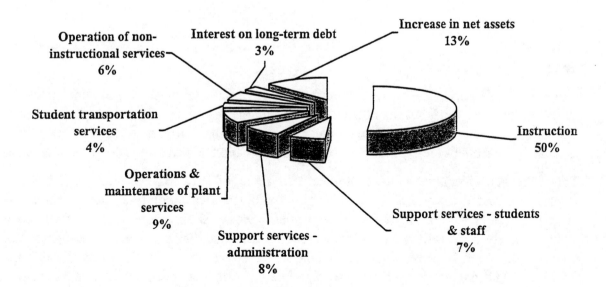

GOVERNMENT-WIDE FINANCIAL ANALYSIS (Concl'd)

Governmental activities. The following table presents the cost of the seven major District functional activities: instruction, support services - students and staff, support services - administration, operation and maintenance of plant services, student transportation services, operation of non-instructional services and interest on long-term debt. The table also shows each function's net cost (total cost less charges for services generated by the activities and intergovernmental aid provided for specific programs). The net cost shows the financial burden that was placed on the State and District's taxpayers by each of these functions.

	Total Expenses	Net (Expense) Revenue
Instruction	$ 9,909,450	$ (8,347,849)
Support services - students and staff	1,403,453	(1,036,826)
Support services - administration	1,531,860	(1,443,583)
Operation and maintenance of plant services	1,661,091	(1,642,649)
Student transportation services	717,784	(612,396)
Operation of non-instructional services	1,180,000	202,437
Interest on long-term debt	580,612	(580,612)
Total expenses	$ 16,984,250	$(13,461,478)

- The cost of all governmental activities this year was $17 million.

- Federal and state governments and charges for services subsidized certain programs with grants and contributions and other local revenues of $3.5 million.

- Net cost of governmental activities ($13.5 million), was financed by general revenues, which are made up of primarily property taxes ($4.0 million) and state and county aid ($11.6 million). Investment earnings accounted for $284,876 of funding.

FINANCIAL ANALYSIS OF THE DISTRICT'S FUNDS

As noted earlier, the District uses fund accounting to ensure and demonstrate compliance with finance-related legal requirements.

Governmental funds. The focus of the District's governmental funds is to provide information on near-term inflows, outflows, and balances of spendable resources. Such information is useful in assessing the District's financing requirements. In particular, unreserved fund balance may serve as a useful measure of the District's net resources available for spending at the end of the fiscal year.

The financial performance of the District as a whole is reflected in its governmental funds. As the District completed the year, its governmental funds reported a combined fund balance of $6.3 million, an increase of $386,891 due primarily to a slight increase in overall revenues. Approximately $1.2 million, or 18.9 percent of the fund balance constitutes unreserved and undesignated fund balance, which is available for spending at the District's discretion. The remaining fund balance is reserved or designated to indicate that it is not available for spending because it has already been committed as follows.

FINANCIAL ANALYSIS OF THE DISTRICT'S FUNDS (Concl'd)

- $601,977 to pay debt service
- $4.1 million for capital projects
- $99,554 for inventory
- $332,099 for prepaid items

The General Fund is the principal operating fund of the District. The decrease in fund balance in the General Fund for the fiscal year was $326,735 a result of an overall utilization of excess beginning fund balance. The fund balance of the Special Revenue Funds showed an increase of $158,807 due primarily to an increase in revenue of the Civic Center Fund. The Debt Service Fund fund balance showed an increase of $342,149 from the prior year. The increase was a result of an increase in property taxes since both the primary and the secondary assessed valuations increased. The Capital Projects Funds showed a fund balance increase of approximately $212,670. The increase was primarily a result of increased revenue in the New School Facilities and Building Renewal Funds.

BUDGETARY HIGHLIGHTS

Over the course of the year, the District revised the annual expenditure budget for student growth. Differences between the original budget and the final amended budget were relatively minor. The $602,252 increase can be briefly summarized as follows:

- $585,924 in increases allocated to regular education in the General Fund.

A schedule showing the original and final budget amounts compared to the District's actual financial activity for the General Fund is provided in this report as required supplementary information.

CAPITAL ASSETS AND DEBT ADMINISTRATION

Capital Assets. As of June 30, 2001, the District had invested $25 million in capital assets, including school buildings, athletic facilities, buses and other vehicles, computers, and other equipment. This amount represents a net increase prior to depreciation of $1.6 million from last year, primarily due to the completion of the final phases of construction on a new school. Total depreciation expense for the year was $634,020.

CAPITAL ASSETS AND DEBT ADMINISTRATION (Concl'd)

The following schedule presents capital asset balances net of depreciation for the fiscal year ended June 30, 2001.

	Amount
Land and improvements	$ 427,659
Buildings and improvements	17,912,543
Vehicles, furniture and equipment	1,005,534
Construction in progress	304,488
Total	**$ 19,650,224**

Additional information on the District's capital assets can be found in Note 5 on page 38 of this report.

Debt Administration. At year-end, the District had $11,443,018 in general obligation bonds and other long-term debt outstanding, of which $1,265,869 is due within one year. The following table presents a summary of the District's outstanding long-term debt for the fiscal year ended June 30, 2001.

	Amount
Leases payable	$ 98,018
School improvement bonds	8,875,000
Refunding and capital appreciation bonds	2,470,000
Total	**$ 11,443,018**

The District maintains a "Baa" rating from Moody's for general obligation debt.

State statutes currently limit the amount of general obligation debt a District may issue to 15 percent of its total assessed valuation. The current debt limitation for the District is $15,062,767, which is more than the District's outstanding general obligation debt.

Additional information on the District's long-term debt can be found in Notes 6-8 on pages 39-41 of this report.

ECONOMIC FACTORS AND NEXT YEAR'S BUDGET AND RATES

Many factors were considered by the District's administration during the process of developing the fiscal year 2001-2002 budget. The primary factor was the District's student population and employee salaries. Also considered in the development of the budget is the local economy.

These indicators were considered when adopting the budget for fiscal year 2001-2002. Budgeted expenditures in the General Fund increased 2.7 percent to $12,368,170 in fiscal year 2001-2002. Increased payroll and employee benefit costs are the primary reason for the increase. No new programs were added to the 2001-2002 budget.

On November 7, 2000, Arizona voters passed Proposition 301, which increased the state sales tax rate from 5% to 5.6%. Annually, approximately $264,000,000 additional dollars raised through the increased sales tax is earmarked for a Classroom Site Fund for K-12 education. Preliminary estimates provided by the state indicated that the District will receive $960,407 in state aid in fiscal year 2001-02 as a result of Proposition 301. However, no assurances can be given as to the ultimate timing of the payments. Additionally, Proposition 301 will fund a two percent inflation factor for each of the next five years and will require the District to add an additional school day for each of the next five years for a total of 180 school days at the end of the five year period.

The tragic events of September 11, 2001 have significantly impacted the economic outlook for everyone, including the District. The economy of the entire State of Arizona, as well as the District includes tourism. The likely immediate economic impact is a reduction in sales tax collections. The District will likely realize lower than projected revenues in fiscal year 2001-02 for its Classroom Site Fund, which was discussed in the previous paragraph.

CONTACTING THE DISTRICT'S FINANCIAL MANAGEMENT

This financial report is designed to provide our citizens, taxpayers, investors and creditors with a general overview of the District's finances and to demonstrate the District's accountability for the resources it receives. If you have questions about this report or need additional information, contact the Business and Finance Department, Avondale Elementary School District No. 44, 235 West Western Avenue, Avondale, Arizona 85323.

(This page intentionally left blank)

BASIC FINANCIAL STATEMENTS

(This page intentionally left blank)

GOVERNMENT-WIDE FINANCIAL STATEMENTS

AVONDALE ELEMENTARY SCHOOL DISTRICT NO. 44
STATEMENT OF NET ASSETS
JUNE 30, 2001

	Governmental Activities
ASSETS	
Current assets:	
Cash and investments	$ 7,508,266
Property taxes receivable	189,631
Due from governmental entities	218,621
Prepaid items	332,099
Inventory, at cost	99,554
Total current assets	8,348,171
Noncurrent assets:	
Land and improvements	446,835
Buildings and improvements	22,491,680
Vehicles, furniture and equipment	1,808,059
Construction in progress	304,488
Accumulated depreciation	(5,400,838)
Total noncurrent assets	19,650,224
Total assets	27,998,395
LIABILITIES	
Current liabilities:	
Accounts payable	178,780
Compensated absences payable	342,078
Accrued interest payable	261,321
Deferred revenues	206,283
Obligations under capital leases	65,869
Construction contracts payable	64,092
Bonds payable	1,200,000
Total current liabilities	2,318,423
Noncurrent liabilities:	
Non-current portion of long-term obligations	10,777,149
Total non-current liabilities	10,777,149
Total liabilities	13,095,572
NET ASSETS	
Invested in capital assets, net of related debt	8,552,181
Restricted for:	
Debt service	656,248
Capital outlay	4,091,619
Unrestricted	1,602,775
Total net assets	$ 14,902,823

The notes to the financial statements are an integral part of this statement.

AVONDALE ELEMENTARY SCHOOL DISTRICT NO. 44
STATEMENT OF ACTIVITIES
YEAR ENDED JUNE 30, 2001

| Functions/Programs | Expenses | Program Revenues | | | Net (Expense) Revenue and Changes in Net Assets |
		Charges for Services	Operating Grants and Contributions	Capital Grants and Contributions	Governmental Activities
Governmental activities:					
Instruction	$ 9,909,450	$ 9,000	$ 1,102,210	$ 450,391	$ (8,347,849)
Support services - students and staff	1,403,453	12,659	336,356	17,612	(1,036,826)
Support services - administration	1,531,860	16,480	59,609	12,188	(1,443,583)
Operation and maintenance of plant services	1,661,091			18,442	(1,642,649)
Student transportation services	717,784	888	4,122	100,378	(612,396)
Operation of non-instructional services	1,180,000	361,238	982,082	39,117	202,437
Interest on long-term debt	580,612				(580,612)
Total governmental activities	$ 16,984,250	$400,265	$2,484,379	$ 638,128	$ (13,461,478)

General revenues:	
Taxes:	
Property taxes, levied for general purposes	1,954,912
Property taxes, levied for debt service	1,903,899
Property taxes, levied for capital outlay	187,629
Investment income	284,876
County aid	850,003
State aid	10,736,591
Total general revenues	15,917,910
Change in net assets	2,456,432
Net assets, beginning of year	12,446,391
Net assets, end of year	$ 14,902,823

The notes to the financial statements are an integral part of this statement.

(This page intentionally left blank)

FUND FINANCIAL STATEMENTS

AVONDALE ELEMENTARY SCHOOL DISTRICT NO. 44
BALANCE SHEET - GOVERNMENTAL FUNDS
JUNE 30, 2001

	General Fund	Debt Service Fund	Bond Building Fund	Other Governmental Funds	Total Governmental Funds
ASSETS					
Cash and investments	$ 13,891	$ 2,031,687	$ 2,160,636	$ 3,302,052	$ 7,508,26
Property taxes receivable	95,967	85,882		7,782	189,63
Due from governmental entities				218,621	218,62
Due from other funds				91,455	91,45
Prepaid items	284,763			47,336	332,09
Inventory, at cost	81,523			18,031	99,55
Total assets	$ 476,144	$ 2,117,569	$ 2,160,636	$ 3,685,277	$ 8,439,62
LIABILITIES AND FUND EQUITY					
Liabilities:					
Accounts payable	$ 118,771	$	$	$ 60,009	$ 178,78
Due to other funds				91,455	91,45
Deferred revenues	65,679	54,271		211,534	331,4
Construction contracts payable				64,092	64,0
Bonds payable		1,200,000			1,200,0
Bond interest payable		261,321			261,3
Total liabilities	184,450	1,515,592		427,090	2,127,1
Fund equity:					
Fund balances (deficits) -					
Reserved for:					
Prepaid items	284,763			47,336	332,0
Inventory	81,523			18,031	99,5
Unreserved	(74,592)	601,977	2,160,636		2,688,0
Unreserved, reported in:					
Special revenue funds				1,267,088	1,267,0
Capital projects funds				1,925,732	1,925,
Total fund equity	291,694	601,977	2,160,636	3,258,187	6,312.
Total liabilities and fund equity	$ 476,144	$ 2,117,569	$ 2,160,636	$ 3,685,277	$ 8,439.

The notes to the financial statements are an integral part of this statement.

Total governmental fund balances $ 6,312,494

Amounts reported for *governmental activities* in the Statement of
Net Assets are different because:

Capital assets used in governmental activities are not financial
resources and therefore are not reported in the funds.

Governmental capital assets	$ 25,051,062	
Less accumulated depreciation	(5,400,838)	19,650,224

Property taxes will not be available to pay for current-period
expenditures and, therefore, are deferred in the funds. 125,201

Long-term liabilities are not due and payable in the
current period and therefore are not reported in
the funds.

Compensated absences payable	(942,078)	
Obligations under capital leases	(98,018)	
Bonds payable	(10,145,000)	(11,185,096)

Net assets of governmental activities $ 14,902,823

The notes to the financial statements are an intergral part of this statement.

	General Fund	Debt Service Fund	Bond Building Fund
Revenues:			
Other local	$ 771,454	$ 89,520	$ 101,354
Property taxes	1,983,196	1,918,964	
State aid and grants	8,767,296		
Federal aid, grants and reimbursements			
Total revenues	11,521,946	2,008,484	101,354
Expenditures:			
Current -			
Instruction	7,520,140		
Support services - students and staff	942,404		
Support services - administration	1,342,284		
Operation and maintenance of plant services	1,579,999		
Student transportation services	455,613		
Operation of non-instructional services	16,005		
Capital outlay			380,030
Debt service -			
Interest, premium and fiscal charges		567,689	
Principal retirement		1,200,000	
Total expenditures	11,856,445	1,767,689	380,030
Excess (deficiency) of revenues over expenditures	(334,499)	240,795	(278,676)
Other financing sources (uses):			
Transfers in		101,354	
Transfers out			(101,354)
Total other financing sources (uses)		101,354	(101,354)
Excess (deficiency) of revenues and other financing sources over expenditures and other financing uses	(334,499)	342,149	(380,030)
Fund balances, beginning of year	618,429	259,828	2,540,666
Increase (decrease) in reserve for inventory	(23,425)		
Increase in reserve for prepaid items	31,189		
Fund balances, end of year	$ 291,694	$ 601,977	$ 2,160,636

The notes to the financial statements are an integral part of this statement.

Other Governmental Funds	Total Governmental Funds
$ 930,194	$ 1,892,522
189,993	4,092,153
2,130,864	10,898,160
2,603,559	2,603,559
5,854,610	19,486,394
1,222,246	8,742,386
402,281	1,344,685
113,357	1,455,641
3,816	1,583,815
4,752	460,365
1,072,014	1,088,019
2,250,337	2,630,367
12,923	580,612
71,032	1,271,032
5,152,758	19,156,922
701,852	329,472
42,677	144,031
(42,677)	(144,031)
701,852	329,472
2,506,680	5,925,603
2,319	(21,106)
47,336	78,525
$ 3,258,187	$ 6,312,494

Net changes in fund balances - total governmental funds $ 386,8

Amounts reported for *governmental activities* in the Statement of Activities are
different because:

Governmental funds report capital outlay as expenditures. However, in the Statement
of Activities, the cost of those assets are allocated over their estimated useful lives
as depreciation expense.

Expenditures for capitalized assets	$ 1,586,801	
Less current year depreciation	(634,020)	952,

Revenues in the Statement of Activities that do not provide current financial
resources are not reported as revenues in the funds. (45,

Repayment of bond principal and capital leases are expenditures in the governmental
funds, but the repayment reduces long-term liabilities in the Statement of Net
Assets.

Bond principal retirement	1,200,000	
Lease retirement	71,032	1,271

Some expenses reported in the Statement of Activities, such as compensated absences,
do not require the use of current financial resources and therefore are not reported as
expenditures in governmental funds. (108

Change in net assets in governmental activities $ 2,456

The notes to the financial statements are an intergral part of this statement.

Page 26

	Agency Funds
ASSETS	
Cash and investments	$ 69,941
Total assets	69,941
LIABILITIES	
Deposits held for others	39,137
Due to student groups	30,804
Total liabilities	$ 69,941
NET ASSETS	$ -

The notes to the financial statements are an integral part of this statement.

NOTE 1 - SUMMARY OF SIGNIFICANT ACCOUNTING POLICIES

The financial statements of the Avondale Elementary School District No. 44 have been prepared in conformity with accounting principles generally accepted in the United States of America as applied to government units. The Governmental Accounting Standards Board (GASB) is the accepted standard-setting body for establishing governmental accounting and financial reporting principles.

In fiscal year 2001, the District adopted GASB Statement No. 34, *"Basic Financial Statements - Management's Discussion and Analysis - for State and Local Governments."* GASB Statement No. 34 requires new basic financial statements for reporting on the District's financial activities. The effect of this change was to include management's discussion and analysis and include the government-wide financial statements prepared on an accrual basis of accounting and fund financial statements which present information on major funds, rather than by fund type.

The more significant of the District's accounting policies are described below.

A. Reporting Entity

The Governing Board is organized under Section 15-321 of the Arizona Revised Statutes (A.R.S.). Management of the District is independent of other state or local governments. The County Treasurer collects taxes for the District, but exercises no control over its expenditures.

The membership of the Governing Board consists of five members elected by the public. Under existing statutes, the Governing Board's duties and powers include, but are not limited to, the acquisition, maintenance and disposition of school property; the development and adoption of a school program; and the establishment, organization and operation of schools.

The Board also has broad financial responsibilities, including the approval of the annual budget, and the establishment of a system of accounting and budgetary controls.

The financial reporting entity consists of a primary government and its component units. The District is a primary government because it is a special-purpose government that has a separately elected governing body, is legally separate, and is fiscally independent of other state or local governments. Furthermore, there are no component units combined with the District for financial statement presentation purposes, and the District is not included in any other governmental reporting entity. Consequently, the District's financial statements include the funds of those organizational entities for which its elected governing board is financially accountable. The District's major operations include education, pupil transportation, construction and maintenance of District facilities, and food services.

NOTE 1 - SUMMARY OF SIGNIFICANT ACCOUNTING POLICIES (Cont'd)

B. Government-Wide and Fund Financial Statements

The government-wide financial statements (i.e., the statement of net assets and the statement of activities) present financial information about the District as a whole. The reported information includes all of the nonfiduciary activities of the District. For the most part, the effect of interfund activity has been removed from these statements. These statements are to distinguish between the *governmental* and *business-type activities* of the District. *Governmental activities* normally are supported by taxes and intergovernmental revenues, and are reported separately from *business-type activities,* which rely to a significant extent on fees and charges for support. The District does not have any business-type activities.

The statement of activities demonstrates the degree to which the direct expenses of a given function or segment are offset by program revenues. *Direct expenses* are those that are clearly identifiable with a specific function or segment. *Program revenues* include 1) charges to customers or applicants who purchase, use, or directly benefit from goods, services, or privileges provided by a given function or segment and 2) grants and contributions that are restricted to meeting the operational or capital requirements of a particular function or segment. Taxes, State and County aid, and other items not included among program revenues are reported instead as *general revenues.*

Separate financial statements are provided for governmental and fiduciary funds, even though the latter are excluded from the government-wide financial statements. Major individual governmental funds are reported as separate columns in the fund financial statements.

C. Measurement Focus, Basis of Accounting, and Financial Statement Presentation

Government-Wide Financial Statements - The government-wide financial statements are reported using the *economic resources measurement focus* and the *accrual basis of accounting,* as is the fiduciary fund financial statement. Revenues are recorded when earned and expenses are recorded when a liability is incurred, regardless of the timing of related cash flows. Property taxes are recognized as revenues in the year for which they are levied. Grants and similar items are recognized as revenue as soon as all eligibility requirements imposed by the grantor or provider have been met. As a general rule the effect of interfund activity has been eliminated from the government-wide financial statements.

NOTE 1 - SUMMARY OF SIGNIFICANT ACCOUNTING POLICIES (Cont'd)

Fund Financial Statements - Governmental fund financial statements are reported using the *current financial resources measurement focus* and the *modified accrual basis of accounting*. Revenues are recognized as soon as they are both measurable and available. Revenues are considered to be *available* when they are collectible within the current period or soon enough thereafter to pay liabilities of the current period. For this purpose, the District considers revenues to be available if they are collected within 60 days of the end of the current fiscal period. Expenditures generally are recorded when a liability is incurred, as under accrual accounting. However, debt service resources are provided during the current year for payment of general long-term debt principal and interest due early in the following year and, therefore, the expenditures and related liabilities have been recognized. Compensated absences are recorded only when payment is due.

Property taxes, State and County aid and investment income associated with the current fiscal period are all considered to be susceptible to accrual and so have been recognized as revenues of the current fiscal period. Food services and miscellaneous revenues are not susceptible to accrual because generally they are not measurable until received in cash. Grants and similar awards are recognized as revenue as soon as all eligibility requirements imposed by the grantor or provider have been met. Deferred revenues also arise when resources are received by the District before it has a legal claim to them, as when grant monies are received prior to meeting all eligibility requirements imposed by the provider.

Delinquent property taxes and property taxes for which there is an enforceable legal claim as of the fiscal year, have been recorded as deferred revenue. Receivables that will not be collected within the available period have also been reported as deferred revenue on the governmental fund financial statements.

The District reports the following major governmental funds:

General Fund - The General Fund accounts for all resources used to finance District maintenance and operation except those required to be accounted for in other funds. It is described as the Maintenance and Operation Fund by A.R.S.

Debt Service Fund - The Debt Service Fund accounts for the accumulation of resources for, and the payment of, general long-term debt principal, interest and related costs.

Bond Building Fund - The Bond Building Fund accounts for monies received from District bond issues that are used to acquire sites, construct or renovate school buildings, supply buildings with furniture and apparatus, improve school grounds, and purchase transportation vehicles.

NOTE 1 - SUMMARY OF SIGNIFICANT ACCOUNTING POLICIES (Cont'd)

Additionally, the District reports the following fund type:

<u>Fiduciary Fund</u> - The Fiduciary Fund accounts for assets held by the District on behalf of others and includes the Student Activities Fund and the Employee Withholding Fund. These Funds account for monies raised by students to finance student clubs and organizations and unremitted payroll deductions temporarily held by the District as an agent.

Private-sector standards of accounting and financial reporting issued prior to December 1, 1989, generally are followed in the government-wide and fiduciary fund financial statements to the extent that those standards do not conflict with or contradict guidance of the Governmental Accounting Standards Board.

When both restricted and unrestricted resources are available for use, it is the District's policy to use restricted resources first, then unrestricted resources as they are needed.

The focus of governmental fund financial statements is on major funds rather than reporting funds by type. Each major fund is presented in a separate column. Non-major funds are aggregated and presented in a single column. Fiduciary funds are reported by fund type.

D. Investments

A.R.S. authorize the District to invest public monies in the State Treasurer's Local government Investment Pool, the County Treasurer's investment pool, interest-bearing savings accounts, certificates of deposit, and repurchase agreements in eligible depositories; bonds or other obligations of the U.S. government that are guaranteed as to principal and interest by the U.S. government; and bonds of the State of Arizona counties, cities, towns, school districts, and special districts as specified by statute.

The State Board of Deposit provides oversight for the State Treasurer's pool, and the Local Government Investment Pool Advisory Committee provides consultation and advice to the Treasurer. The fair value of a participant's position in the pool approximates the value of that participant's pool shares. No comparable oversight is provided for the County Treasurer's investment pool, and the structure of that pool does not provide for shares.

NOTE 1 - SUMMARY OF SIGNIFICANT ACCOUNTING POLICIES (Cont'd)

A.R.S. require the District to deposit certain cash with the County Treasurer. That cash is pooled for investment purposes, except for cash of the Debt Service and Bond Building Funds that may be invested separately. Interest earned from investments purchased with pooled monies is allocated to each of the District's funds based on their average balances. As required by statute, interest earnings of the Bond Building Fund are recorded initially in that Fund, but then transferred to the Debt Service Fund.

All investments are stated at fair value.

E. Investment Income

Investment income is composed of interest and net changes in the fair value of applicable investments. Investment income is included in other local revenue in the fund financial statements.

F. Receivables and Payables

Activity between funds that are representative of lending/borrowing arrangements outstanding at the end of the fiscal year are referred to as either "due to/from other funds" (i.e., the current portion of interfund loans) or "advances to/from other funds" (i.e., the non-current portion of interfund loans). All other outstanding balances between funds are reported as "due to/from other funds."

All receivables, including property taxes receivable, are shown net of an allowance for uncollectibles.

Property tax levies are obtained by applying tax rates against either the primary assessed valuation or the secondary assessed valuation. Primary and secondary valuation categories are composed of the exact same properties. However, the primary category limits the increase in property values to 10% from the previous year, while there is no limit to the increase in property values for secondary valuation. Override and debt service tax rates are applied to secondary assessed valuation and all other tax rates are applied to the primary assessed valuation.

The County levies real property taxes on or before the third Monday in August, which become due and payable in two equal installments. The first installment is due on the first day of October and becomes delinquent after the first business day of November. The second installment is due on the first day of March of the next year and becomes delinquent after the first business day of May. The billings are considered past due after these dates, at which time the applicable property is subject to penalties and interest.

NOTE 1 - SUMMARY OF SIGNIFICANT ACCOUNTING POLICIES (Cont'd)

The County also levies various personal property taxes during the year, which are due the second Monday of the month following receipt of the tax notice, and become delinquent 30 days thereafter.

Pursuant to ARS, a lien against assessed real and personal property attaches on the first day of January preceding assessment and levy; however according to case law, an enforceable legal claim to the asset does not arise.

G. Inventory

All inventories are valued at cost using the first-in/first-out (FIFO) method. Inventories are recorded as expenses when consumed in the government-wide financial statements. Inventories are recorded as expenditures when purchased in the fund financial statements and are offset by a reserve of fund balance.

The United States Department of Agriculture (USDA) commodity portion of the food services inventory consists of food donated by the USDA. It is valued at estimated market prices paid by the USDA.

H. Prepaid Items

Certain payments to vendors reflect costs applicable to future accounting periods and are recorded as prepaid items in both the government-wide and fund financial statements. Prepaid items are recorded as expenses when consumed in the government-wide financial statements. Prepaid items are recorded as expenditures when purchased in the fund financial statements and are offset by a reserve of fund balance.

I. Capital Assets

Capital assets which include land and improvements, buildings and improvements, vehicles, furniture, equipment and construction in progress, are reported in the government-wide financial statements.

Capital assets are defined by the District as assets with an initial, individual cost in excess of $5,000 and an estimated useful life of more than one year. Such assets are recorded at historical cost, or estimated historical cost if purchased or constructed. Donated capital assets are recorded at the estimated fair market value at the date of donation.

The costs of normal maintenance and repairs that do not add to the value of the asset or materially extend assets lives are not capitalized.

NOTE 1 - SUMMARY OF SIGNIFICANT ACCOUNTING POLICIES (Cont'd)

Capital assets are depreciated using the straight line method over the following estimated useful lives:

Land improvements	20-25 years
Buildings and improvements	20-50 years
Vehicles, furniture and equipment	5-15 years

J. Compensated Absences

The District's employee vacation and sick leave policies generally provide for granting vacation and sick leave with pay. Accrued sick leave is earned by all full-time employees working at least 10 months a year, at a rate of 1 day a month. All twelve-month employees earn vacation, at a rate of one week of vacation after one year of employment, two weeks after three years, three weeks after 8 years, and four weeks after 18 years. The current and long-term liabilities for accumulated vacation and sick leave are reported on the government-wide financial statements. A liability for these amounts is reported in governmental funds only if they have matured, for example, as a result of employee leave, resignations and retirements.

K. Long-term Obligations

In the government-wide financial statements, long-term debt and other long-term obligations are reported as liabilities on the statement of net assets. Bond premiums and discounts, as well as issuance costs, are deferred and amortized over the life of the bonds using the effective interest method. Bonds payable are reported net of the applicable bond premium or discount. Bond issuance costs are reported as deferred charges and amortized over the term of the related debt.

In the fund financial statements, governmental fund types recognize bond premiums and discounts, as well as bond issuance costs, during the current period. The face amount of debt issued is reported as other financing sources. Premiums received on debt issuances are reported as other financing sources while discounts on debt issuances are reported as other financing uses. Issuance costs, whether or not withheld from the actual debt proceeds received, are reported as debt service expenditures.

L. Fund Equity

In the fund financial statements, governmental funds report reservations of fund balance for amounts that are not available for expenditures or are legally restricted by outside parties for use for a specific purpose. Designations of fund balance represent tentative management plans that are subject to change.

NOTE 1 - SUMMARY OF SIGNIFICANT ACCOUNTING POLICIES (Concl'd)

M. Interfund Activity

Flows of cash from one fund to another without a requirement for repayment are reported as interfund transfers. Interfund transfers between governmental funds are eliminated in the Statement of Activities. Interfund transfers in the fund financial statements are reported as other financing sources/uses.

N. Estimates

The preparation of the financial statements in conformity with accounting principles generally accepted in the United States of America requires management to make estimates and assumptions that affect the amounts reported in the financial statements and accompanying notes. Actual results may differ from those estimates.

NOTE 2 - STEWARDSHIP, COMPLIANCE AND ACCOUNTABILITY

Budgetary Information - The District operates within the budget requirements for school districts as specified by State law and as interpreted by the Arizona Department of Education and the Auditor General. The financial reports reflect the following budgetary standards.

- For the fiscal year beginning July 1, a proposed expenditure budget is presented by the Governing Board to the County School Superintendent and/or the Superintendent of Public Instruction on or before July 5.

- The proposed expenditure budget is advertised in the local newspaper, together with a notice of public hearing.

- Once adopted, the expenditure budget can be revised only by the Governing Board for specific reasons set forth in the A.R.S. The budget was increased in fiscal year 2000-2001 for sudden growth in average daily membership. However, the revision was insignificant. Budget amendments and budget transfers between District funds by management are not allowed without Governing Board approval. However overexpenditures by line items are allowable as long as fund totals are not exceeded.

- Although it is not adopted or published, a budget of revenue from all sources for the fiscal year is prepared by the District and transmitted to the County School Superintendent and/or the Superintendent of Public Instruction on or before September 15. The revenue budget can not be revised.

- Budgets are prepared on the modified accrual basis of accounting, except as explained in Note 10.

NOTE 2 - STEWARDSHIP, COMPLIANCE AND ACCOUNTABILITY (Concl'd)

- All appropriations, including encumbered appropriations, lapse at year-end.

- The legal level of budgetary control (that is, the level at which expenditures cannot legally exceed the appropriated amount) is established at the individual fund level for all funds.

Excess Expenditures Over Budget - The following individual non-major fund had expenditures which exceeded the revised budget for the year ended June 30, 2001:

	Budget	Expenditures	Excess
Governmental Funds:			
Special Revenue:			
E-Rate	$ -0-	$ 296,568	$ 296,568

However, resources were available to cover expenditures of this fund.

NOTE 3 - CASH AND INVESTMENTS

The captions and amounts of cash and investments on the balance sheet in the District's individual major funds and non-major and fiduciary funds in the aggregate consist of the following.

	General Fund	Debt Service Fund	Bond Building Fund	Non-major and other Funds	Total
Cash in bank	$	$	$	$ 69,941	$ 69,9
Cash and investments held by County Treasurer	13,891	2,031,687	2,160,636	3,302,052	7,508,2
Total	$ 13,891	$ 2,031,687	$ 2,160,636	$ 3,371,993	$ 7,578,2

The District's deposits at June 30, 2001, were entirely covered by Federal depository insurance.

Investments are reported at fair value. At June 30, 2001, the District's investments consisted of the following.

	Fair Value
Cash and investments held by the County Treasurer	$ 7,508,266
Total	$ 7,508,266

The District's investment in the County Treasurer's investment pool represents a proportionate interest in the pool's portfolio; however the District's portion is not identified with specific investments and are not subject to custodial credit risk.

NOTE 4 - RECEIVABLES

Receivables, net of allowance for uncollectibles, as of year end for the District's individual major funds and non-major funds in the aggregate are as follows:

	General Fund	Debt Service Fund	Non-major Funds	Total
Property taxes	$ 95,967	$ 85,882	$ 7,782	$ 189,631
Due from other governments:				
Due from Federal government			171,143	171,143
Due from State government			47,478	47,478
Total Receivables	$ 95,967	$ 85,882	$ 226,403	$ 408,252

Governmental funds report deferred revenue in connection with receivables for revenues that are not considered to be available to liquidate liabilities of the current period. Governmental funds also defer revenue recognition in connection with resources that have been received, but not yet earned. At the end of the current fiscal year, the various components of deferred revenue reported in the governmental funds were as follows:

	Unavailable	Unearned
Delinquent property taxes receivable (General Fund)	$ 65,679	$
Delinquent property taxes receivable (Debt Service Fund)	54,271	
Delinquent property taxes receivable (Non-major governmental funds)	5,251	
Grant drawdowns prior to meeting all eligibility requirements (Non-major governmental funds)		206,283
Total deferred revenue for governmental funds	$ 125,201	$ 206,283

NOTE 5 - CAPITAL ASSETS

A summary of capital asset activity for the fiscal year ended June 30, 2001 follows.

Governmental Activities	Beginning Balance	Increase	Decrease	Ending Balance
Capital assets, not being depreciated:				
Land	$ 176,321	$	$	$ 176,32
Construction in progress	1,222,622	300,449	1,218,583	304,48
Total capital assets, not being depreciated	1,398,943	300,449	1,218,583	480,80
Capital assets, being depreciated:				
Land improvements	134,720	135,794		270,51
Buildings and improvements	20,308,281	2,183,399		22,491,68
Vehicles, furniture and equipment	1,622,317	185,742		1,808.05
Total capital assets being depreciated	22,065,318	2,504,935		24,570,25
Less accumulated depreciation for:				
Land improvements	(11,902)	(7,274)		(19,17
Buildings and improvements	(4,080,077)	(499,060)		(4,579,13
Vehicles, furniture and equipment	(674,839)	(127,686)		(802,52
Total accumulated depreciation	(4,766,818)	(634,020)		(5,400,83
Total capital assets, being depreciated, net	17,298,500	1,870,915		19,169.4
Governmental activities capital assets, net	$ 18,697,443	$ 2,171,364	$ 1,218.583	$ 19,650,2

Depreciation expense was charged to governmental functions as follows:

Instruction	$ 490,736
Support services - students and staff	19,798
Support services - administration	18,282
Operation and maintenance of plant services	10,679
Student transportation services	81,949
Operation of non-instructional services	12,576
Total depreciation expense - governmental activities	$ 634,020

The beginning balances for capital assets do not agree to the June 30, 2000 financial statements due to a change in capitalization policy.

Construction Commitments - As of June 30, 2001, the District was involved in several construction projects. The estimated cost to complete the construction projects is $6,907,484.

NOTE 6 - OBLIGATIONS UNDER CAPITAL LEASES

The District has acquired copiers under the provisions of long-term lease agreements classified as capital leases. These lease agreements qualify as capital leases for accounting purposes and, therefore, have been recorded at the present value of their future minimum lease payments as of the inception date.

The assets acquired through capital leases over $5,000 are as follows:

	Governmental Activities
Assets:	
Vehicles, furniture and equipment	$ 93,020
Less: Accumulated depreciation	(50,119)
Total	$ 42,901

The future minimum lease obligations and the net present value of these minimum lease payments as of June 30, 2001 were as follows:

Year Ending June 30:	Governmental Activities
2002	$ 71,780
2003	19,179
2004	9,501
2005	5,543
Total minimum lease payments	106,003
Less: amount representing interest	7,985
Present value of minimum lease payments	$ 98,018

NOTE 7 - BONDS PAYABLE

Bonds payable at June 30, 2001, consisted of the outstanding school improvement and refunding bonds. The bonds are both callable and noncallable with interest payable semiannually.

Purpose	Interest Rates	Maturity	Outstanding Principal June 30, 2001	Due Within One Year
Refunding, Capital Appreciation Bonds, Series 1993	4.0-4.3%	7/1/2000-02	$ 2,470,000	$ 1,200,000
School Improvement Bonds of 1998, Series A, 1998	4.0-4.7%	7/1/2003-13	4,350,000	
School Improvement Bonds of 1998, Series B, 1999	4.0-5.25%	7/1/2003-13	4,525,000	
Total			$ 11,345,000	$ 1,200,000

Annual debt service requirements to maturity on general obligation and refunding bonds at June 30, 2001, are summarized as follows.

Year ending June 30:	Governmental Activities Principal	Interest	Total
2002	$ 1,200,000	$ 497,741	$ 1,697,741
2003	1,270,000	445,537	1,715,537
2004	650,000	404,257	1,054,257
2005	675,000	375,353	1,050,353
2006	700,000	344,588	1,044,588
2007-2011	3,975,000	1,126,717	5,101,717
2012-2013	2,875,000	287,394	3,162,394
Total	$ 11,345,000	$ 3,481,587	$ 14,826,587

NOTE 8 - CHANGES IN LONG-TERM LIABILITIES

Long-term liability activity for the year ended June 30, 2001 was as follows:

	Beginning Balance	Additions	Reductions	Ending Balance	Due Within One Year
Governmental activities:					
Bonds payable	$12,770,000	$	$1,425,000	$11,345,000	$1,200,000
Obligations under capital leases	169,050		71,032	98,018	65,869
Compensated absences	833,519	145,795	37,236	942,078	342,078
Governmental activity long-term liabilities	$ 13,772,569	$ 145,795	$ 1,533,268	$ 12,385,096	$ 1,607,947

NOTE 9 - INTERFUND RECEIVABLES, PAYABLES, AND TRANSFERS

At June 30, 2001, interfund balances were as follows:

Due to/from other funds:

	Due from
	Non-major Governmental
Due to Non-major governmental funds	$ 91,455
Total	$ 91,455

At June 30, 2001, the Title I - Educationally Disadvantaged, Title I - Migrant and Title III - Goals 2000 Funds (Non-major governmental funds) had negative cash balances in the Treasurer's pooled cash accounts. Negative cash on deposit with the County Treasurer was reduced by interfund borrowing with the Medicaid Reimbursement Fund (a non-major governmental fund). All interfund balances are expected to be paid within one year.

NOTE 9 - INTERFUND RECEIVABLES, PAYABLES, AND TRANSFERS (Concl'd)

Interfund transfers:

Transfer out	Debt Service	Non-major Governmental	Total
Bond Building	$ 101,354	$	$ 101,354
Non-major governmental funds		42,677	42,677
Total	$ 101,354	$ 42,677	$ 144,031

Transfers between funds are used to (1) move investment income earned in the Bond Building Fund, that is required by statute to be expended in the Debt Service Fund (2) to move Federal and State grant funds restricted for indirect costs to the Indirect Cost Fund (a non-major governmental fund).

NOTE 10 - CONTINGENT LIABILITIES

Compliance - Amounts received or receivable from grantor agencies are subject to audit and adjustment by grantor agencies, principally the federal government. Any disallowed claims, including amounts already collected, may constitute a liability of the applicable funds. The amount, if any, of expenditures/expenses that may be disallowed by the grantor cannot be determined at this time, although the District expects such amounts, if any, to be immaterial.

Lawsuits - The District is a defendant in various lawsuits. Although the outcome of these lawsuits is not presently determinable, in the opinion of the District's counsel, the resolution of these matters will not have a material adverse effect on the financial condition of the District.

NOTE 11 - RISK MANAGEMENT

The District is exposed to various risks of loss related to torts; theft of, damage to, and destruction of assets; errors and omissions; injuries to employees; and natural disasters. The District was unable to obtain general property and liability insurance at a cost it considered to be economically justifiable. Therefore, the District joined the Arizona School Risk Retention Trust, Inc. (ASRRT), together with other school districts in the State. ASRRT is a public entity risk pool currently operating as a common risk management and insurance program for 182 member school districts. The District pays an annual premium to ASRRT for its general insurance coverage. The agreement provides that ASRRT will be self-sustaining through member premiums and will reinsure through commercial companies for claims in excess of the following amounts for each category listed below.

Insurance Category	Reinsurance
Property Insurance	$100,000,000 per occurrence
Automobile Physical Damage	$2,000,000 per occurrence as well as amounts in excess of Trust annual aggregate limit $100,000
General, Professional and Automobile Liability	$4.5 million in excess of $500,000 per occurrence
Excess General, Automobile and Professional Liability	$5,000,000 excess of $5,000,000 or $10,000,000 limit of liability
Excess General Public, Automobile and Professional Liability	$10,000,000 excess of $15,000,000 limit of liability
Crime Insurance	$500,000 Public Employee Dishonesty; $500,000 Forgery or Alteration; $150,000 Money and Securities; $500,000 Computer Fraud
Boiler and Machinery	$10,000,000 comprehensive form
Underground Storage Tank	$1,000,000 per release/$2,000,000 annual aggregate
Special Risk Insurance	$5,000,000 per occurrence, $100,000 death or dismemberment benefit each person/$500,000 aggregate
Non-Owned Aircraft	$10,000,000 per occurrence

The District continues to carry commercial insurance for all other risks of loss, including workers' compensation and employee health and accident insurance. Settled claims resulting from these risks have not exceeded commercial insurance coverage in any of the past three fiscal years.

NOTE 12 - RETIREMENT PLAN

Plan Description - The District contributes to a cost-sharing multiple-employer defined benefit pension plan administered by the Arizona State Retirement System. Benefits are established by state statute and generally provide retirement, death, long-term disability, survivor, and health insurance premium benefits. The System is governed by the Arizona State Retirement System Board according to the provisions of A.R.S. Title 38, Chapter 5, Article 2.

The System issues a comprehensive annual financial report that includes financial statements and required supplementary information. The most recent report may be obtained by writing the System, 3300 North Central Avenue, P.O. Box 33910, Phoenix, Arizona 85067-3910 or by calling (602) 240-2001 or (800) 621-3778.

Funding Policy - The Arizona State Legislature establishes and may amend active plan members' and the District's contribution rate. For the year ended June 30, 2001, active plan members and the District were each required by statute to contribute at the actuarially determined rate of 2.66 percent (2.17 percent retirement and 0.49 percent long-term disability) of the members' annual covered payroll. The District's contributions to the System for the years ended June 30, 2001, 2000, and 1999 were $261,163, $231,143 and $282,002, respectively, which were equal to the required contributions for the year.

NOTE 13 - SUBSEQUENT EVENT - INCREASE IN FUTURE STATE AID

Arizona voters passed Proposition 301, which increased the State sales tax rate from 5.0% to 5.6%. Approximately $264 million additional dollars raised through this increase in Arizona sales taxes is earmarked for a Classroom Site Fund for K-12 education. These funds are to be used for performance-based teacher compensation, increases in teachers' base salaries, and classroom enhancements such as reductions in class size, additional teachers and aides, teacher training and dropout prevention. In addition, these funds will be used to adjust the basic State aid formula that will include a 2% inflation factor for each of the next five years, as well as provide an additional school day each year for the next five years, for a total of 180 school days at the end of the five years. Preliminary estimates provided by the State indicate that the District will receive approximately $960,407 more in State aid funding in fiscal year 2001-02, due to this change in the law.

BUDGETARY COMPARISON SCHEDULE
(REQUIRED SUPPLEMENTARY INFORMATION)

(This page intentionally left blank)

| | Budgeted Amounts | | Non-GAAP | Variance with Final Budget - Favorable (Unfavorable) |
	Original	Final	Actual	
Revenues:				
Other local	$ 764,574	$ 764,574	$ 771,454	$ 6,880
Property taxes	2,005,350	2,005,350	1,983,196	(22,154)
State aid and grants	8,573,567	8,573,567	8,767,296	193,729
Total revenues	11,343,491	11,343,491	11,521,946	178,455
Expenditures:				
Current -				
Regular Education				
Instruction	5,782,312	6,264,850	6,065,153	199,697
Support services - students and staff	712,925	760,925	778,888	(17,963)
Support services - administration	1,231,725	1,264,225	1,227,093	37,132
Operation and maintenance of plant services	1,522,297	1,545,183	1,569,686	(24,503)
Operation of non-instructional services	16,623	16,623	16,005	618
Total regular education	9,265,882	9,851,806	9,656,825	194,981
Special Education				
Instruction	1,439,335	1,455,727	1,382,696	73,031
Support services - students and staff	163,420	149,528	156,090	(6,562)
Support services - administration	130,969	128,469	105,416	23,053
Student transportation services			17,152	(17,152)
Total special education	1,733,724	1,733,724	1,661,354	72,370
Student Transportation Services				
Pupil transportation	462,611	462,611	434,335	28,276
Total student transportation services	462,611	462,611	434,335	28,276
Total expenditures	11,462,217	12,048,141	11,752,514	295,627
Excess (deficiency) of revenues over expenditures	(118,726)	(704,650)	(230,568)	474,082
Fund balances, July 1, 2000	118,726	118,726	514,498	395,772
Increase (decrease) in reserve for inventory			(23,425)	(23,425)
Increase in reserve for prepaid items			31,189	31,189
Fund balances (deficits), June 30, 2001	$ -	$ (585,924)	$ 291,694	$ 877,618

See accompanying notes to schedule.

NOTE 1 - BUDGETARY BASIS OF ACCOUNTING

The adopted budget of the District is prepared on a basis consistent with accounting principles generally accepted in the United States of America with the following exception: a portion of fiscal year 2000-01 insurance payments were charged against the fiscal year 1999-2000 budget. Consequently, the following adjustment is necessary to present actual expenditures and fund balance at July 1, 2000 on a budgetary basis in order to provide a meaningful comparison.

	General Fund	
	Total Expenditures	Fund Balance, July 1, 2000
Statement of Revenues, Expenditures and Changes in Fund Balances - Governmental Funds	$ 11,856,445	$ 618,429
Fiscal year 2000-01 insurance payments charged against fiscal year 1999-2000 budget	(103,931)	(103,931)
Budgetary Comparison Schedule for the General Fund	$ 11,752,514	$ 514,498

OTHER MAJOR GOVERNMENTAL FUNDS
BUDGETARY COMPARISON SCHEDULES

AVONDALE ELEMENTARY SCHOOL DISTRICT NO. 44
BUDGETARY COMPARISON SCHEDULE FOR THE DEBT SERVICE FUND
YEAR ENDED JUNE 30, 2001

	Budgeted Amounts			Variance with Final Budget - Favorable
	Original	Final	Actual	(Unfavorable)
Revenues:				
Other local	$ 5,466	$ 5,466	$ 89,520	$ 84,054
Property taxes	1,929,119	1,929,119	1,918,964	(10,155)
Total revenues	1,934,585	1,934,585	2,008,484	73,899
Expenditures:				
Debt service -				
Interest, premium and fiscal charges	658,560	658,560	567,689	90,871
Principal retirement	1,399,440	1,399,440	1,200,000	199,440
Total expenditures	2,058,000	2,058,000	1,767,689	290,311
Excess (deficiency) of revenues over expenditures	(123,415)	(123,415)	240,795	364,210
Other financing sources (uses):				
Transfers in			101,354	101,354
Total other financing sources (uses)			101,354	101,354
Excess (deficiency) of revenues and other financing sources over expenditures and other financing uses	(123,415)	(123,415)	342,149	465,564
Fund balances, July 1, 2000	2,028,044	2,028,044	259,828	(1,768,216)
Fund balances, June 30, 2001	$ 1,904,629	$ 1,904,629	$ 601,977	$ (1,302,652)

AVONDALE ELEMENTARY SCHOOL DISTRICT NO. 44
BUDGETARY COMPARISON SCHEDULE FOR THE BOND BUILDING FUND
YEAR ENDED JUNE 30, 2001

| | Budgeted Amounts | | | Variance with Final Budget - Favorable |
	Original	Final	Actual	(Unfavorable)
Revenues:				
Other local	$ 59,334	$ 59,334	$ 101,354	$ 42,020
Total revenues	59,334	59,334	101,354	42,020
Expenditures:				
Capital outlay	8,500,000	8,500,000	380,030	8,119,970
Total expenditures	8,500,000	8,500,000	380,030	8,119,970
Excess (deficiency) of revenues over expenditures	(8,440,666)	(8,440,666)	(278,676)	8,161,990
Other financing sources (uses):				
Proceeds from sale of bonds	5,900,000	5,900,000		(5,900,000)
Transfers out			(101,354)	(101,354)
Total other financing sources (uses)	5,900,000	5,900,000	(101,354)	(6,001,354)
Excess (deficiency) of revenues and other financing sources over expenditures and other financing uses	(2,540,666)	(2,540,666)	(380,030)	2,160,636
Fund balances, July 1, 2000	2,540,666	2,540,666	2,540,666	
Fund balances, June 30, 2001	$	$	$ 2,160,636	$ 2,160,636

(This page intentionally left blank)

NON-MAJOR GOVERNMENTAL FUNDS

AVONDALE ELEMENTARY SCHOOL DISTRICT NO. 44
COMBINING BALANCE SHEET - ALL NON-MAJOR GOVERNMENTAL FUNDS - BY FUND TYPE
JUNE 30, 2001

	Special Revenue	Capital Projects	Total Non Major Governmental Funds
ASSETS			
Cash and investments	$ 1,276,298	$ 2,025,754	$ 3,302,052
Property taxes receivable		7,782	7,782
Due from governmental entities	218,621		218,621
Due from other funds	91,455		91,455
Prepaid items	47,336		47,336
Inventory, at cost	18,031		18,031
Total assets	$ 1,651,741	$ 2,033,536	$ 3,685,277
LIABILITIES AND FUND EQUITY			
Liabilities:			
Accounts payable	$ 21,548	$ 38,461	$ 60,009
Due to other funds	91,455		91,455
Deferred revenues	206,283	5,251	211,534
Construction contracts payable		64,092	64,092
Total liabilities	319,286	107,804	427,090
Fund equity:			
Fund balances -			
Reserved for:			
Prepaid items	47,336		47,336
Inventory	18,031		18,031
Unreserved:			
Undesignated	1,267,088		1,267,088
Designated for capital outlay		1,925,732	1,925,732
Total equity	1,332,455	1,925,732	3,258,187
Total liabilities and fund equity	$ 1,651,741	$ 2,033,536	$ 3,685,277

	Special Revenue	Capital Projects	Total Non Major Governmental Funds
Revenues:			
Other local	$ 467,044	$ 463,150	$ 930,194
Property taxes		189,993	189,993
State aid and grants	161,569	1,969,295	2,130,864
Federal aid, grants and reimbursements	2,603,559		2,603,559
Total revenues	3,232,172	2,622,438	5,854,610
Expenditures:			
Current -			
Instruction	1,222,246		1,222,246
Support services - students and staff	402,281		402,281
Support services - administration	113,357		113,357
Operation and maintenance of plant services	3,816		3,816
Student transportation services	4,752		4,752
Operation of non-instructional services	1,072,014		1,072,014
Capital outlay	304,554	1,945,783	2,250,337
Debt service -			
Interest, premium and fiscal charges		12,923	12,923
Principal retirement		71,032	71,032
Total expenditures	3,123,020	2,029,738	5,152,758
Excess (deficiency) of revenues over expenditures	109,152	592,700	701,852
Other financing sources (uses):			
Transfers in	42,677		42,677
Transfers out	(42,677)		(42,677)
Total other financing sources (uses)			
Excess (deficiency) of revenues and other financing sources over expenditures and other financing uses	109,152	592,700	701,852
Fund balances, beginning of year	1,173,648	1,333,032	2,506,680
Increase in reserve for inventory	2,319		2,319
Increase in reserve for prepaid items	47,336		47,336
Fund balances, end of year	$ 1,332,455	$ 1,925,732	$ 3,258,187

The following Special Revenue Funds are maintained by the District. Arizona Revised Statutes (A.R.S.) and the Uniform System of Financial Records (USFR) required the establishment of these funds for the specified activities.

Classroom Site - to account for the financial activity of the six-tenths of one percent increase in the state sales tax due to the passage of Proposition 301.

Title I - Educationally Disadvantaged - to account for financial assistance to local educational agencies for supplementary instructional programs for educationally disadvantaged students.

Title I - Migrant - to account for financial assistance to local educational agencies for supplementary instructional programs for migrant students.

Title II - Eisenhower Grant - to account for financial assistance for supplementary math and science programs.

Technology Literacy Grant - to account for financial assistance for technology literacy programs.

Title IV - Safe and Drug Free Schools - to account for financial assistance for chemical abuse awareness programs funded by the Federal government.

Title VI - Innovative Education Program - to account for financial assistance for supplementary writing programs.

EHA Title VI-B Entitlement - to account for supplemental financial assistance to State and local educational agencies in providing a free, appropriate public education to disabled children.

Federal Preschool - to account for financial assistance for instructional programs for disabled preschool students

Emergency Immigrant Education - to account for financial assistance to local educational agencies for educational services and costs for immigrant children.

Medicaid Reimbursement - to account for financial assistance for Medicaid programs.

Title III - Goals 2000 - to account for financial assistance for the state and local education systemic improvement grants funded by the Federal government.

E-Rate - to account for Federal assistance administered by the Schools and Libraries Corporation (SLC) to provide discounts to schools and libraries on the cost of telecommunications (local and long-distance phone service), Internet access, and network wiring within buildings.

Class Size Reduction - to account for financial assistance received from the State for the preparation of individuals for employment.

Early Childhood - to account for financial assistance from the state for instructional programs for kindergarten through third grade students.

State Chemical Abuse - to account for financial assistance for chemical abuse awareness.

Gifted Education - to account for financial assistance received from the State for programs for gifted students.

Other State Projects - to account for financial assistance for other state projects.

School Plant - to account for proceeds from the sale or lease of school property.

Food Services - to account for the financial activity of the food services program. This program provides for regular and incidental meals, lunches and snacks in connection with school functions.

Civic Center - to account for monies received from the rental of school facilities for civic activities.

Community School - to account for revenues and expenditures for the purposes of academic and skill development for all citizens.

Extracurricular Activities Fees Tax Credit - to account for revenues and expenditures of monies collected in support of extracurricular activities to be taken as a tax credit by the taxpayer in accordance with A.R.S. 43-1089.01.

Gifts and Donations - to account for the revenues and expenditures of gifts, donations, bequests and private grants made to the District.

District Services - to account for the financial activity of providing goods and services to departments or schools within the District, or other districts on a cost reimbursement basis.

Fingerprinting - to account for the revenues and expenditures of fingerprinting new employees as mandated by the State.

School Opening - to account for revenues received for opening new schools.

Insurance Proceeds - to account for the monies received from insurance companies to be used for repair or replacement of lost, stolen or damaged property.

Textbooks - to account for monies received from students to replace or repair lost or damaged textbooks.

Indirect Costs - to account for monies transferred from Federal or State projects for administrative costs.

Unemployment Insurance - to account for unemployment insurance payments to the Department of Economic Security.

Insurance Refund - to account for insurance premium refunds.

Grants and Gifts to Teachers - to account for financial assistance for the funding of grants and gifts to teachers.

Intergovernmental Agreements - to account for the financial activities relating to agreements with other governments.

AVONDALE ELEMENTARY SCHOOL DISTRICT NO. 44
COMBINING BALANCE SHEET - NON-MAJOR SPECIAL REVENUE FUNDS
JUNE 30, 2001

	Classroom Site	Title I - Educationally Disadvantaged	Title I - Migrant	Title II - Eisenhower Grant
ASSETS				
Cash and investments	$	$	$	$ 816
Due from governmental entities	47,478	6,838	28,338	
Due from other funds				
Prepaid items		22,895		
Inventory, at cost				
Total assets	$ 47,478	$ 29,733	$ 28,338	$ 816
LIABILITIES AND FUND EQUITY				
Liabilities:				
Accounts payable	$	$ 6,612	$ 303	$ 607
Due to other funds		23,121	28,035	
Deferred revenues	47,478			209
Total liabilities	47,478	29,733	28,338	816
Fund equity:				
Fund balances (deficits) -				
Reserved for:				
Prepaid items		22,895		
Inventory				
Unreserved:				
Undesignated		(22,895)		
Total fund equity				
Total liabilities and fund equity	$ 47,478	$ 29,733	$ 28,338	$ 816

Technology Literacy Grant	Title IV - Safe and Drug Free Schools	Title VI - Innovative Education Program	EHA Title VI-B Entitlement	Federal Preschool	Emergency Immigrant Education
$ 2,430	$ 16,515	$ 441	$ 74,559	$ 3,468	$ 22,349
			6,496		
$ 2,430	$ 16,515	$ 441	$ 81,055	$ 3,468	$ 22,349
$ 214	$ 611	$ 19	$ 4,453	$ 29	$ 977
2,216	15,904	422	76,602	3,439	21,372
2,430	16,515	441	81,055	3,468	22,349
			6,496		
			(6,496)		
$ 2,430	$ 16,515	$ 441	$ 81,055	$ 3,468	$ 22,349

(Continued)

	Medicaid Reimbursement	Title III - Goals 2000	E - Rate	Class Size Reduction
ASSETS				
Cash and investments	$ 8,695	$	$ 2,504	$ 11,141
Due from governmental entities		40,779		
Due from other funds	91,455			
Prepaid items				1,238
Inventory, at cost				
Total assets	$ 100,150	$ 40,779	$ 2,504	$ 12,379
LIABILITIES AND FUND EQUITY				
Liabilities:				
Accounts payable	$	$ 480	$	$ 545
Due to other funds		40,299		
Deferred revenues				11,834
Total liabilities		40,779		12,379
Fund equity:				
Fund balances (deficits) -				
Reserved for:				
Prepaid items				1,238
Inventory				
Unreserved:				
Undesignated	100,150		2,504	(1,238)
Total fund equity	100,150		2,504	
Total liabilities and fund equity	$ 100,150	$ 40,779	$ 2,504	$ 12,379

	Early Childhood	State Chemical Abuse	Gifted Education	Other State Projects	School Plant	Food Services
	$ 11,074	$ 5,466	$ 227	$ 11,238	$ 119,638	$ 94,718
						95,188
	3,094					13,613
						18,031
	$ 14,168	$ 5,466	$ 227	$ 11,238	$ 119,638	$ 221,550
	$ 4,292	$	$	$	$	$ 1,076
	9,876	5,466	227	11,238		
	14,168	5,466	227	11,238		1,076
	3,094					13,613
						18,031
	(3,094)				119,638	188,830
					119,638	220,474
	$ 14,168	$ 5,466	$ 227	$ 11,238	$ 119,638	$ 221,550

(Continued)

AVONDALE ELEMENTARY SCHOOL DISTRICT NO. 44
COMBINING BALANCE SHEET - NON-MAJOR SPECIAL REVENUE FUNDS
JUNE 30, 2001
(Continued)

	Civic Center	Community School	Extracurricular Activities Fees Tax Credit	Gifts and Donations
ASSETS				
Cash and investments	$ 126,138	$ 2,999	$ 5,028	$ 7,642
Due from governmental entities				
Due from other funds				
Prepaid items				
Inventory, at cost				
Total assets	$ 126,138	$ 2,999	$ 5,028	$ 7,642
LIABILITIES AND FUND EQUITY				
Liabilities:				
Accounts payable	$ 263	$	$	$ 5
Due to other funds				
Deferred revenues				
Total liabilities	263			5
Fund equity:				
Fund balances (deficits) -				
Reserved for:				
Prepaid items				
Inventory				
Unreserved:				
Undesignated	125,875	2,999	5,028	7,637
Total fund equity	125,875	2,999	5,028	7,637
Total liabilities and fund equity	$ 126,138	$ 2,999	$ 5,028	$ 7,642

District Services	Fingerprinting	Insurance Proceeds	Textbooks	Indirect Costs	Unemployment Insurance
$ 63,121	$ 1,391	$ 37,778	$ 6,556	$ 72,168	$ 543,337
$ 63,121	$ 1,391	$ 37,778	$ 6,556	$ 72,168	$ 543,337
$	$	$	$	$ 49	$ 188
				49	188
63,121	1,391	37,778	6,556	72,119	543,149
63,121	1,391	37,778	6,556	72,119	543,149
$ 63,121	$ 1,391	$ 37,778	$ 6,556	$ 72,168	$ 543.337

(Continued)

AVONDALE ELEMENTARY SCHOOL DISTRICT NO. 44
COMBINING BALANCE SHEET - NON-MAJOR SPECIAL REVENUE FUNDS
JUNE 30, 2001
(Concluded)

	Insurance Refund	Grants and Gifts to Teachers	Inter governmental Agreements	Totals
ASSETS				
Cash and investments	$ 9,859	$ 3,266	$ 11,736	$ 1,276,298
Due from governmental entities				218,621
Due from other funds				91,455
Prepaid items				47,336
Inventory, at cost				18,031
Total assets	$ 9,859	$ 3,266	$ 11,736	$ 1,651,741
LIABILITIES AND FUND EQUITY				
Liabilities:				
Accounts payable	$	$ 819	$ 6	$ 21,548
Due to other funds				91,455
Deferred revenues				206,283
Total liabilities		819	6	319.286
Fund equity:				
Fund balances (deficits) -				
Reserved for:				
Prepaid items				47,336
Inventory				18,031
Unreserved:				
Undesignated	9,859	2,447	11,730	1,267,088
Total fund equity	9,859	2,447	11,730	1,332,455
Total liabilities and fund equity	$ 9,859	$ 3,266	$ 11,736	$ 1,651,741

(This page intentionally left blank)

AVONDALE ELEMENTARY SCHOOL DISTRICT NO. 44
COMBINING STATEMENT OF REVENUES, EXPENDITURES AND CHANGES IN FUND BALANCES-
NON-MAJOR SPECIAL REVENUE FUNDS
YEAR ENDED JUNE 30, 2001

	Title I - Educationally Disadvantaged	Title I - Migrant	Title II - Eisenhower Grant
Revenues:			
Other local	$	$	$
State aid and grants			
Federal aid, grants and reimbursements	794,926	81,020	47,693
Total revenues	794,926	81,020	47,693
Expenditures:			
Current -			
Instruction	665,003	47,094	
Support services - students and staff	84,487	27,134	46,662
Support services - administration	50,648	2,784	
Operation and maintenance of plant services			
Student transportation services			
Operation of non-instructional services		2,344	
Capital outlay			
Total expenditures	800,138	79,356	46,662
Excess (deficiency) of revenues over expenditures	(5,212)	1,664	1,031
Other financing sources (uses):			
Transfers in			
Transfers out	(17,683)	(1,664)	(1,031)
Total other financing sources (uses)	(17,683)	(1,664)	(1,031)
Excess (deficiency) of revenues and other financing sources over expenditures and other financing uses	(22,895)		
Fund balances, beginning of year			
Increase in reserve for inventory			
Increase in reserve for prepaid items	22,895		
Fund balances, end of year	$	$	$

	Technology Literacy Grant	Title IV - Safe and Drug Free Schools	Title VI - Innovative Education Program	EHA Title VI-B Entitlement	Federal Preschool	Emergency Immigrant Education
	$	$	$	$	$	$
	12,985	14,439	19,665	276,119	22,208	21,437
	12,985	14,439	19,665	276,119	22,208	21,437
		2,904	19,265	178,477	21,728	13,442
	2,531	11,286		97,899		5,201
				150		
	10,454					2,302
	12,985	14,190	19,265	276,526	21,728	20,945
		249	400	(407)	480	492
		(249)	(400)	(6,089)	(480)	(492)
		(249)	(400)	(6,089)	(480)	(492)
				(6,496)		
				6,496		
	$	$	$	$	$	$

(Continued)

	Medicaid Reimbursement	Title III - Goals 2000	E - Rate
Revenues:			
Other local	$	$	$
State aid and grants			
Federal aid, grants and reimbursements	35,703	68,135	299,072
Total revenues	35,703	68,135	299,072
Expenditures:			
Current -			
Instruction			17,127
Support services - students and staff		66,784	
Support services - administration			11,081
Operation and maintenance of plant services			3,816
Student transportation services	2,127		
Operation of non-instructional services			
Capital outlay			264,544
Total expenditures	2,127	66,784	296,568
Excess (deficiency) of revenues over expenditures	33,576	1,351	2,504
Other financing sources (uses):			
Transfers in			
Transfers out		(1,351)	
Total other financing sources (uses)		(1,351)	
Excess (deficiency) of revenues and other financing sources over expenditures and other financing uses	33,576		2,504
Fund balances, beginning of year	66,574		
Increase in reserve for inventory			
Increase in reserve for prepaid items			
Fund balances, end of year	$ 100,150	$	$ 2,504

	Class Size Reduction	Early Childhood	State Chemical Abuse	Gifted Education	Other State Projects	School Plant
	$	$ 147,969	$ 8,301	$ 5,299	$	$ 12,192
	93,647					
	93,647	147,969	8,301	5,299		12,192
	92,833	136,807		987		
		11,981	8,301	2,610		
		2,275				
				1,702		
	92,833	151,063	8,301	5,299		
	814	(3,094)				12,192
	(2,052)					
	(2,052)					
	(1,238)	(3,094)				12,192
						107,446
	1,238	3,094				
	$	$	$	$	$	$ 119,638

(Continued)

	Food Services	Civic Center	Community School
Revenues:			
Other local	$ 284,668	$ 70,900	$ 553
State aid and grants			
Federal aid, grants and reimbursements	816,510		
Total revenues	1,101,178	70,900	553
Expenditures:			
Current -			
Instruction			
Support services - students and staff		10,558	
Support services - administration			
Operation and maintenance of plant services			
Student transportation services		2,625	
Operation of non-instructional services	1,063,078	4,100	
Capital outlay	25,552		
Total expenditures	1,088,630	17,283	
Excess (deficiency) of revenues over expenditures	12,548	53,617	553
Other financing sources (uses):			
Transfers in			
Transfers out	(11,186)		
Total other financing sources (uses)	(11,186)		
Excess (deficiency) of revenues and other financing sources over expenditures and other financing uses	1,362	53,617	553
Fund balances, beginning of year	203,180	72,258	2,446
Increase in reserve for inventory	2,319		
Increase in reserve for prepaid items	13,613		
Fund balances, end of year	$ 220,474	$ 125,875	$ 2,999

Extracurricular Activities Fees Tax Credit	Gifts and Donations	District Services	Fingerprinting	Insurance Proceeds	Textbooks
$ 9,798	$ 8,556	$ 3,616	$ 2,097	$ 4,538	$ 1,615
9,798	8,556	3,616	2,097	4,538	1,615
11,586	2,403				3,914
	3,963			357	
			730		
	217				
11,586	6,583		730	357	3,914
(1,788)	1,973	3,616	1,367 ·	4,181	(2,299)
(1,788)	1,973	3,616	1,367	4,181	(2,299)
6,816	5,664	59,505	24	33,597	8,855
$ 5,028	$ 7,637	$ 63,121	$ 1,391	$ 37,778	$ 6,556

	Indirect Costs	Unemployment Insurance	Insurance Refund
Revenues:			
Other local	$ 3,571	$ 31,414	$ 565
State aid and grants			
Federal aid, grants and reimbursements			
Total revenues	3,571	31,414	565
Expenditures:			
Current -			
Instruction			
Support services - students and staff			
Support services - administration	38,508	9,456	
Operation and maintenance of plant services			
Student transportation services			
Operation of non-instructional services			
Capital outlay			
Total expenditures	38,508	9,456	
Excess (deficiency) of revenues over expenditures	(34,937)	21,958	565
Other financing sources (uses):			
Transfers in	42,677		
Transfers out			
Total other financing sources (uses)	42,677		
Excess (deficiency) of revenues and other financing sources over expenditures and other financing uses	7,740	21,958	565
Fund balances, beginning of year	64,379	521,191	9,294
Increase in reserve for inventory			
Increase in reserve for prepaid items			
Fund balances, end of year	$ 72,119	$ 543,149	$ 9,859

Grants and Gifts to Teachers		Inter governmental Agreements		Totals	
$	7,990	$	24,971	$	467,044
					161,569
					2,603,559
	7,990		24,971		3,232,172
	8,676				1,222,246
			22,527		402,281
					113,357
					3,816
					4,752
					1,072,014
					304,554
	8,676		22,527		3,123,020
	(686)		2,444		109,152
					42,677
					(42,677)
	(686)		2,444		109,152
	3,133		9,286		1,173,648
					2,319
					47,336
$	2,447	$	11,730	$	1,332,455

	Title I - Educationally Disadvantaged		
	Budget	Actual	Variance - Favorable (Unfavorable)
Revenues:			
Other local	$	$	$
State aid and grants			
Federal aid, grants and reimbursements	863,237	794,926	(68,311)
Total revenues	863,237	794,926	(68,311)
Expenditures:			
Current -			
Instruction	682,822	665,003	17,819
Support services - students and staff	98,995	84,487	14,508
Support services - administration	62,820	50,648	12,172
Operation and maintenance of plant services			
Student transportation services			
Operation of non-instructional services			
Capital outlay			
Total expenditures	844,637	800,138	44,499
Excess (deficiency) of revenues over expenditures	18,600	(5,212)	(23,812)
Other financing sources (uses):			
Transfers in			
Transfers out	(18,600)	(17,683)	917
Total other financing sources (uses)	(18,600)	(17,683)	917
Excess (deficiency) of revenues and other financing sources over expenditures and other financing uses		(22,895)	(22.895)
Fund balances (deficits), July 1, 2000			
Increase in reserve for inventory			
Increase in reserve for prepaid items		22,895	22,895
Fund balances (deficits), June 30, 2001	$	$	$

	Title I - Migrant				Title II - Eisenhower Grant		
	Budget	Actual	Variance - Favorable (Unfavorable)		Budget	Actual	Variance - Favorable (Unfavorable)
	$	$	$		$	$	$
	82,196	81,020	(1,176)		47,802	47,693	(109)
	82,196	81,020	(1,176)		47,802	47,693	(109)
	45,818	47,094	(1,276)				
	28,306	27,134	1,172		46,769	46,662	107
	3,204	2,784	420				
	3,191	2,344	847				
	80,519	79,356	1,163		46,769	46,662	107
	1,677	1,664	(13)		1,033	1,031	(2)
	(1,677)	(1,664)	13		(1,033)	(1,031)	2
	(1,677)	(1,664)	13		(1,033)	(1,031)	2
	$	$	$		$	$	$

(Continued)

| | Technology Literacy Grant | | |
	Budget	Actual	Variance - Favorable (Unfavorable)
Revenues:			
Other local	$	$	$
State aid and grants			
Federal aid, grants and reimbursements	13,088	12,985	(103)
Total revenues	13,088	12,985	(103)
Expenditures:			
Current -			
Instruction			
Support services - students and staff	2,692	2,531	161
Support services - administration			
Operation and maintenance of plant services			
Student transportation services			
Operation of non-instructional services			
Capital outlay	10,396	10,454	(58)
Total expenditures	13,088	12,985	103
Excess (deficiency) of revenues over expenditures			
Other financing sources (uses):			
Transfers in			
Transfers out			
Total other financing sources (uses)			
Excess (deficiency) of revenues and other financing sources over expenditures and other financing uses			
Fund balances (deficits), July 1, 2000			
Increase in reserve for inventory			
Increase in reserve for prepaid items			
Fund balances (deficits), June 30, 2001	$	$	$

Title IV - Safe and Drug Free Schools			Title VI - Innovative Education Program		
Budget	Actual	Variance - Favorable (Unfavorable)	Budget	Actual	Variance - Favorable (Unfavorable)
$	$	$	$	$	$
29,198	14,439	(14,759)	20,087	19,665	(422)
29,198	14,439	(14,759)	20,087	19,665	(422)
5,274	2,904	2,370	19,687	19,265	422
23,644	11,286	12,358			
28,918	14,190	14,728	19,687	19,265	422
280	249	(31)	400	400	
(280)	(249)	31	(400)	(400)	
(280)	(249)	31	(400)	(400)	
$	$	$	$	$	$

(Continued)

AVONDALE ELEMENTARY SCHOOL DISTRICT NO. 44
COMBINING SCHEDULE OF REVENUES, EXPENDITURES AND CHANGES IN
FUND BALANCES - BUDGET AND ACTUAL - NON-MAJOR SPECIAL REVENUE FUNDS
YEAR ENDED JUNE 30, 2001
(Continued)

| | EHA Title VI-B Entitlement | | |
	Budget	Actual	Variance - Favorable (Unfavorable)
Revenues:			
Other local	$	$	$
State aid and grants			
Federal aid, grants and reimbursements	352,621	276,119	(76,502)
Total revenues	352,621	276,119	(76,502)
Expenditures:			
Current -			
Instruction	222,081	178,477	43,604
Support services - students and staff	120,650	97,899	22,751
Support services - administration	2,398	150	2,248
Operation and maintenance of plant services			
Student transportation services			
Operation of non-instructional services			
Capital outlay			
Total expenditures	345,129	276,526	68,603
Excess (deficiency) of revenues over expenditures	7,492	(407)	(7,899)
Other financing sources (uses):			
Transfers in			
Transfers out	(7,492)	(6,089)	1,403
Total other financing sources (uses)	(7,492)	(6,089)	1,403
Excess (deficiency) of revenues and other financing sources over expenditures and other financing uses		(6,496)	(6,496)
Fund balances (deficits), July 1, 2000			
Increase in reserve for inventory			
Increase in reserve for prepaid items		6,496	6,496
Fund balances (deficits), June 30, 2001	$	$	$

	Federal Preschool			Emergency Immigrant Education		
	Budget	Actual	Variance - Favorable (Unfavorable)	Budget	Actual	Variance - Favorable (Unfavorable)
	$	$	$	$	$	$
	25,574	22,208	(3,366)	43,911	21,437	(22,474)
	25,574	22,208	(3,366)	43,911	21,437	(22,474)
	25,024	21,728	3,296	13,379	13,442	(63)
				16,113	5,201	10,912
				13,768	2,302	11,466
	25,024	21,728	3,296	43,260	20,945	22,315
	550	480	(70)	651	492	(159)
	(550)	(480)	70	(651)	(492)	159
	(550)	(480)	70	(651)	(492)	159
	$	$	$	$	$	$

(Continued)

AVONDALE ELEMENTARY SCHOOL DISTRICT NO. 44
COMBINING SCHEDULE OF REVENUES, EXPENDITURES AND CHANGES IN
FUND BALANCES - BUDGET AND ACTUAL - NON-MAJOR SPECIAL REVENUE FUNDS
YEAR ENDED JUNE 30, 2001
(Continued)

| | Medicaid Reimbursement | | |
	Budget	Actual	Variance - Favorable (Unfavorable)
Revenues:			
Other local	$	$	$
State aid and grants			
Federal aid, grants and reimbursements	34,000	35,703	1,703
Total revenues	34,000	35,703	1,703
Expenditures:			
Current -			
Instruction			
Support services - students and staff			
Support services - administration			
Operation and maintenance of plant services			
Student transportation services	34,000	2,127	31,873
Operation of non-instructional services			
Capital outlay			
Total expenditures	34,000	2,127	31,873
Excess (deficiency) of revenues over expenditures		33,576	33,576
Other financing sources (uses):			
Transfers in			
Transfers out			
Total other financing sources (uses)			
Excess (deficiency) of revenues and other financing sources over expenditures and other financing uses		33,576	33,576
Fund balances (deficits), July 1, 2000		66,574	66,574
Increase in reserve for inventory			
Increase in reserve for prepaid items			
Fund balances (deficits), June 30, 2001	$	$ 100,150	$ 100,150

* The E-Rate Fund was included in the District's budget, however, the budget was -0-.

	Title III - Goals 2000				E - Rate	
Budget	Actual	Variance - Favorable (Unfavorable)	Budget*	Actual	Variance - Favorable (Unfavorable)
$	$	$	$	$	$
72,838	68,135	(4,703)		299,072	299,072
72,838	68,135	(4,703)		299,072	299,072
36		36		17,127	(17,127)
71,263	66,784	4,479			
				11,081	(11,081)
				3,816	(3,816)
				264,544	(264,544)
71,299	66,784	4,515		296,568	(296,568)
1,539	1,351	(188)		2,504	2,504
(1,539)	(1,351)	188			
(1,539)	(1,351)	188			
				2,504	2,504
$	$	$	$	$ 2,504	$ 2,504

(Continued)

| | Class Size Reduction | | |
	Budget	Actual	Variance - Favorable (Unfavorable)
Revenues:			
Other local	$	$	$
State aid and grants			
Federal aid, grants and reimbursements	105,381	93,647	(11,734)
Total revenues	105,381	93,647	(11,734)
Expenditures:			
Current -			
Instruction	103,106	92,833	10,273
Support services - students and staff			
Support services - administration			
Operation and maintenance of plant services			
Student transportation services			
Operation of non-instructional services			
Capital outlay			
Total expenditures	103,106	92,833	10,273
Excess (deficiency) of revenues over expenditures	2,275	814	(1,461)
Other financing sources (uses):			
Transfers in			
Transfers out	(2,275)	(2,052)	223
Total other financing sources (uses)	(2,275)	(2,052)	223
Excess (deficiency) of revenues and other financing sources over expenditures and other financing uses		(1,238)	(1,238)
Fund balances (deficits), July 1, 2000			
Increase in reserve for inventory			
Increase in reserve for prepaid items		1,238	1,238
Fund balances (deficits), June 30, 2001	$	$	$

| | Early Childhood | | | | State Chemical Abuse | |
	Budget	Actual	Variance - Favorable (Unfavorable)		Budget	Actual	Variance - Favorable (Unfavorable)
$	155,489	$ 147,969	$ (7,520)	$	10,158	$ 8,301	$ (1,857)
	155,489	147,969	(7,520)		10,158	8,301	(1,857)
	141,325	136,807	4,518				
	11,979	11,981	(2)		10,158	8,301	1,857
	2,185	2,275	(90)				
	155,489	151,063	4,426		10,158	8,301	1,857
		(3,094)	(3,094)				
		(3,094)	(3,094)				
		3,094	3,094				
$		$	$		$	$	$

(Continued)

AVONDALE ELEMENTARY SCHOOL DISTRICT NO. 44
COMBINING SCHEDULE OF REVENUES, EXPENDITURES AND CHANGES IN
FUND BALANCES - BUDGET AND ACTUAL - NON-MAJOR SPECIAL REVENUE FUNDS
YEAR ENDED JUNE 30, 2001
(Continued)

| | Gifted Education | | |
	Budget	Actual	Variance - Favorable (Unfavorable)
Revenues:			
Other local	$	$	$
State aid and grants	5,299	5,299	
Federal aid, grants and reimbursements			
Total revenues	5,299	5,299	
Expenditures:			
Current -			
Instruction	1,100	987	113
Support services - students and staff	2,467	2,610	(143)
Support services - administration			
Operation and maintenance of plant services			
Student transportation services			
Operation of non-instructional services			
Capital outlay	1,732	1,702	30
Total expenditures	5,299	5,299	
Excess (deficiency) of revenues over expenditures			
Other financing sources (uses):			
Transfers in			
Transfers out			
Total other financing sources (uses)			
Excess (deficiency) of revenues and other financing sources over expenditures and other financing uses			
Fund balances (deficits), July 1, 2000			
Increase in reserve for inventory			
Increase in reserve for prepaid items			
Fund balances (deficits), June 30, 2001	$	$	$

	School Plant			Food Services		
	Budget	Actual	Variance - Favorable (Unfavorable)	Budget	Actual	Variance - Favorable (Unfavorable)
$		$ 12,192	$ 12,192	$ 258,844	$ 284,668	$ 25,824
				843,748	816,510	(27,238)
		12,192	12,192	1,102,592	1,101,178	(1,414)
				1,280,000	1,063,078	216,922
					25,552	(25,552)
				1,280,000	1,088,630	191,370
		12,192	12,192	(177,408)	12,548	189,956
					(11,186)	(11,186)
					(11,186)	(11,186)
		12,192	12,192	(177,408)	1,362	178,770
	107,447	107,446	(1)	177,408	203,180	25,772
					2,319	2,319
					13,613	13,613
$	107,447	$ 119,638	$ 12,191	$	$ 220,474	$ 220,474

(Continued)

	Civic Center		
	Budget	Actual	Variance - Favorable (Unfavorable)
Revenues:			
Other local	$	$ 70,900	$ 70,900
State aid and grants			
Federal aid, grants and reimbursements			
Total revenues		70,900	70,900
Expenditures:			
Current -			
Instruction			
Support services - students and staff	55,000	10,558	44,442
Support services - administration			
Operation and maintenance of plant services			
Student transportation services		2,625	(2,625)
Operation of non-instructional services		4,100	(4,100)
Capital outlay			
Total expenditures	55,000	17,283	37,717
Excess (deficiency) of revenues over expenditures	(55,000)	53,617	108,617
Other financing sources (uses):			
Transfers in			
Transfers out			
Total other financing sources (uses)			
Excess (deficiency) of revenues and other financing sources over expenditures and other financing uses	(55,000)	53,617	108,617
Fund balances (deficits), July 1, 2000	72,258	72,258	
Increase in reserve for inventory			
Increase in reserve for prepaid items			
Fund balances (deficits), June 30, 2001	$ 17,258	$ 125,875	$ 108,617

	Community School			Extracurricular Activities Fees Tax Credit		
	Budget	Actual	Variance - Favorable (Unfavorable)	Budget	Actual	Variance - Favorable (Unfavorable)
	$ 2,554	$ 553	$ (2,001)	$ 8,184	$ 9,798	$ 1,614
	2,554	553	(2,001)	8,184	9,798	1,614
				16,100	11,586	4,514
	5,000		5,000			
	5,000		5,000	16,100	11,586	4,514
	(2,446)	553	2,999	(7,916)	(1,788)	6,128
	(2,446)	553	2,999	(7,916)	(1,788)	6,128
	2,446	2,446		6,816	6,816	
	$	$ 2,999	$ 2,999	$ (1,100)	$ 5,028	$ 6,128

(Continued)

AVONDALE ELEMENTARY SCHOOL DISTRICT NO. 44
COMBINING SCHEDULE OF REVENUES, EXPENDITURES AND CHANGES IN
FUND BALANCES - BUDGET AND ACTUAL - NON-MAJOR SPECIAL REVENUE FUNDS
YEAR ENDED JUNE 30, 2001
(Continued)

| | Gifts and Donations | | |
	Budget	Actual	Variance - Favorable (Unfavorable)
Revenues:			
Other local	$ 29,336	$ 8,556	$ (20,780)
State aid and grants			
Federal aid, grants and reimbursements			
Total revenues	29,336	8,556	(20,780)
Expenditures:			
Current -			
Instruction		2,403	(2,403)
Support services - students and staff		3,963	(3,963)
Support services - administration			
Operation and maintenance of plant services			
Student transportation services			
Operation of non-instructional services	35,000	217	34,783
Capital outlay			
Total expenditures	35,000	6,583	28,417
Excess (deficiency) of revenues over expenditures	(5,664)	1,973	7,637
Other financing sources (uses):			
Transfers in			
Transfers out			
Total other financing sources (uses)			
Excess (deficiency) of revenues and other financing sources over expenditures and other financing uses	(5,664)	1,973	7,637
Fund balances (deficits), July 1, 2000	5,664	5,664	
Increase in reserve for inventory			
Increase in reserve for prepaid items			
Fund balances (deficits), June 30, 2001	$	$ 7,637	$ 7,637

District Services				Fingerprinting			
Budget		Actual	Variance - Favorable (Unfavorable)	Budget		Actual	Variance - Favorable (Unfavorable)
$	$ 3,616	$ 3,616		$ 976	$ 2,097	$ 1,121	
	3,616	3,616		976	2,097	1,121	
16,000		16,000		5,000	730	4,270	
16,000		16,000		5,000	730	4,270	
(16,000)	3,616	19,616		(4,024)	1,367	5,391	
(16,000)	3,616	19.616		(4,024)	1,367	5,391	
59,905	59,505	(400)		24	24		
$ 43,905	$ 63,121	$ 19,216		$ (4,000)	$ 1,391	$ 5,391	

(Continued)

	School Opening		
	Budget	Actual	Variance - Favorable (Unfavorable)
Revenues:			
Other local	$ 36,727	$	$ (36,727)
State aid and grants			
Federal aid, grants and reimbursements			
Total revenues	36,727		(36,727)
Expenditures:			
Current -			
Instruction			
Support services - students and staff			
Support services - administration			
Operation and maintenance of plant services			
Student transportation services			
Operation of non-instructional services			
Capital outlay			
Total expenditures			
Excess (deficiency) of revenues over expenditures	36,727		(36,727)
Other financing sources (uses):			
Transfers in			
Transfers out			
Total other financing sources (uses)			
Excess (deficiency) of revenues and other financing sources over expenditures and other financing uses	36,727		(36,727)
Fund balances (deficits), July 1, 2000	(36,727)		36,727
Increase in reserve for inventory			
Increase in reserve for prepaid items			
Fund balances (deficits), June 30, 2001	$	$	$

	Insurance Proceeds				Textbooks		
	Budget	Actual	Variance - Favorable (Unfavorable)		Budget	Actual	Variance - Favorable (Unfavorable)
$		$ 4,538	$ 4,538	$	6,145	$ 1,615	$ (4,530)
		4,538	4,538		6,145	1,615	(4,530)
					15,000	3,914	11,086
	30,000	357	29,643				
	30,000	357	29,643		15,000	3,914	11,086
	(30,000)	4,181	34,181		(8,855)	(2,299)	6,556
	(30,000)	4,181	34,181		(8,855)	(2,299)	6,556
	33,597	33,597			8,855	8,855	
$	3,597	$ 37,778	$ 34,181	$		$ 6,556	$ 6,556

(Continued)

AVONDALE ELEMENTARY SCHOOL DISTRICT NO. 44
COMBINING SCHEDULE OF REVENUES, EXPENDITURES AND CHANGES IN
FUND BALANCES - BUDGET AND ACTUAL - NON-MAJOR SPECIAL REVENUE FUNDS
YEAR ENDED JUNE 30, 2001
(Continued)

| | Indirect Costs | | |
	Budget	Actual	Variance - Favorable (Unfavorable)
Revenues:			
Other local	$	$ 3,571	$ 3,571
State aid and grants			
Federal aid, grants and reimbursements			
Total revenues		3,571	3,571
Expenditures:			
Current -			
Instruction			
Support services - students and staff			
Support services - administration	80,000	38,508	41,492
Operation and maintenance of plant services			
Student transportation services			
Operation of non-instructional services			
Capital outlay			
Total expenditures	80,000	38,508	41,492
Excess (deficiency) of revenues over expenditures	(80,000)	(34,937)	45,063
Other financing sources (uses):			
Transfers in	15,621	42,677	27,056
Transfers out			
Total other financing sources (uses)	15,621	42,677	27,056
Excess (deficiency) of revenues and other financing sources over expenditures and other financing uses	(64,379)	7,740	72,119
Fund balances (deficits), July 1, 2000	64,379	64,379	
Increase in reserve for inventory			
Increase in reserve for prepaid items			
Fund balances (deficits), June 30, 2001	$	$ 72,119	$ 72,119

	Unemployment Insurance				Insurance Refund		
	Budget	Actual	Variance - Favorable (Unfavorable)		Budget	Actual	Variance - Favorable (Unfavorable)
	$	$ 31,414	$ 31,414		$	$ 565	$ 565
		31,414	31,414			565	565
	20,000	9,456	10,544		1,000		1,000
	20,000	9,456	10,544		1,000		1,000
	(20,000)	21,958	41,958		(1,000)	565	1,565
	(20,000)	21,958	41,958		(1,000)	565	1,565
	521,191	521,191			9,294	9,294	
	$ 501,191	$ 543,149	$ 41,958		$ 8,294	$ 9,859	$ 1,565

(Continued)

AVONDALE ELEMENTARY SCHOOL DISTRICT NO. 44
COMBINING SCHEDULE OF REVENUES, EXPENDITURES AND CHANGES IN
FUND BALANCES - BUDGET AND ACTUAL - NON-MAJOR SPECIAL REVENUE FUNDS
YEAR ENDED JUNE 30, 2001
(Concluded)

| | Grants and Gifts to Teachers | | |
	Budget	Actual	Variance - Favorable (Unfavorable)
Revenues:			
Other local	$ 8,866	$ 7,990	$ (876)
State aid and grants			
Federal aid, grants and reimbursements			
Total revenues	8,866	7,990	(876)
Expenditures:			
Current -			
Instruction	12,000	8,676	3,324
Support services - students and staff			
Support services - administration			
Operation and maintenance of plant services			
Student transportation services			
Operation of non-instructional services			
Capital outlay			
Total expenditures	12,000	8,676	3,324
Excess (deficiency) of revenues over expenditures	(3,134)	(686)	2,448
Other financing sources (uses):			
Transfers in			
Transfers out			
Total other financing sources (uses)			
Excess (deficiency) of revenues and other financing sources over expenditures and other financing uses	(3,134)	(686)	2,448
Fund balances (deficits), July 1, 2000	3,134	3,133	(1)
Increase in reserve for inventory			
Increase in reserve for prepaid items			
Fund balances (deficits), June 30, 2001	$	$ 2,447	$ 2,447

| Inter governmental Agreements | | | | Totals | | |
Budget	Actual	Variance - Favorable (Unfavorable)		Budget	Actual	Variance - Favorable (Unfavorable)
$ 5,713	$ 24,971	$ 19,258		$ 357,345	$ 467,044	$ 109,699
				170,946	161,569	(9,377)
				2,533,681	2,603,559	69,878
5,713	24,971	19,258		3,061,972	3,232,172	170,200
				1,302,752	1,222,246	80,506
24,400	22,527	1,873		547,436	402,281	145,155
				190,422	113,357	77,065
					3,816	(3,816)
				34,000	4,752	29,248
				1,320,376	1,072,014	248,362
				25,896	304,554	(278,658)
24,400	22,527	1,873		3,420,882	3,123,020	297,862
(18,687)	2,444	21,131		(358,910)	109,152	468,062
				15,621	42,677	27,056
				(34,497)	(42,677)	(8,180)
				(18,876)		18,876
(18,687)	2,444	21,131		(377,786)	109,152	486,938
9,287	9,286	(1)		1,044,978	1,173,648	128,670
					2,319	2,319
					47,336	47,336
$ (9,400)	$ 11,730	$ 21,130		$ 667,192	$ 1,332,455	$ 665,263

(This page intentionally left blank)

NON-MAJOR CAPITAL PROJECTS FUNDS

The following Capital Projects Funds are maintained by the District. Arizona Revised Statutes (A.R.S.) and the Uniform System of Financial Records (USFR) require the establishment of these funds for the specified activities.

Unrestricted Capital Fund - to account for transactions relating to the acquisition of capital items other than Soft Capital by purchase or lease as prescribed by A.R.S.

Adjacent Ways Fund - to account for monies received to finance improvements on property adjacent to the school, such as public streets or alleys, or improvements on school property that provide safe access for buses and fire equipment.

Soft Capital Fund - to account for transactions relating to the acquisition of capital items that are capital materials and equipment needed to assist students in mastering Arizona's Academic Standards.

Gifts and Donations Fund - to account for gifts and donations to be expended for capital acquisition.

Capital Equity Fund - to account for monies received from the State for capital improvements.

Deficiencies Correction Fund - to account for monies received from the School Facilities Board that are used to correct deficiencies in square footage and in quality of facilities and equipment.

New School Facilities Fund - to account for monies received from the School Facilities Board that are used to purchase land, to construct new school buildings, and related architectural and engineering fees.

Building Renewal Fund - to account for monies received from the School Facilities Board that are used for infrastructure or for major upgrades, repairs, or renovations to areas, systems or buildings that will maintain or extend their useful life.

	Unrestricted Capital	Adjacent Ways	Soft Capital	Gifts and Donations
ASSETS				
Cash and investments	$ 143,002	$ 100,426	$ 302,792	$ 461,249
Property taxes receivable		104	7,678	
Total assets	$ 143,002	$ 100,530	$ 310,470	$ 461,249
LIABILITIES AND FUND EQUITY				
Liabilities:				
Accounts payable	$ 10,874	$	$ 2,265	$ 25,322
Deferred revenues		104	5,147	
Construction contracts payable				
Total liabilities	10,874	104	7,412	25,322
Fund equity:				
Fund balances -				
Unreserved:				
Designated for capital outlay	132,128	100,426	303,058	435,927
Total fund equity	132,128	100,426	303,058	435,927
Total liabilities and fund equity	$ 143,002	$ 100,530	$ 310,470	$ 461,249

Capital Equity	Deficiencies Correction	New School Facilities	Building Renewal	Totals
$ 339	$ 3,619	$ 522,549	$ 491,778	$ 2,025,754
				7,782
$ 339	$ 3,619	$ 522,549	$ 491,778	$ 2,033,536
$	$	$	$	$ 38,461
				5,251
		4,731	59,361	64,092
		4,731	59,361	107,804
339	3,619	517,818	432,417	1,925,732
339	3,619	517,818	432,417	1,925,732
$ 339	$ 3,619	$ 522,549	$ 491,778	$ 2,033,536

	Unrestricted Capital	Adjacent Ways	Soft Capital
Revenues:			
Other local	$ 40,318	$ 4,994	$ 59,238
Property taxes	227	24,584	165,182
State aid and grants	154,823	10	745,256
Total revenues	195,368	29,588	969,676
Expenditures:			
Capital outlay	473,168	6,634	657,911
Debt service -			
Interest, premium and fiscal charges	12,923		
Principal retirement	71,032		
Total expenditures	557,123	6,634	657,911
Excess (deficiency) of revenues over expenditures	(361,755)	22,954	311,765
Fund balances (deficits), beginning of year	493,883	77,472	(8,707)
Fund balances, end of year	$ 132,128	$ 100,426	$ 303,058

Gifts and Donations	Capital Equity	Deficiencies Correction	New School Facilities	Building Renewal	Totals
$ 358,270	$ 329	$	$	$ 1	$ 463,150
					189,993
		253,281	515,785	300,140	1,969,295
358,270	329	253,281	515,785	300,141	2,622,438
25,322	23,200	249,662	305,788	204,098	1,945,783
					12,923
					71,032
25,322	23,200	249,662	305,788	204,098	2,029,738
332,948	(22,871)	3,619	209,997	96,043	592,700
102,979	23,210		307,821	336,374	1,333,032
$ 435,927	$ 339	$ 3,619	$ 517,818	$ 432,417	$ 1,925,732

AVONDALE ELEMENTARY SCHOOL DISTRICT NO. 44
COMBINING SCHEDULE OF REVENUES, EXPENDITURES AND CHANGES IN
FUND BALANCES - BUDGET AND ACTUAL - NON-MAJOR CAPITAL PROJECTS FUNDS
YEAR ENDED JUNE 30, 2001

| | Unrestricted Capital | | |
	Budget	Actual	Variance - Favorable (Unfavorable)
Revenues:			
Other local	$ 25,000	$ 40,318	$ 15,318
Property taxes		227	227
State aid and grants	46,784	154,823	108,039
Total revenues	71,784	195,368	123,584
Expenditures:			
Capital outlay	666,126	473,168	192,958
Debt service -			
Interest, premium and fiscal charges		12,923	(12,923)
Principal retirement		71,032	(71,032)
Total expenditures	666,126	557,123	109,003
Excess (deficiency) of revenues over expenditures	(594,342)	(361,755)	232,587
Fund balances (deficits), July 1, 2000	530,610	493,883	(36,727)
Fund balances (deficits), June 30, 2001	$ (63,732)	$ 132,128	$ 195,860

	Adjacent Ways				Soft Capital		
	Budget	Actual	Variance - Favorable (Unfavorable)		Budget	Actual	Variance - Favorable (Unfavorable)
$	5,094	$ 4,994	$ (100)	$	51,632	$ 59,238	$ 7,606
	30,434	24,584	(5,850)		167,190	165,182	(2,008)
		10	10		511,057	745,256	234,199
	35,528	29,588	(5,940)		729,879	969,676	239,797
	113,000	6,634	106,366		707,121	657,911	49,210
	113,000	6,634	106,366		707,121	657,911	49,210
	(77,472)	22,954	100,426		22,758	311,765	289,007
	77,472	77,472			(12,084)	(8,707)	3,377
$		$ 100,426	$ 100,426	$	10,674	$ 303,058	$ 292,384

(Continued)

| | Gifts and Donations | | |
	Budget	Actual	Variance - Favorable (Unfavorable)
Revenues:			
Other local	$	$ 358,270	$ 358,270
Property taxes			
State aid and grants			
Total revenues		358,270	358,270
Expenditures:			
Capital outlay	100,000	25,322	74,678
Debt service -			
Interest, premium and fiscal charges			
Principal retirement			
Total expenditures	100,000	25,322	74,678
Excess (deficiency) of revenues over expenditures	(100,000)	332,948	432,948
Fund balances (deficits), July 1, 2000	102,979	102,979	
Fund balances (deficits), June 30, 2001	$ 2,979	$ 435,927	$ 432,948

	Capital Equity				Deficiencies Correction		
	Budget	Actual	Variance - Favorable (Unfavorable)		Budget	Actual	Variance - Favorable (Unfavorable)
$	1,790	$ 329	$ (1,461)	$		$	$
						253,281	253,281
	1,790	329	(1,461)			253,281	253,281
	25,000	23,200	1,800		250,000	249,662	338
	25,000	23,200	1,800		250,000	249,662	338
	(23,210)	(22,871)	339		(250,000)	3,619	253,619
	23,210	23,210					
$		$ 339	$ 339	$	(250,000)	$ 3,619	$ 253,619

(Continued)

| | New School Facilities | | |
	Budget	Actual	Variance - Favorable (Unfavorable)
Revenues:			
Other local	$	$	$
Property taxes			
State aid and grants	442,179	515,785	73,606
Total revenues	442,179	515,785	73,606
Expenditures:			
Capital outlay	750,000	305,788	444,212
Debt service -			
Interest, premium and fiscal charges			
Principal retirement			
Total expenditures	750,000	305,788	444,212
Excess (deficiency) of revenues over expenditures	(307,821)	209,997	517,818
Fund balances (deficits), July 1, 2000	307,821	307,821	
Fund balances (deficits), June 30, 2001	$	$ 517,818	$ 517,818

Building Renewal			Totals		
Budget	Actual	Variance - Favorable (Unfavorable)	Budget	Actual	Variance - Favorable (Unfavorable)
$	$ 1	$ 1	$ 83,516	$ 463,150	$ 379,634
			197,624	189,993	(7,631)
131,701	300,140	168,439	1,131,721	1,969,295	837,574
131,701	300,141	168,440	1,412,861	2,622,438	1,209,577
468,075	204,098	263,977	3,079,322	1,945,783	1,133,539
				12,923	(12,923)
				71,032	(71,032)
468,075	204,098	263,977	3,079,322	2,029,738	1,049,584
(336,374)	96,043	432,417	(1,666,461)	592,700	2,259,161
336,374	336,374		1,366,382	1,333,032	(33,350)
$	$ 432,417	$ 432,417	$ (300,079)	$ 1,925,732	$ 2,225,811

(This page intentionally left blank)

AGENCY FUNDS

Student Activities Fund - to account for monies raised by students to finance student clubs and organizations but held by the District as an agent.

Employee Withholding Fund - to account for unremitted payroll deductions temporarily held by the District as an agent.

	Student Activities	Employee Withholding	Total
ASSETS			
Cash and investments	$ 30,804	$ 39,137	$ 69,941
Total assets	30,804	39,137	69,941
LIABILITIES			
Deposits held for others		39,137	39,137
Due to student groups	30,804		30,804
Total liabilities	$ 30,804	$ 39,137	$ 69,941
NET ASSETS	$ -	$ -	$ -

AVONDALE ELEMENTARY SCHOOL DISTRICT NO. 44
COMBINING STATEMENT OF CHANGES IN ASSETS AND LIABILITIES - AGENCY FUNDS
YEAR ENDED JUNE 30, 2001

	Balance July 1, 2000	Additions	Deductions	Balance June 30, 2001
STUDENT ACTIVITIES FUND				
Assets				
Cash and investments	$ 23,892	$ 195,750	$ 188,838	$ 30,804
Total assets	$ 23,892	$ 195,750	$ 188,838	$ 30,804
Liabilities				
Due to student groups	$ 23,892	$ 195,750	$ 188,838	$ 30,804
Total liabilities	$ 23,892	$ 195,750	$ 188,838	$ 30,804
EMPLOYEE WITHHOLDING FUND				
Assets				
Cash and investments	$ 28,448	$ 753,691	$ 743,002	$ 39,137
Total assets	$ 28,448	$ 753,691	$ 743,002	$ 39,137
Liabilities				
Deposits held for others	$ 28,448	$ 753,691	$ 743,002	$ 39,137
Total liabilities	$ 28,448	$ 753,691	$ 743,002	$ 39,137
TOTAL AGENCY FUNDS				
Assets				
Cash and investments	$ 52,340	$ 949,441	$ 931,840	$ 69,941
Total assets	$ 52,340	$ 949,441	$ 931,840	$ 69,941
Liabilities				
Deposits held for others	$ 28,448	$ 753,691	$ 743,002	$ 39,137
Due to student groups	23,892	195,750	188,838	30,804
Total liabilities	$ 52,340	$ 949,441	$ 931,840	$ 69,941

(This page intentionally left blank)

CAPITAL ASSETS USED IN THE OPERATION OF GOVERNMENTAL FUNDS

Governmental funds capital assets

Land and improvements	$	446,835
Buildings and improvements		22,491,680
Vehicles, furniture and equipment		1,808,059
Construction in progress		304,488
Total governmental funds capital assets	$	25,051,062

Investments in governmental funds capital assets by source

Special Revenue Funds	$	3,006,127
Capital Projects Funds		21,919,680
Donations		125,255
Total governmental funds capital assets	$	25,051,062

AVONDALE ELEMENTARY SCHOOL DISTRICT NO. 44
CAPITAL ASSETS USED IN THE OPERATION OF GOVERNMENTAL FUNDS
SCHEDULE BY FUNCTION AND ACTIVITY
JUNE 30, 2001

Function and Activity	Land and Improvements	Buildings and Improvements	Vehicles, Furniture and Equipment	Construction In Progress	Total
Instruction	$ 446,835	$ 20,838,519	$ 201,051	$ 304,488	$ 21,790,893
Support services - students and staff		489,143	159,188		648,331
Support services - administration		303,946	34,679		338,625
Operation and maintenance of plant services		551,531	111,735		663,266
Student transportation services		86,366	1,193,062		1,279,428
Operation of non-instructional services		222,175	108,344		330,519
Total	$ 446,835	$ 22,491,680	$ 1,808,059	$ 304,488	$ 25,051,062

AVONDALE ELEMENTARY SCHOOL DISTRICT NO. 44
CAPITAL ASSETS USED IN THE OPERATION OF GOVERNMENTAL FUNDS
SCHEDULE OF CHANGES BY FUNCTION AND ACTIVITY
YEAR ENDED JUNE 30, 2001

Function and Activity	General Fixed Assets July 1, 2000	Additions	Deletions	General Fixed Assets June 30, 2001
Instruction	$ 20,568,792	2,440,684	1,218,583	21,790,893
Support service - students and staff	564,169	84,162		648,331
Support services - administration	310,572	28,053		338,625
Operation and maintenance of plant services	578,077	85,189		663,266
Student transportation services	1,139,159	140,269		1,279,428
Operation of non-instructional services	303,492	27,027		330,519
Total	23,464,261	2,805,384	1,218,583	25,051,062

STATISTICAL SECTION

Fiscal Year	Support Services - Administration	Instruction & Support Services - Students & Staff	Operation & Maintenance of Plant Services	Student Transportation Services	Operation of Non-Instructional Services	Interest on Long-term Debt	Total
2000-01	$ 1,531,860	$ 11,312,903	$ 1,661,091	$ 717,784	$ 1,180,000	$ 580,612	$ 16,984,250

* The provisions of the Governmental Accounting Standards Board (GASB) Statement No. 34 were adopted in fiscal year 2001 therefore only one year is shown. The source of this information is District records.

Government-wide Expenses

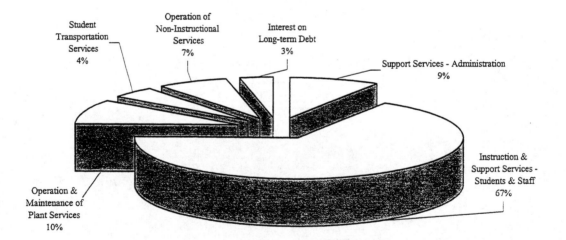

	PROGRAM REVENUES			GENERAL REVENUES				
Fiscal Year	Charges for Services	Operating Grants & Contributions	Capital Grants & Contributions	Property Taxes	Investment Income	County Aid	State Aid	Total
2000-01	$ 400,265	$ 2,484,379	$ 638,128	$ 4,046,440	$ 284,876	$ 850,003	$ 10,736,591	$ 19,440,682

* The provisions of the Governmental Accounting Standards Board (GASB) Statement No. 34 were adopted in fiscal year 2001 therefore only one year is shown. The source of this information is District records.

Government-wide Revenues

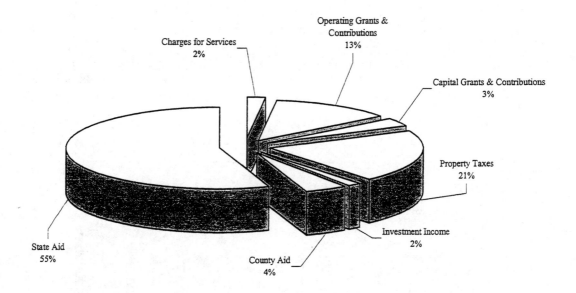

Fiscal Year		Instruction & Suppport Services - Student & Staff	Support Services - Administration	Operation & Maintenance of Plant Services	Student Transportation Services	Operation of Non-instructional Services	Capital Outlay	Debt Service	Total
2000-01		$ 10,087,071	$ 1,455,641	$ 1,583,815	$ 460,365	$ 1,088,019	$ 304,554	$ 1,767,689	$ 16,747,1:
1999-00		8,838,282	1,350,388	1,475,065	426,006	1,052,299	411,512	2,031,109	15,584,6
1998-99	**	8,340,427	1,411,422	1,443,340	415,185	1,016,181	370,167	1,565,996	14,562,7
1997-98		8,358,524	581,542	1,276,229	363,183	972,503	24,798	1,309,163	12,885,9
1996-97		7,981,868	567,969	1,420,716	339,412	925,872	75,233	1,216,583	12,527,6
1995-96		7,904,668	541,311	1,339,203	327,601	928,929	92,227	1,232,121	12,366,0
1994-95		8,007,782	555,053	1,391,550	310,228	886,939	41,599	1,306,187	12,499,3
1993-94		7,446,225	531,566	1,305,905	297,744	811,039	54,556	1,216,631	11,663,6
1992-93		7,148,905	525,147	1,380,377	284,509	729,127	33,409	1,314,596	11,416,0
1991-92		6,759,874	568,914	1,400,004	255,067	700,185	43,254	1,376,043	11,103,3

* Funds included are General, Special Revenue and Debt Service. The source of this information is District records.
** New functional categories were adopted in fiscal year 1998-99.

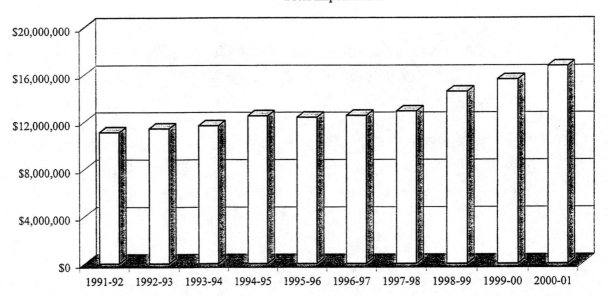

Total Expenditures

AVONDALE ELEMENTARY SCHOOL DISTRICT NO. 44
GENERAL SCHOOL SYSTEM REVENUES BY SOURCE*
LAST 10 FISCAL YEARS
(UNAUDITED)

Fiscal Year	Investment Income	Other Local County Aid & Grants	Other Local Food Services Sales	Other Local Other	Property Taxes	State Aid and Grants	Federal Aid, Grants & Reimbursements	Total
2000-01	$ 145,955	$ 770,360	$ 280,712	$ 130,991	$ 3,902,160	$ 8,928,865	$ 2,603,559	$ 16,762,602
1999-00	91,632	642,906	236,955	95,320	3,527,168	8,081,261	2,326,543	15,001,785
1998-99	176,912	628,778	197,910	108,782	3,115,881	8,199,740	2,259,837	14,687,840
1997-98	120,647	608,499	210,488	228,274	2,575,581	7,585,880	1,899,521	13,228,890
1996-97	128,050	578,004	176,995	148,905	2,566,489	7,207,526	1,865,949	12,671,918
1995-96	95,530	604,450	171,646	105,093	2,456,107	7,100,635	1,878,858	12,412,319
1994-95	72,463	636,833	143,687	75,710	2,496,286	7,155,204	1,845,949	12,426,132
1993-94	70,113	623,092	139,752	47,990	2,447,334	6,450,721	1,879,580	11,658,582
1992-93	142,406	619,509	137,629	45,424	2,208,711	6,345,265	1,482,078	10,981,022
1991-92	206,983	766,363	143,570	21,515	2,390,533	6,232,903	1,391,580	11,153,447

* Funds included are General, Special Revenue and Debt Service. The source of this information is District records.

Total Revenues

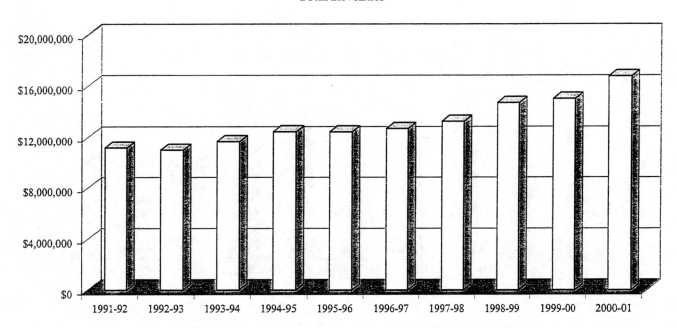

AVONDALE ELEMENTARY SCHOOL DISTRICT NO. 44
PROPERTY TAX LEVIES AND COLLECTIONS*
LAST 10 FISCAL YEARS
(UNAUDITED)

Fiscal Year	Real Property Tax Levy	Collected to June 30th End of Tax Fiscal Year		Collected to June 30, 2001	
		Amount	Percent of Levy	Amount	Percent of Levy
2000-01	$ 3,935,515	$ 3,702,921	94.09 %	$ 3,702,921	94.09 %
1999-00	3,541,198	3,332,627	94.11	3,524,359	99.52
1998-99	3,152,012	2,975,814	94.41	3,116,562	98.88
1997-98	2,687,195	2,502,551	93.13	2,680,353	99.75
1996-97	2,454,434	2,345,150	95.55	2,443,401	99.55
1995-96	2,640,143	2,490,713	94.34	2,622,155	99.32
1994-95	2,562,802	2,370,099	92.48	2,510,283	97.95
1993-94	2,475,482	2,318,899	93.67	2,396,469	96.81
1992-93	2,442,469	2,293,549	93.90	2,374,998	97.24
1991-92	2,735,908	2,460,336	89.93	2,669,451	97.57

* Unsecured personal property taxes are not included in this schedule because the dates of the monthly rolls vary each year.
On the average, 93% of unsecured property taxes are collected within 90 days after the due date.

Amounts collected are on a cash basis.

The source of this information is the Maricopa Treasurer's records.

Property Taxes Collected to End of Fiscal Year

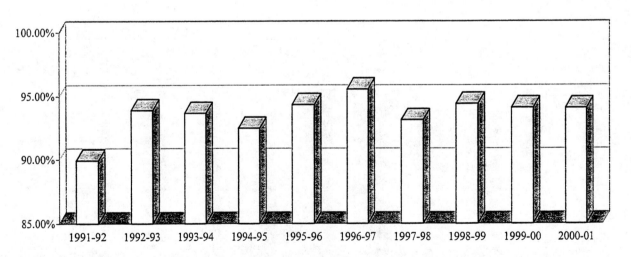

AVONDALE ELEMENTARY SCHOOL DISTRICT NO. 44
ASSESSED AND ESTIMATED ACTUAL VALUE OF TAXABLE PROPERTY*
LAST 10 YEARS
(UNAUDITED)

Fiscal Year	Net Secondary Assessed Value	Estimated Actual Value	Ratio of Net Assessed to Estimated Actual Value
2000-01	$ 100,418,449	$ 796,149,091	12.61 %
1999-00	82,226,968	536,882,332	15.32
1998-99	74,734,634	489,494,533	15.27
1997-98	65,889,795	443,319,384	14.86
1996-97	58,793,130	387,631,683	15.17
1995-96	56,570,881	361,821,939	15.64
1994-95	55,530,078	372,714,972	14.90
1993-94	59,670,064	342,268,831	17.43
1992-93	63,406,929	359,195,883	17.65
1991-92	66,584,190	376,186,369	17.70

* The source of this information is State and County Abstract of the Assessment Roll, Arizona Department of Revenue.

Ratio of Net Assessed to Estimated Actual Value

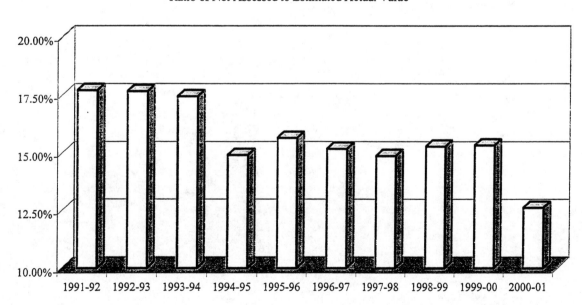

AVONDALE ELEMENTARY SCHOOL DISTRICT NO. 44
COMPARATIVE TAX RATES*
(PER $100 OF ASSESSED VALUE)
(UNAUDITED)

	2000-2001		1999-2000	
	Valuation	**Rate**	**Valuation**	**Rate**
Primary	$ 93,445,436		$ 76,594,232	
Maintenance & Operation		$ 2.3341		$ 2.6466
Adjacent Ways		0.0330		0.0021
Soft Capital		0.1955		0.2127
		$ 2.5626		$ 2.8614
Secondary	$ 100,418,449		$ 82,226,968	
Bond Interest & Redemption		$ 1.9292		$ 2.0986
		$ 1.9292		$ 2.0986

* The source of this information is District records.

2000-01 Tax Rates

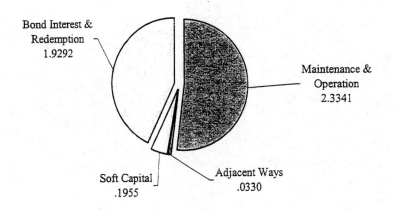

Bond Interest & Redemption 1.9292

Maintenance & Operation 2.3341

Soft Capital .1955

Adjacent Ways .0330

AVONDALE ELEMENTARY SCHOOL DISTRICT NO. 44
PROPERTY TAX RATES - DIRECT AND OVERLAPPING GOVERNMENTS*
(PER $100 OF ASSESSED VALUE)
LAST 10 FISCAL YEARS
(UNAUDITED)

| | | Maricopa County | | | | | | | |
Fiscal Year	State of Arizona	County-wide	Community College District	Flood Control District	Central AZ Water Conservation District	City of Avondale	City of Goodyear	Agua Fria Union High School District No. 216	Avondale Elementary School District No. 44
2000-01	0.00	1.27	1.11	0.23	0.13	1.28	1.95	3.88	4.49
1999-00	0.00	1.30	1.13	0.29	0.14	1.64	2.10	4.49	4.96
1998-99	0.00	1.28	1.11	0.33	0.14	1.78	2.09	4.63	4.82
1997-98	0.00	1.26	1.13	0.34	0.14	1.35	2.11	4.15	4.53
1996-97	0.00	1.78	1.05	0.34	0.14	1.58	2.13	4.14	4.56
1995-96	0.47	1.83	1.11	0.33	0.14	1.35	2.09	4.53	5.18
1994-95	0.47	1.77	0.89	0.36	0.14	1.32	2.10	4.59	5.24
1993-94	0.47	1.79	0.85	0.39	0.14	0.64	2.14	3.78	4.66
1992-93	0.47	1.74	0.85	0.39	0.14	0.60	2.04	4.35	4.30
1991-92	0.47	1.69	0.84	0.44	0.14	0.56	2.09	3.58	4.79

---

* The combined tax rate includes the tax rate for debt service payments, which is based on the secondary assessed valuation of the entity, and the tax rate for all other purposes such as maintenance and operation and capital outlay, which is based on the primary assessed valuation of the municipality.

The source of this information is the Maricopa County Treasurer's records.

AVONDALE ELEMENTARY SCHOOL DISTRICT NO. 44
RATIO OF NET GENERAL BONDED DEBT
TO ASSESSED VALUE AND NET BONDED DEBT PER CAPITA*
LAST 10 FISCAL YEARS
(UNAUDITED)

Fiscal Year	Population	Net Secondary Assessed Value	Net Bonded Debt	Ratio of Net General Bonded Debt to Assessed Value	Net Bonded Debt Per Capita
2000-01	33,600	$ 100,418,449	$ 9,543,023	9.50 %	$ 284
1999-00	32,000	82,226,968	11,085,172	13.48	346
1998-99	28,650	74,734,634	8,287,346	11.09	289
1997-98	26,020	65,889,795	8,818,003	13.38	339
1996-97	25,111	58,793,130	5,394,438	9.18	215
1995-96	24,000	56,570,881	6,419,378	11.35	267
1994-95	23,040	55,530,078	7,378,199	13.29	320
1993-94	22,839	59,670,064	8,160,016	13.68	357
1992-93	21,505	63,406,929	8,419,619	13.28	392
1991-92	18,837	66,584,190	9,705,816	14.58	515

* The source of this information is District records.

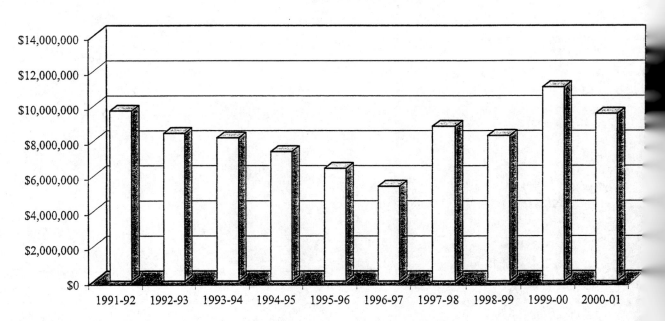

Net Bonded Debt

District General Obligation and Refunding Bonds:

Net secondary assessed value		$ 100,418,449
Debt limit - 15% of net assessed value		$ 15,062,767
Amount of debt applicable to debt limit:		
General Obligation and Refunding Bonds Outstanding (Class A)	$ 10,145,000	
Less:		
Assets in Debt Service Fund available for payment of principal	601,977	
Total amount of debt applicable to debt limit		9,543,023
Legal debt margin		$ 5,519,744

---

* The source of this information is District records.

The State of Arizona now provides funds for construction and maintenance of school facilities
to meet the minimum capital facilities standards. Due to this change in funding, a school district was
able to issue Class A school construction bonds until December 31, 1999. Beginning January 1, 2000,
school districts may issue Class B bonds to enhance facilities beyond the minimum standards
established by the State. Districts may issue Class B bonds up to an amount not exceeding 5% of the
secondary assessed valuation or $1500 per student, whichever is greater. In addition, the Class B bonds,
together with outstanding Class A bonds previously issued, cannot exceed the constitutional debt limit of
15% of the secondary assessed valuation. The District currently has no Class B bonds outstanding.

Jurisdiction	Net Assessed Value	Net Debt Outstanding	Percentage Applicable to School District	Amount Applicable School Dist
Overlapping:				
Maricopa County	$ 21,138,917,389	$ 79,595,000	0.43 %	$ 342,2
Community College District	21,138,917,389	269,990,000	0.43	1,160,9
City of Avondale	104,461,872	12,884,000	28.07	3,616,5
City of Goodyear	136,713,813	12,200,000	50.40	6,148,8
Wildflower Ranch Community Facilities District	3,598,387	650,000	89.88	584,2
Community Facilities General District No.1 of the City of Goodyear	20,429,623	2,850,000	25.61	729,
Community Facilities Utilities District No.1 of the City of Goodyear	37,279,466	8,515,000	14.07	1,198,
Agua Fria Union High School District No. 216	247,777,298	25,750,000	40.09	10,323,
Total Overlapping:				24,103,
Direct:				
Avondale Elementary School District No. 44	100,418,449	9,543,023	100.00	9,543,
Total Direct and Overlapping General Obligation Bonded Debt				$ 33,646,

* The source of this information is District records and the State and County Abstract of the Assessment Roll, Arizona Department of Revenue.

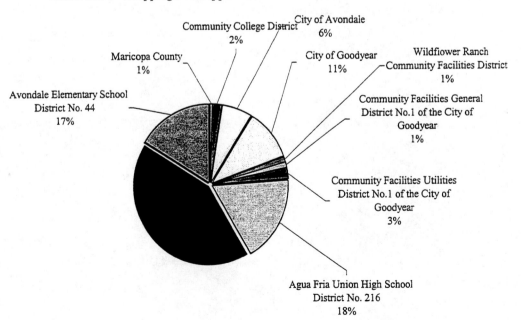

Direct and Overlapping Debt Applicable to School District

Community College District 2%
City of Avondale 6%
Maricopa County 1%
City of Goodyear 11%
Wildflower Ranch Community Facilities District 1%
Avondale Elementary School District No. 44 17%
Community Facilities General District No.1 of the City of Goodyear 1%
Community Facilities Utilities District No.1 of the City of Goodyear 3%
Agua Fria Union High School District No. 216 18%

AVONDALE ELEMENTARY SCHOOL DISTRICT NO. 44
RATIO OF ANNUAL DEBT SERVICE FOR
GENERAL BONDED DEBT TO TOTAL GENERAL EXPENDITURES*
LAST 10 FISCAL YEARS
(UNAUDITED)

Fiscal Year	Principal	Interest and Fiscal Charges	Total Debt Service	Total Expenditures*	Ratio of Debt Service To Total Expenditures
2000-01	$ 1,200,000	$ 567,689	$ 1,767,689	$ 16,747,154	10.56 %
1999-00	1,425,000	606,109	2,031,109	15,584,661	13.03
1998-99	170,000	1,395,996	1,565,996	14,562,718	10.75
1997-98	1,115,000	194,163	1,309,163	12,885,942	10.16
1996-97	975,000	241,583	1,216,583	12,527,653	9.71
1995-96	925,000	307,121	1,232,121	12,366,060	9.96
1994-95	935,000	371,187	1,306,187	12,499,338	10.45
1993-94	860,000	356,631	1,216,631	11,663,666	10.43
1992-93	655,000	659,596	1,314,596	11,416,070	11.52
1991-92	550,000	826,043	1,376,043	11,103,341	12.39

* Funds included are General, Special Revenue and Debt Service. The source of this information is District records.

Ratio of Debt Service to Total Expenditures

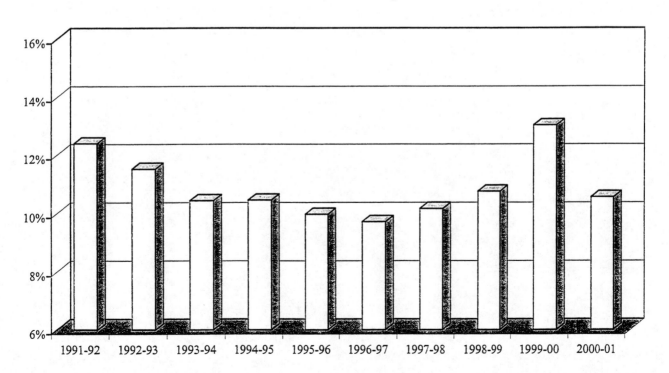

AVONDALE ELEMENTARY SCHOOL DISTRICT NO. 44
COUNTY-WIDE DEMOGRAPHIC STATISTICS*
LAST 10 YEARS
(UNAUDITED)

Calendar Year	Population as of July 1	Per Capita Income	Average Daily School Membership (through Grade 12)	College and University Enrollment	Unemployment Rate (June)
2000	3,072,149	$ **	539,430	**	2.6 %
1999	2,913,500	28,205	519,261	151,139	3.0
1998	2,806,100	27,254	499,949	149,247	2.7
1997	2,720,600	24,601	474,820	141,414	3.0
1996	2,634,600	23,435	428,541	152,373	3.6
1995	2,528,700	22,274	418,226	151,102	3.4
1994	2,355,900	21,364	378,283	153,898	4.7
1993	2,291,200	20,195	364,281	147,189	5.0
1992	2,233,700	19,367	351,280	140,479	6.4
1991	2,180,000	18,551	338,384	135,519	4.9

---

* Information is County-wide, since it is not available at District level. The source of this information is the Arizona Economic Indicators.

** Information is not available.

AVONDALE ELEMENTARY SCHOOL DISTRICT NO. 44
COUNTY-WIDE BUILDING PERMITS, BANK DEPOSITS AND RETAIL SALES*
LAST 10 YEARS
(UNAUDITED)

Calendar Year	Value of Building Permits Issued	New Housing Units Authorized	Bank Deposits	Retail Sales
2000	$ 4,774,188,000	42,205	$ 27,336,883,000	$ 25,881,116,287
1999	6,555,264,000	36,997	25,213,758,000	23,704,579,962
1998	8,488,426,000	47,801	24,940,253,000	21,504,574,000
1997	7,111,311,000	42,568	20,568,058,000	19,900,822,680
1996	6,793,533,000	39,626	17,806,183,000	18,547,512,000
1995	5,637,579,000	37,091	21,171,950,000	18,001,702,137
1994	3,877,559,000	26,733	20,017,167,000	15,446,000,000
1993	3,529,540,000	24,147	19,485,966,000	13,384,000,000
1992	3,228,423,000	20,489	19,358,015,000	12,756,889,000
1991	2,501,786,000	15,140	19,448,091,000	13,407,000,000

* Information is County-wide, since it is not available at the District level. The source of this information is the Arizona Department of Revenue and the Arizona Bankers Association.

AVONDALE ELEMENTARY SCHOOL DISTRICT NO. 44
NET SECONDARY ASSESSED VALUATION BY PROPERTY CLASSIFICATION*
JUNE 30, 2001
(UNAUDITED)

Legal Class	Description		Net Secondary Assessed Valuation	Percent of Total	
2	Mining and Utilities	$	7,519,761	7.49	%
3	Commercial & Industrial		51,049,180	50.84	
4	Agricultural & Vacant		11,338,868	11.29	
5	Residential (Owner Occupied)		22,664,170	22.57	
6	Residential (Rented)		7,402,253	7.37	
7	Railroad, Private Car, Airline Flight Properties		328,357	0.32	
8	Properties (Governmental)		115,860	0.12	
	Total	$	100,418,449	100.00	%

* The source of this information is the State and County Abstract of the Assessment Roll, Arizona Department of Revenue.

Net Secondary Assessed Valuation By Property Classification

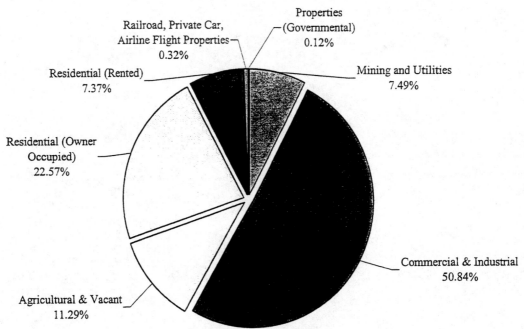

Taxpayer	Actual Assessed Valuation	As Percent of District's Net Assessed Valuation
Arizona Public Service Company	$ 5,126,703	4.79 %
Loral Corporation	3,981,490	3.72
Wigwam Outlet Stores	3,478,452	3.25
McLane Company	2,964,711	2.77
U.S. West Corporation	2,622,218	2.45
Rubbermaid, Inc.	2,311,833	2.16
SunCor Development Co.	2,236,912	2.09
Wal-Mart Stores, Inc.	1,519,816	1.42
Goodyear Hotel Partners	1,369,975	1.28
Unidynamics Phoenix, Inc.	1,102,402	1.03
	$ 26,714,512	24.96 %

* The source of this information is the Maricopa County Assessors' records.

2000-01 Principal Taxpayers

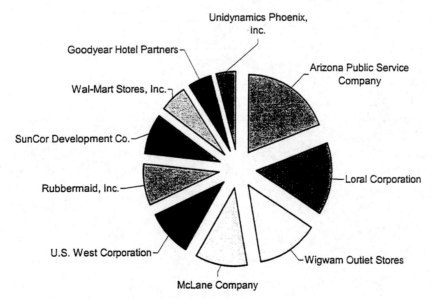

AVONDALE ELEMENTARY SCHOOL DISTRICT NO. 44
AVERAGE DAILY MEMBERSHIP (ADM)*
LAST 10 FISCAL YEARS
(UNAUDITED)

Fiscal Year	Total ADM
2000-01	3,168
1999-00	2,849
1998-99	2,823
1997-98	2,748
1996-97	2,699
1995-96	2,593
1994-95	2,585
1993-94	2,560
1992-93	2,524
1991-92	2,474

---

* The source of this information is District records.

Average Daily Membership

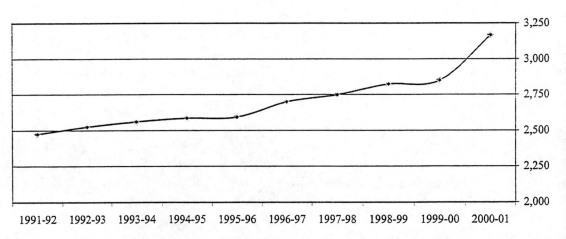

Date established	1894	
Area	30	square miles
Population	33,600	

Number of schools:

	Elementary	5
	Middle Schools	1

Employees:

	Certified	190
	Classified	191

Teacher/Student Ratio	1 : 18
Student Count	3,168

---

* The source of this information is District records.

(This page intentionally left blank)